MENTAL RETARDATION: ITS SOCIAL AND LEGAL CONTEXT

STANLEY J. VITELLO
Rutgers University

RONALD M. SOSKIN
Bose, McKinney and Evans

Prentice-Hall, Inc., Englewood Cliffs, New Jersey 07632

Library of Congress Cataloging in Publication Data

Vitello, Stanley J.
    Mental retardation.

    Bibliography: p. 170
    Includes index.
    1. Mentally handicapped—United States. 2. Mentally
handicapped—Government policy—United States. 3. Mental
health laws—United States. I. Soskin, Ronald M.
II. Title.
HV3006.A4V57   1985   362.3'0973   84-9815
ISBN 0-13-576521-8

© 1985 by Prentice-Hall, Inc., Englewood Cliffs, New Jersey 07632

Printed in the United States of America

10 9 8 7 6 5 4 3 2 1

Editorial/production supervision and
    interior design: Virginia Cavanagh Neri
Cover design: Wanda Lubelska Design
Manufacturing buyer: Ron Chapman

ISBN 0-13-576521-8   01

Prentice-Hall International, Inc., *London*
Prentice-Hall of Australia Pty. Limited, *Sydney*
Editora Prentice-Hall do Brasil, Ltda., *Rio de Janiero*
Prentice-Hall Canada Inc., *Toronto*
Prentice-Hall of India Private Limited, *New Delhi*
Prentice-Hall of Japan, Inc., *Tokyo*
Prentice-Hall of Southeast Asia Pte. Ltd., *Singapore*
Whitehall Books Limited, *Wellington, New Zealand*

This book is dedicated to **Ron and Travis Guidry**,
and to other loving brothers and sisters

New York Yankees pitcher **Ron Guidry**, on the 16th birthday of his retarded younger brother, was named yesterday the winner of baseball's **Roberto Clemente** Award for his work with the Special Olympics. Guidry expressed gratitude, but added, "I'd trade every significant achievement I've ever had to see **Travis** continue to progress and be able to lead a reasonably normal life. He's the one who has made the truly significant achievements."

The Star-Ledger
February 14, 1984, p. 2.

CONTENTS

Foreword   vii

Preface   ix

ONE   Definition, Classification, and Epidemiology   1

The Clinical Perspective 2
The Social System Perspective 13
The Developmental Perspective 15
Epidemiology 17
Summary 22

TWO   Deinstitutionalization   23

Deinstitutionalization Defined 23
Historical Precursors 24
Impetus for Deinstitutionalization 28
Impact of Deinstitutionalization 38
Deinstitutionalization Backlash 41

THREE   Mainstreaming   48

Mainstreaming Defined 48
Historical Precursors 49
Impetus for Mainstreaming 50
Impact of Mainstreaming 57
Mainstreaming Backlash 62
Summary 69

FOUR   Families   70

Diagnosis   71
Home Care   78
Alternative Placement   84
Family Care: A Shift in Social Policy   87
Familial Rights of Mentally Retarded Persons   89

FIVE   Residential, Social, and Advocacy Services   96

Residential Services   97
Social Services   108
Advocacy Services   121
Summary   132

SIX   Prevention   133

Biogenic Determinants: Medical Interventions   134
New Advances in Medical Diagnoses and Treatment   142
Economic and Legal Issues   144
Sociocultural Determinants: Social Interventions   147
Large Scale Social Interventions   155
A Synergistic Approach to Prevention   157

SEVEN   Futures   159

Technology   159
Integration/Segregation   161
Professional and Community Education   161
International Developments   163
Research   163
Social Vulnerability   164
National Leadership   166
Summary   166

Glossary   167

References   170

Index   205

FOREWORD

The field of mental retardation has experienced sharp swings between moods of optimism and pessimism. On one end of the pendulum, the people labeled as deficient in intelligence have been perceived as uneducable, a menace to public safety, and burdens to be sequestered away. On the other extreme, the same people—stripped of their labels, limitations, and liabilities—have at times been portrayed in a false light as holy innocents or curable children. Although it is tempting to suggest alternating cycles of optimism and pessimism, the historical record is more complex than that. Every era has had its theorists and practitioners viewing mental retardation as capable of being ameliorated to some degree by interventions at the level of the individual, the family, and the environment. As this book makes clear, there is now a professional and scientific consensus which provides a solid basis for a prognosis of hope, for believing in the efficacy of such interventions.

As a result, this is an age of rising, but realistic expectations for disabled consumers, their families, and their professional advisors and helpers. Those expectations have also been fueled by the legitimizing and politicizing effects of human rights declarations such as the Declaration on the Special and General Rights of Mentally Retarded Persons promulgated by the International League of Societies for Persons with Mental Handicap, the United Nations Declaration on the Rights of Mentally Retarded Persons that drew upon the League's work, and the U.N. Declaration on the Rights of Disabled Persons that refined and expanded those earlier sets of principles. Activists have taken such universal principles and transformed them into laws and policies, which offer the promise of a decent and dignified life for every disabled person.

But promise and practice have too often diverged. Out of that experience, as the authors of this book explain, militant (and no so militant) parents, self-advocates, and other advocates have turned to the courts and to public opinion to claim the rights of retarded persons. Their well-publicized successes in those forums helped to stimulate additional advocacy for retarded persons in particular and an ethic of assertiveness on behalf of disabled persons in general.

These developments have introduced new complexities and new possibilities in the field of mental retardation. Its students and practitioners must not only master a primary discipline, but must also understand the legal and social context in which habilitation decisions are made, and have access to the relevant research from the psychological, medical, and sociological literatures. Recalling Clausewitz's dictum that war is too important to be left to generals, the lives of mentally retarded people are too important to be left to a narrowly trained or intellectually isolated cadre of habilitation specialists. We need new curriculums, training materials, and clinical training experiences that reflect that recognition. Indeed, this text is both an appeal for, and a means to, a broadened perspective and cross-disciplinary training.

The authors of *Mental Retardation: Its Social and Legal Context* identify the tensions between this society's ideals and its willingness to make the day-to-day accommodations to realize its egalitarian goals. They describe America's willingness to embrace policies of normalization, deinstitutionalization, and mainstreaming, as well as the constraints of budget, training, and public attitudes that hamper full implementation of such policies. They recognize the heretofore neglected strengths and capabilities of retarded people as well as their vulnerabilities. We possess the information needed for richer and more autonomous futures for these fellow citizens of ours, but lack the means to disseminate this knowledge to those who might make a difference. Although this society of affluence can afford unique freedoms and service possibilities, we seem to lack the political will to reduce the ravages of poverty that so intensify the problem of mental retardation in the United States. Pointing to the sensitivity of care providers to trends in governmental funding, the authors criticize the current instabilities in federal funding that threaten to undermine progress achieved in the 1960s and 1970s and to plunge retarded people into a growing underclass.

In sum, this book is a thoroughly researched, balanced, and thoughtful survey of the field. As a text, it brings together a variety of perspectives, observations, and intriguing facts. As a reference work, it marshalls the data for persuasive advocacy on a variety of topics, including prevention, the familial rights of mentally retarded persons, and the need for a range of supportive services. Vitello and Soskin have rendered a valuable accounting of not only the social and legal norms, but progress to date in achieving those norms in an interdisciplinary field in transition.

Stanley S. Herr
University of Maryland School of Law

PREFACE

A number of professionals who write about mental retardation have urged students to examine this disability within a larger social context. Such an approach will not only enrich (and hopefully enliven) one's studies, but will also enable the student to fully grasp what it means to be a mentally retarded person in American society. Indeed, "the field of mental retardation is a window through which to study our society" (Sarason & Doris, 1979, p. 19).

The intent of this text is to provide the student with an understanding of how social and legal events have shaped (and continue to shape) the lives of mentally retarded people. We include and elaborate on information that is given limited attention in most mental retardation texts. For example, we give considerable emphasis to judicial activism and social policies that have had a profound impact on the lives of mentally retarded people in recent decades.

In understanding the position of mentally retarded people in our society, we urge, too, that students acquire a broadened perspective. We have selected some information from the disciplines of history, economics, and sociology that we hope will assist the student in the development of a broader perspective. Our wish is that the student will begin to appreciate what A. Bartlett Giamatti, the president of Yale University, refers to as the "connectedness" of the disciplines that enables us to reach an understanding of complex social problems, in this case mental retardation.

The student of mental retardation will know that no manuscript provides the final answers, but raises more compelling questions. Without being apologetic, this primer on the social and legal context of mental retardation demands further analysis, inquiry, and synthesis. Our reward for the completion of the text was the realization of the truth expressed by Daniel Boorstin: "[t] he great obstacle to progress is not ignorance, but the illusion of knowledge."

The notion to write this text came to the authors as a consequence of their interest and involvement in the field of mental retardation. One author an educator, the other an attorney, we have had an ongoing dialogue on the legal and social issues affecting mentally retarded people over a 10-year period. We have learned much from each other as well as from other colleagues and students with whom we shared our thinking as the text took form. Professor Michael K. McCormack of the University of Medicine and Dentistry of New Jersey—Rutgers Medical School, contributed substantially to the material in Chapter Six. To these many individuals we express our appreciation.

We are grateful to Susan Willig, our editor at Prentice-Hall, for her encouragement and patience; to Ginny Neri, our production editor, who gave much care and light to these pages—thank you; and to Genevieve Vaughn, our copy editor, who performed a superb job in making the text technically correct and readable. Special appreciation is due our families for their support and understanding.

Stanley J. Vitello
Ronald M. Soskin
January 13, 1984

CHAPTER ONE
DEFINITION, CLASSIFICATION, AND EPIDEMIOLOGY

Mental retardation is a social phenomenon that has existed since the beginning of time. It will undoubtedly be a part of humankind for some time to come. From the beginning of recorded history, there have always been persons whose marked intellectual limitations have made it difficult for them to meet the demands of their social environment. What has changed over time is our understanding of the nature of the construct to explain limited intellectual functioning and its consequence—social incompetence. As will be noted below, the terms we use to label the construct have also varied over the centuries.

A construct may be defined as a term applied to an abstract set of qualities or characteristics which go together to make up a particular phenomenon. Since mental retardation is not a unitary phenomenon, the many definitions which have been formulated over the centuries embody concepts that give this multifaceted construct additional clarity and meaning. Definitions to a large extent reflect our present understanding of the mental retardation construct. As our understanding of the construct changes, it can be expected that the definition of mental retardation will be revised. In fact, since 1921 there have been eight revisions of the definition adopted by the American Association on Mental Deficiency. The latest 1983 revision will be presented in this chapter.

Early definitions of mental retardation represented theoretical statements about the underlying nature of the condition. More recent definitions have operationalized these theoretical concepts (e.g., intelligence, adaptive behavior), in terms of the presence or absence of specific behaviors or cognitive processes, an approach that makes possible the use of technical means (i.e., testing) to assess the existence of the condition. In the following sections we will discuss three theoretical perspectives on mental retardation: the clinical, social systems and developmental perspectives. When considered together, these perspectives elucidate our understanding of mental retardation construct. Finally, the chapter will examine the role of epidemiology in determining the scope of mental retardation, and as a factor in social planning.

THE CLINICAL PERSPECTIVE

According to Mercer (1973a), the clinical perspective "classifies mental retardation as a handicapping condition, which exists in the individual and can be diagnosed by clinically trained professionals using properly standardized assessment techniques" (p. 2). Definitions reflecting the clinical perspective have been formulated by professionals in medicine and psychology. Whereas psychologists define mental retardation in terms of limited mental development as measured by a person's performance on a psychometric test, those in the biological sciences define retardation as the presence of observable or inferred brain pathology. Both disciplines offer concepts that are important to our understanding of mental retardation as a construct.

Biological Concepts

Organic impairment.   The scientific study of mental retardation has its roots in the medical and biological sciences, where the focus is on the etiology (or cause) of severe forms of mental retardation. *The medical or pathological model* posits the presence of organic impairment (i.e., observed anatomical, neurological, or biochemical abnormality) as the essential criterion that defines mental retardation. Early definitions attributed *idiocy* or *mental deficiency* to "disturbances of the central brain systems" (Seguin, 1866), "malnutrition or disease of the nervous centers" (Ireland, 1900), and "defective development of the brain" (Tredgold & Soddy, 1956, pp. 1-2). This impairment resulted in "incomplete mental development," (Tredgold, 1937) manifested in social incompetence (Doll, 1941).

More recent definitions continue to link mental retardation to a central nervous system impairment. Jervis (1952) states:

> Mental retardation may be defined, from a medical point of view, as a condition of arrested or incomplete mental development induced by disease or injury before adolescence or arising from genetic causes. (p. 175)

Benoit (1959) views mental retardation as:

> ...a deficit of intellectual function resulting from varied intrapersonal and/or extrapersonal determinants, but having as a common proximate cause a diminished efficiency of the nervous system thus entailing a lessened general capacity for growth in perceptual and conceptual interpretations and consequently in environmental adjustment. (p. 54)

According to Luria (1963):

> Mentally retarded children . . . have suffered from a severe brain disease while in uterus or in early childhood, and this has disturbed the normal development of their brain and produced serious anomalies in mental development. (p. 5)

Unlike earlier definitions, these later definitions attribute mild as well as severe forms of mental retardation to central nervous system impairments. Tarjan (1970) estimated that about 20 percent of mildly retarded persons have some organic impairment. Neurological impairment is viewed along a continuum in which marked impairment results in severe retardation and minimal impairment results in mild mental retardation or other learning disorders (Baumeister & MacLean, 1979). Proponents of this view argue that our inability to detect organic elements in mild mental retardation is due to the insensitivity of our diagnostic tools, and not to the absence of pathology. Salvia (1978) regards those cases where structural abnormality is *inferred* but not observable as "quasi-biological" cases of mental retardation. He explains:

> No one seriously doubts that structural abnormality within the central nervous system (CNS) can have an adverse effect on behavioral development. However, a one-to-one correspondence between CNS structure and behavior has rarely been demonstrated. What has been demonstrated repeatedly is that (1) some persons classified as mentally retarded evidence CNS pathology; (2) some persons classified as mentally retarded do not evidence CNS pathology, even in autopsy; and (3) some persons not classified as mentally retarded evidence CNS pathology. (p. 33)

In summary, the definitions cited above are derived from a clinical perspective in which mental retardation is conceptualized as a biological deficit (i.e., brain pathology) within the individual. While biological concepts are plausible in explaining the behavior of profoundly, severely, and some moderately retarded persons in whom there is evidence of organic impairment, a biological explanation becomes more problematic in explaining the behavior of mildly retarded persons whenever such evidence is generally absent (Kushlick & Blunden, 1974). Until advances in psychophysiological research provide more sensitive techniques to directly measure not only the subtle pathological functioning of the central nervous system but also its behavioral effects, additional concepts are needed to explain mental retardation (Karrer, Nelson, & Galbraith, 1979).

Psychological Concepts

Intelligence. During the first half of the 20th century the mental testing movement pioneered by the work of Alfred Binet, Lewis Terman, and David Wechsler introduced *intelligence* as a concept to explain cognitive development. Operationally, a person's level of cognitive development is determined by the score he obtains on a standardized intelligence test (e.g., the Stanford-Binet or the Wechsler Scales). On the basis of a *statistical model* (which posits a normal distribution of intelligence), a person whose intelligence-quotient (IQ) score deviates significantly from an arbitrarily defined norm is judged to be mentally retarded. Degree of retardation is measured by the magnitude to which the obtained IQ score deviates from the norm. In the early 1900s, *feebleminded* persons obtaining an IQ score below 25 were classified as *idiots*; those obtaining an IQ score between 25 and 50 were classified as *imbeciles*. Goddard later introduced the term *moron* to classify persons whose IQ scores fell between 50 and 70. As will be discussed later in this chapter, other terms are now used to designate the degree of mental retardation.

Proponents of the pathological model discussed above interpreted a low IQ score as another symptom of an underlying physiological deficit. According to Blanton (1976), "The 'scientific reality' of test scores now supplemented the 'scientific reality' of brain disease as the basis for definition of feeblemindedness" (p. 172). Moreover, in keeping with the pathological model, where clear evidence of brain disease was absent, feeblemindedness (particularly among morons) was attributed to the inheritance of defective genetic material. As early as 1908, Tredgold distinguished between *intrinsic* and *extrinsic* etiological forms of mental retardation. Mental retardation caused by genetic factors was referred to as intrinsic retardation, whereas damage to the central nervous system was the cause of extrinsic retardation.

The invention of intelligence tests dramatically increased the statistical prevalence of feeblemindedness, owing to the large number of persons now classified as morons (Gould, 1981). Then, as today, there was considerable debate as to whether, in fact, these persons should be classified as feebleminded (Davies, 1959). Unlike idiots and imbeciles, most morons were capable of functioning independently in many areas of community life. The only basis for labeling them feebleminded was their poor performance on the newly constructed intelligence test. Despite this observation, as the testing movement gained frantic momentum, increasing numbers of persons were classified as morons. It was argued that the increase in the number of morons was attributable to the high fecundity rate among persons whose feeblemindedness was genetically inherited (Dugdale, 1910; Goddard, 1912). As will be discussed in Chapter 2, evidence supporting the hereditarian theory of feeble-mindedness was to have adverse consequences for these individuals (Gould, 1981).

Before long, however, the studies of Dugdale and Goddard came under scientific attack for their erroneous explanation of the Mendelian laws of heredity and for their failure to consider the influence of an individual's social environment as a major etiologic factor in mental retardation. Beginning in the 1930s, environmentalists argued that social conditions that deprived children of early cognitive stimulation resulted in poor performance on intelligence tests. Moreover, IQ scores could be increased if environmental conditions were improved (Skeels & Dye, 1939; Hunt, 1961). While the nature-nurture issue continues to be lively debated with regard to the causes of mild mental retardation, it is widely accepted that both genetic and environmental factors interact to determine an individual's intellectual ability (Ramey & Finkelstein, 1981). The debate is now centered on the relative contribution of each of these factors in the etiology of mental retardation (Jensen, 1969; Hernstein, 1973; Kamin & Eysenck, 1981).

In summary, what needs to be emphasized here is that the introduction of the concept of *IQ* helped explain forms of mental retardation where there was no evidence of brain pathology. Thus within the clinical perspective, *mental retardation* means that an individual has less of an attribute called intelligence (as measured on an intelligence test). The genetic and environmental theories that have been posited to explain low intelligence, while still incomplete, nevertheless further our understanding of mental retardation as a construct.

Adaptive behavior.   The definitions of mental retardation mentioned earlier (Tredgold, 1937; Doll, 1941) include social incompetence as a salient characteristic of mentally retarded persons. According to Jastak, MacPhee, and Whiteman (1963), "Biological and psychological criteria are only as good as their ability to predict social competence by multiple measures of achievement." Since neither biological measures of organic impairment nor psychological measures (low IQ scores) adequately predict social competence or level of adaptive behavior, it was necessary to measure this attribute as a separate entity. Furthermore, it was recognized that intelligence tests measure only a small sample of behavior, and that measures of a wider range of behavior should be obtained before an individual is diagnosed as mentally retarded. Consequently, in 1959 Rick Heber and his associates introduced the concept of *adaptive behavior* into the official definition of mental retardation adopted by the American Association on Mental Deficiency (AAMD).

Heber defined adaptive behavior as "the effectiveness with which the individual copes with the nature and social demands of his environment" (1961, p. 61). In a later revision of the definition, Grossman (1973) defined adaptive behavior as "the effectiveness or degree with which the individual meets the standards of personal independence and social responsibility expected of his age and cultural group" (p. 41). A number of standardized tests have been developed to measure an individual's level of adaptive behavior. The *Vineland Social Maturity Scale* (Doll, 1964) and the *AAMD Adaptive Behavior Scale* (Nihira, Foster, Shellhaas, & Leland, 1969) are the most widely used. As with intelligence testing, the adaptive behavior tests use a statistical model to determine an individual's current level of adaptive behavior, which is described in terms of the number of standard deviations from the norm. Clinically, individuals who lack specific social skills typical for their age group may be labeled mentally retarded.

In the following sections, the current AAMD definition of mental retardation will be discussed at length. This operational definition can be described as clinical, in that it includes measures of both intelligence and adaptive behavior in determining the presence of mental retardation *within* the person; however, as will be pointed out later in this chapter, the definition also reflects the measurement of those human attributes which are valued in our society—intelligence and social competence (Ramey & Finkelstein, 1981).

AAMD Definition of Mental Retardation

Although the definition has been revised four times since 1959, the two dimensions of low intelligence and impaired adaptive behavior have been retained as criteria in the official AAMD definition of mental retardation. The current definition reads:

> Mental retardation refers to significantly subaverage general intellectual functioning existing concurrently with deficits in adaptive behavior and manifested during the developmental period. (Grossman, 1983, p. 1)

The Grossman manual operationalizes the terms used in the definition:

> *Significantly Subaverage Intellectual Functioning* is defined as approximately IQ 70 or below.

> *Adaptive Behavior* is defined as the effectiveness or degree with which individuals meet the standards of personal independence and social responsibility expected for age and cultural group. Expectations of adaptive behavior vary for different age groups; DEFICITS IN ADAPTIVE BEHAVIOR will vary at different ages. These may be reflected in the following areas:

During *Infancy and Early Childhood* in:

1. Sensorimotor Skills Development
2. Communication Skills (including speech and language)
3. Self-Help Skills
4. Socialization (development of ability to interact with others)

During *Childhood and Early Adolescence* in Areas 1 through 4 and/or:

5. Application of Basic Academic Skills in Daily Life Activities
6. Application of Appropriate Reasoning and Judgment in Mastery of the Environment

7. Social Skills (participation in group activities and interpersonal relationships)

During *Late Adolescence and Adult Life* in Areas 1 through 7 and/or:

8. Vocational and Social Responsibilities and Performance

Developmental Period is defined as the period of time between birth and the 18th birthday.[1]

Several features of the AAMD definition need to be highlighted.

1. The use of the IQ score alone is not acceptable in the diagnosis of mental retardation. Clinically measured subaverage intellectual functioning *and* deficits in adaptive behavior must coexist (see Figure 1–1).

   Mental retardation is differentiated from other types of mental disabilities (e.g., autism, emotional disturbance, and learning disabilities). These differential diagnoses are often difficult to determine and often rely on clinical judgment. The characteristics of autistic children overlap with the characteristics of severely and profoundly retarded children (e.g., low intelligence, behavioral impairment). Similarly, some would argue that there is little difference in those characteristics among children labeled mildly retarded, emotionally disturbed, and learning-disabled (Hallahan & Kauffman, 1977). Nevertheless, children who manifest deficits in adaptive behavior (e.g., social behavior or a discrepancy in expected levels of academic performance) but whose IQ scores fall within the normal IQ range are usually labeled emotionally disturbed or learning-disabled. This should not suggest that a child who is labeled mentally retarded cannot have a concomitant emotional disturbance or specific learning disability in addition to general mental retardation. In fact, this is often the case rather than the exception among the "dually diagnosed" (Reiss, Levitan, & McNally, 1982).

INTELLECTUAL FUNCTIONING

		Retarded	Not Retarded
ADAPTIVE BEHAVIOR	Retarded	Mentally Retarded	Not Mentally Retarded (Emotionally Disturbed or Learning Disabled)
	Not Retarded	Not Mentally Retarded (Bi-cultural Children)	Not Mentally Retarded

FIGURE 1–1 Possible Combinations of Measured Intellectual Functioning and Adaptive Behavior. (Adapted from H. J. Grossman (Ed.), *Classification in Mental Retardation*, p. 12, 1983. Copyright, 1983, American Association on Mental Deficiency.)

[1] From H.G. Grossman (ed.), *Classification in Mental Retardation*, pp. 11, 26, 1983. Copyright, 1983, American Association on Mental Deficiency.

2. Low intelligence and behavioral deficits must be manifested during the developmental period, which is arbitrarily set from birth to 18 years of age. An earlier revision set the upper limit of the developmental period at 16 years of age (Heber, 1961). Since age 18 corresponds with the approximate age for the completion of high school, it provides a convenient cutoff for the division between adolescence and adulthood.

    Under the AAMD definition, a person who sustains brain injury after 18 years of age resulting in retarded functioning cannot be labeled mentally retarded. Baumeister and Muma (1975) question the relevancy of the chronological age criteria in the definition. They contend that the relevant criterion is behavior, and that to include age adds little.

3. The definition avoids mentioning of the etiology of mental retardation; instead, it emphasizes *present* behavioral functioning and offers no prognosis about the future. Although the intent of the authors was to protect a person who was once labeled mentally retarded from bearing that label forever, any significant change in an individual's intellectual status should lead the observer to question the assessment that was made in the first instance. In fact, not enough protection is provided for those who are misclassified as mentally retarded. More will be said about this later.

According to the Grossman manual, the severity of mental retardation is determined by the magnitude to which a person's intelligence scores and adaptive behavior scores deviate from the norm. On the basis of the IQ score that a person obtains on the Stanford-Binet or Wechsler Scales, one is classified as mildly, moderately, severely, or profoundly retarded (see Table 1-1). Similarly, on the basis of measures of adaptive behavior on the AAMD Adaptive Behavior Scales, these four levels of mental retardation can also be determined (see Table 1-2).

Although the above classification system, based on degree of mental retardation, is useful in facilitating communication and research activities (and even in these instances, one should be more explicit), one should be particularly careful in using these rather gross demarcations in making decisions about the programatic needs of mentally retarded individuals. *Mentally retarded persons represent an extremely heterogeneous group of individuals.* Two individuals classified at the same level of mental retardation may be quite different in many attributes. Simi-

TABLE 1-1   Levels of Retardation by IQ Range Obtained on Measure of General Intellectual Functioning

TERM	IQ RANGE FOR LEVEL
Mild mental retardation	50–55 to approximately 70
Moderate mental retardation	35–40 to 50–55
Severe mental retardation	20–25 to 35–40
Profound mental retardation	Below 20 or 25
Unspecified	

From H. J. Grossman (Ed), *Classification in Mental Retardation*, p. 13, 1983. Copyright, 1983, American Association on Mental Deficiency.

TABLE 1-2   Illustration of Highest Level of Adaptive Behavior
Functioning by Chronological Age and Level

6 years: MILD
9 years: MODERATE
12 years and above: SEVERE
15 years and above: PROFOUND

Independent functioning: Feeds self with spoon and/or fork, may spill occasionally; puts on clothing but needs help with small buttons and jacket zippers; tries to bathe self but needs help; can wash and dry hands but not very efficiently; toilet trained but may have accidents, wet bed, or may need reminders and help with cleaning and clothes.

Physical: Hops or skips; climbs steps with alternating feet; rides tricycle (or bicycle over 8 years); climbs trees or jungle gym; plays dance games; throws ball and may hit target.

Communication: Has speaking vocabulary of over 300 to 400 words and uses grammatically correct sentences. If nonverbal, may use many gestures for communication. Understands simple verbal communications, including directions and questions ("Put it on the shelf." "Where do you live?"). May have some articulation problems. May recognize advertising words and signs (Ice cream, STOP, EXIT, MEN, LADIES). Relates experiences in simple language.

Social: Participates in group activities and simple group games; interacts with others in simple play ("Store," "House") and expressive activities (art, dance).

From H. J. Grossman (Ed.), *Classification in Mental Retardation*, p. 205, 1983. Copyright, 1983, American Association on Mental Deficiency.

larly, retarded persons at two different levels of retardation may exhibit overlapping characteristics.

The IQ-cutoff debate.   Prior to 1959, an IQ of 70 was widely accepted as the cutoff score in defining mental retardation. In 1959 the Heber committee set the cutoff point for subaverage intellectual functioning (i.e., mental retardation) at *1* standard deviation (s.d.) below the mean. Thus, those persons whose obtained IQ score was between 68 and 83 on the Stanford-Binet (s.d. = 16) and between 70 and 84 on the Wechsler Scales (s.d. = 15) were classified as *borderline retarded*. The use of a higher IQ cutoff point undoubtedly reflected the social and political climate of the 1960s, when affirmative action was taken to identify disadvantaged children for the purpose of providing compensatory and special education programs. Before long, however, civil rights activists questioned the legitimacy of the use of intelligence tests in the labeling of a disproportionate number of minority group children as retarded. Moreover, there was growing concern about the negative consequences that followed this classification—stigmatization and the separation of children into ineffective special education programs. These developments influenced the 1973 Grossman revision of the AAMD definition.

The Grossman committee defined mental retardation as *significantly* sub-average general intellectual functioning. In order to satisfy this criteria for a diagnosis of mental retardation, an individual must obtain an IQ score *2* standard deviations below the mean (i.e., a 67 IQ on the Stanford-Binet or a 69 IQ on the Wechsler Scales). With the swoop of a pen, the Grossman committee decreased the prevalence of mental retardation by 13.5 percent (Polloway & Payne, 1975). Thirty million individuals with IQ scores between 70 and 84 were no longer mentally retarded; they were now referred to as persons with borderline intelligence. That is, they constituted the lower end of the normal range of intelligence. The 1973 revision again reflects how sensitive the designation of an arbitrary IQ cutoff score is to influences in the social and political environment (Ramey & Finkelstein, 1981).

The 1983 Grossman revision emphasizes the importance of both clinical judgment and the concept of standard error of measurement in the diagnosis of mental retardation. The IQ of 70 or "approximately 70" is suggested as a guideline for determining the presence of mental retardation. According to H. J. Grossman (1983):

> The employment of two specific numbers, 67 and 69, implied a degree of precision in IQ assessment that was not intended. The use of the statement "IQ approximately 70" avoids the implication of such precision. (p. 23)

A consideration of a particular test's standard error of measurement recognizes the "zone of uncertainty" surrounding an obtained IQ score. For example, the standard error of measurement on the Stanford-Binet and Wechsler is 3 and 4 respectively. Thus, the "true" IQ score should be within 3 or 4 points of the obtained IQ score two-thirds of the time, and within about 6 to 8 points 95 times out of 100. An individual with an obtained IQ of 70 is considered to represent a band or zone of about 66 to 74 (2/3 probability) or 60 to 78 (95/100 probability). H. J. Grossman (1983) points out:

> Treating the IQ with some flexibility permits the inclusion of persons having higher IQs than 70 who truly need special education or other programs. It also permits exclusion of those with somewhat lower IQs than 70 if the complete clinical judgment is that they are not mentally retarded. (pp. 23, 24)

These changes in the cutoff point in defining mental retardation have been met with mixed reactions among mental retardation professionals. Those supporting a lowering of the IQ score argue that the term *mentally retarded* should only be used to label persons whose retardation is marked (Baroff, 1974; Clausen, 1972; Mercer, 1973a). It has even been suggested that it may be unjustifiable to label persons with IQ scores between 55 and 70 as retarded, if their only difficulties are encountered in school learning (Mercer, 1973a). A narrower definition would only include the "truly retarded" or "obviously retarded," whose incompetence is comprehensive, permanent, and caused by a biological defect (Reschly, 1981; Edgerton, 1979); these individuals would fall within the present *developmental disabilities* definition.

The term *developmental disability*, as defined in the Rehabilitation, Comprehensive Services, and Developmental Disabilities Amendments of 1978 (P.L. 95-602), refers to those individuals whose disability (1) is attributable to a mental and/or physical impairment; (2) is manifest before the person reaches 22 years of age; (3) is likely to continue indefinitely; (4) reflects the person's need for special care or treatment or other services for an extended duration; and (5) results in substantial functional limitations in three or more of the following areas: self-care, receptive and expressive language, learning, mobility, self-direction, capacity for independent living, and economic self-sufficiency. Under the learning area, the law specifies that for the classification *developmentally disabled,* substantial intellectual functioning must be within the moderately, severely, or profoundly mentally retarded ranges. Those individuals who would be classified as mildly retarded would not be considered developmentally disabled, unless they possessed other handicaps that substantially limit their ability to function. Jacobson and Janicki (1983) found that 58.4 percent of their sample of mentally retarded persons would be classified as developmentally disabled. Clearly, the inclusion of mental retardation within the developmental disabilities parameters would result in a definitional shift toward the more severe end of the intellectual continuum, with services available to significantly fewer low-intelligence persons (Summers, 1981; Baroff, 1982; Lubin, Jacobson, & Kiely, 1982; Jacobson & Janicki, 1983). (This position appeals to proponents of the "truly needy" policies of the Reagan administration and efforts to tighten the eligibility requirements for the receipt of disability benefits.)

For this reason, a number of mental retardation professionals have expressed some reservations regarding the narrowing of the IQ criterion for defining mental retardation (Robinson & Robinson, 1976; Maloney & Ward, 1979; Zigler & Balla, 1983). These authors fear that the narrowing of the criterion will make it difficult for some persons with low intelligence to receive needed services. They argue that cutoff points for mental retardation are arbitrary and do not necessarily indicate which persons have difficulty coping as a result of low intelligence. Many individuals with IQ scores above 70 will have adaptive deficits that make it difficult for them to function in our increasingly complex society. This view is reflected in the need for flexibility and clinical judgment in the diagnosis of mental retardation. Zigler and Balla (1982) conclude:

> The heart of the matter remains: Is it better to label an individual with an IQ between 50 and 70 mentally retarded or should the label be avoided if at all possible? The nature of the labeling debate in our nation has commonly emphasized the downward use of labeling. There should be little disagreement that if nothing of value benefits the labeled individual, then the label

should never be employed. What is underemphasized is that the label may result in advantageous consequences such as helpful interventions and social services. Thus, the potential liabilities of labeling must be weighed against potential assets. (p. 38)

Adaptive behavior emphasis. As discussed earlier, while deficits in adaptive behavior have always been regarded as the sine qua non of mental retardation, it is only recently that the importance of such deficits has been accentuated in the official definition of mental retardation. This can be attributed to the widely recognized fallibility of intelligence tests as the sole determinant of mental retardation, and to improvements in the development of standardized measures of adaptive behavior (Nihira, Foster, Shelhaas, & Leland, 1974, Sparrow, Balla, & Cichetti, 1984). A number of writers, however, still regard adaptive behavior as too elusive a concept to measure validly. Salvia (1978) contends that the cultural and ethnic heterogeneity of the United States population is a major impediment to formulating the concept of adaptive behavior in operational terms. Clausen (1972) has argued that because available measures of adaptive behavior still remain imprecise, subjective judgments, they should not be relied on in the diagnosis of mental retardation. Similarly, Zigler and Balla (1982) regard adaptive behavior as too vague a construct to have any validity for use in a classification system. They propose that measures of adaptive behavior be considered as correlates of mental retardation rather than as defining features of the condition. Clausen as well as Zigler and Balla recognize the limitations of intelligence testing, but they argue that it is the most valid measure we have to measure the essence of mental retardation—limited cognitive functioning.

D. L. MacMillan (1977) predicted that despite the growing emphasis on measures of adaptive behavior in the diagnosis of mental retardation, there would continue to be a heavy reliance on the sole use of the IQ score. This prediction was realized in a study by Huberty, Koller, and Ten Brink (1980), where it was found that most states continue to emphasize intelligence-test scores in the definition and diagnosis of mental retardation and to deemphasize or totally exclude measures of adaptive behavior. More recently, however, Patrick and Reschly (1982) reported progress among the states in the inclusion of adaptive behavior measures in the definition and classification of mental retardation, although many problems remain:

Consensus has not been achieved in the domains of adaptive behavior that are most important, much work is needed in the development of instruments, and, finally, additional guidance is needed in the form of decision rules for combining information on intelligence and adaptive behavior. (pp. 357–358)

The failure to consider measures of adaptive behavior not only violates the requirements of the AAMD definition but also contributes to the misclassification of children, particularly those from minority backgrounds. The social system perspective places major emphasis on the adaptive behavior of children in a number of social settings in order to reduce errors in classification.

THE SOCIAL SYSTEM PERSPECTIVE

The social system perspective on mental retardation is derived from the sociological study of deviance and labeling theory (Becker, 1963; Erikson, 1966). According to Erikson (1966):

> Deviance is not a property inherent in a particular kind of behavior, it is a property conferred upon that behavior by the people who come into direct individual contact with it. (p. 6)

Jane Mercer has applied the concepts used by deviancy theorists (i.e., status, role expectation, and social norms) in her formulation of the social system perspective of *mild* retardation. While she regards the clinical perspective as applicable for explaining severe retardation, it is unsatisfactory in the explanation of mild retardation. In distinguishing the social system perspective from the clinical perspective, Mercer (1973a) states:

> From a social system perspective, "mental retardation" is an achieved social status and mental retardation is the role associated with that status . . . From a social system perspective, the term mental retardation does not describe individual pathology, but rather refers to the label applied to a person because he occupies the position of mentally retarded in some social system. (pp. 27–28)

Sarason and Doris (1979) view the social system perspective this way:

> Mental retardation is not a "thing," not a set of characteristics inherent in an individual, but a concept that both describes and judges interactions of an individual, a social content, and the culturally determined values, traditions, and expectations that give shape and substance to the context at a particular time. (p. 17)

In short, the social system perspective emphasizes the judgments of others that leads to the labeling of a person as retarded in a particular social setting. The basis of this judgment is the lack of intelligent behavior observed by those who make the judgment (i.e., the labeler). Since it is derived from deviancy theory, the social system perspective focuses its attention on (1) the social norms that define mental retardation, (2) the labeling process, and (3) the consequences of being labeled *retarded*.

Social Norms

In our meritocracy, a high value is placed on intellectual competence. Our social institutions sort out people on the basis of their intelligence and provide opportunities to enhance the productivity and life chances of the brightest (Kirp, 1973; Jencks, 1979). To be bright is to command social desirability and to be held in high esteem. Dexter (1964) observed, "A society which increasingly focuses on 'excellence' meaning thereby intellectual excellence, as does ours, tends more and more to discriminate against stupidity" (p. 42). Thus, persons judged to be lacking intellectual competence in our culture are labeled mentally retarded. According to Maloney and Ward (1979), to be labeled mentally retarded is the "ultimate stigma" in an intellectually oriented society.

Labeling Process

As noted above, the social system perspective is applicable to the labeling of mildly retarded persons. It is not until they enter a school system that a large number of children "achieve" the mentally retarded status. Mercer (1973a) has traced the stages a child passes through in achieving this status. Typically, a child's failure to meet the social and academic expectations of the regular classroom setting results in a referral by the teacher for psychological testing, the attainment of a low IQ score, and the classification as educable mentally retarded (EMR). (Children labeled EMR are mildly retarded but able to achieve academically.)

Studies have revealed that a disproportionate number of children labeled EMR come from various minority groups (e.g., black, Hispanic). Mercer (1973a) attributes these findings not to genetic intellectual inferiority among minority-group children, but to Anglocentric schools and intelligence testing procedures that embody the values of the core culture. A vicious cycle ensues when many children from different cultural backgrounds perform poorly on school tasks and subsequently obtain low IQ scores; they then receive poor education programs that further retard their academic performance. Mercer argues that the intelligence testing of minority children is culturally biased, which results in their misclassification as mentally retarded. In addition, Mercer contends that the diagnosis of mental retardation is based on the failure of the child to meet the expectations of one social system (i.e., the school); little consideration is given to the child's adjustment in other social systems (e.g., the family and the neighborhood).

In an effort to correct these discriminatory practices in the intellectual assessment of children from different cultural backgrounds, Mercer and Lewis (1978) have developed a System of Multicultural Pluralistic Assessment (SOMPA). Their multidimensional assessment procedures include: (1) an identification of the socialization milieu in which the child is reared; (2) an assessment of the child's adaptive behavior in nonacademic activities (e.g., social development); (3) an inventory of the child's health history; and (4) a screening for physical impairments (e.g., verbal and auditory acuity). The child's performance on the WISC-R intelligence test (referred to as the achievement level) is adjusted using the sociocultural scales developed for children from each different socioethnic group (i.e., Hispanic, black, white). This pluralistic model yields a measure of the child's estimated learning potential (ELP). Children with high ELP for their cultural group should not be labeled mentally retarded, even though their IQ scores fall below the cutoff for diagnosing mental retardation using the WISC-R norms. Thus, the pluralistic assessment system emphasizes ELP rather than IQ in the determination of whether a child from a different cultural group should be labeled mentally retarded. Reschly (1981) reported that the use of the SOMPA measures significantly decreased the number of children who would have been classified as mildly mentally retarded.

Consequences of Labeling

Deviancy theorists emphasize the negative consequences of labeling a person mentally retarded (Goffman, 1961). Labels create a stereotype that overshadows the wide range of individual differences found among mentally retarded persons. The prevailing stereotype regarding retarded people is that they are totally incompetent and dependent, and that they reside (or should reside) in institutions. This stereotype contributes to the low expectation that many have of retarded persons. Persons labeled retarded come to accept the low expectations of themselves; this contributes to a self-fulfilling prophesy, resulting in even lower self-esteem and achievement (Edgerton, 1967; Bogdan, 1980). The label of mentally retarded is also stigmatizing and has detrimental consequences. (This view of the direct effects of labeling has been challenged by D. L. MacMillan, Jones & Aloia, 1974). Retarded persons have been devalued, discredited, and regarded as superfluous in our society (Goffman, 1961; Farber, 1968; Wolfensberger, 1972). They have been segregated, have been stripped of legal rights, and have become the victims of subhuman treatment.

In summary, the social system perspective shifts attention away from the individual to the characteristics of the social settings in which a person is labeled mentally retarded. Moreover, this perspective tells us something about a society's tolerance for intellectual differences and the methods it has developed to manage those who are judged to be mentally retarded.

THE DEVELOPMENTAL PERSPECTIVE

Many educators and other professionals involved in the habilitation of mentally retarded persons have adopted a developmental perspective of mental retardation. In a way, this perspective is an outgrowth of the social system perspective, where the emphasis is on external factors that influence an individual's cognitive development. This view holds that mentally retarded persons are not innately "uneducable," "untrainable," or "nonteachable"; the focus is on the individual's educability and the manipulation of the environment to enhance development. According to Roos (1979a), the *developmental model* holds that

> each retarded person should be approached with the positive expectation that he can learn, grow and develop. Like all human beings retarded persons are greatly influenced by their environment. In order to learn and grow they need conditions which foster their development. The goals of development are increasing the complexity of behavior . . . improving capacity to cope with the environment, and . . . enhancing culturally defined human qualities. (p. 613)

Mental retardation is not regarded as a fixed, static condition, but as a condition that is responsive to *active treatment*. Active treatment entails designing development-enhancing programs for every retarded person, regardless of the severity of the mental retardation. (This objective has resulted in a controversy within the field; more will be said about the nature of the controversy later.) For profoundly and severely retarded persons, the developmental model calls for the application of behavior analysis strategies to increase levels of social and motor development. Educational programs to enhance the development of cognitive and vocational skills should be made available for moderately and mildly retarded persons. Advocates of the developmental perspective point to the significant behavioral gains that have been made among retarded persons when expectations are raised and instructional programs are appropriately designed.

Developmental
and Difference Theories

Psychometrics, which introduced the IQ and MA (mental age) concepts, has generated two major psychological theories used to explain the limitations in cognitive functioning characteristic of mentally retarded persons—the developmental theory and the difference theory. Briefly, the *developmental position* holds that the cognitive functioning of retarded persons is similar to that of younger non-retarded persons. That is, when MA is used as an estimate of present cognitive ability, a retarded person (older and with a lower IQ) and a nonretarded person (younger with a higher IQ), when matched on MA, should not differ in performance on a given learning task. When differences in performance do occur, they are attributable to experiential and/or motivational factors, not to cognitive ability (Zigler, 1969). Piaget's developmental theory of intelligence gives additional support to this position. Retarded and nonretarded children progress through the same developmental stages described by Piaget. However, the retarded progress at a slower rate and, depending on the degree of retardation, asymptote at a given stage. According to Inhelder (1968), the severely and profoundly retarded asymptote at the sensori-motor state (MA < 2), the moderately retarded at the preoperational stage (MA 2 to 7), and the mildly retarded at the concrete operational stage (MA 7 to 11). Mentally retarded persons, by definition, are incapable of formal operational thought. Although their *rate* of mental development is slower, there is some evidence that mental maturity may occur at a later chronological age among mentally retarded persons, compared to nonretarded persons (Fisher & Zeaman, 1970; Kushlich & Blunden, 1974). The implications for continued educational programming among adult retarded persons is promising.

Unlike the developmental position, which attributes experience and motivation as influences on cognitive performance, the *difference position* holds that differences in IQ account for the variance between the performance of retarded and nonretarded persons who are matched on MA. Lower IQs among retarded persons explain both the quantitative and qualitative differences in performance which is attributed to cognitive deficits that have a neurological basis. These cognitive deficits include defects in short-term memory (Ellis, 1970), input organization

(Spitz, 1966), attention (Zeaman & House, 1963), inhibition (Luria, 1959), and incidental learning (Denny, 1964). Although such cognitive defects were once thought to be irreversible, recent research has demonstrated that mentally retarded persons can be trained to improve these cognitive processes (Ellis, 1979a).

Summary

The clinical, social system, and developmental perspectives embody concepts that enhance our understanding of the mental retardation construct. Rather than being viewed as incompatible perspectives, they can be considered complementary to one another. Whereas the clinical perspective focuses on the characteristics of the individual, the social system and developmental perspectives focus on the influence of external factors. The clinical perspective is most applicable to those who have been referred to as clinically retarded.

> In clinical retardation, the degree of intellectual deficit ranges from moderate to profound, that is, less than IQ 55. The diagnosis of clinical retardation is typically made at birth or in the first years of life. Moreover, the condition is largely unchanging throughout life. Clinical retardation can usually be shown to have concomitant organic deficits of a neurological, metabolic, or physiological sort (Edgerton, 1979, pp. 3–4).

Most forms of clinical retardation are obvious to the untrained observer and have been described by Kanner (1949) as the "absolute" type of mental retardation, in that the person would stand out as intellectually limited in any existing culture. On the other hand, there are the socioculturally retarded, whom Edgerton (1979) describes as those persons

> with mild intellectual impairment with IQs ranging from 55 to 69. The condition is not diagnosed until the child enters school, has academic difficulty, and undergoes psychological assessment. There are seldom marked physical handicaps and laboratory tests for physical abnormalities are usually negative. (p. 4)

Sociocultural retardation is best understood within the social system perspective. Individuals are labeled mentally retarded "relative" to the standards of a particular setting of which they are a part (Kanner, 1949). The developmental perspective holds that both groups of mentally retarded persons are capable of behavioral change through appropriate programs of education and habilitation.

EPIDEMIOLOGY

Epidemiology is a science that studies the distribution and determinants of disease and other health problems as they occur in populations. In the formulation of mental retardation policies, it is extremely important that accurate epidemiological data be available. By projecting the number of persons who are mentally retarded at birth, at school age, and in adulthood, epidemiology makes it possible to plan for services. For example, screening at birth, genetic counseling, and prenatal and routine health-care services can be provided to prevent mental retardation. Under P.L. 94-142 (Education for All Handicapped Children Act of 1975), accurate epidemiological data gathered by local school districts must be collected for use in the planning and financing of educational programs for mentally retarded children. Population-based information can provide vital statistics for the development of community residential and social services for adult retarded persons who are being deinstitutionalized. Two interrelated measures, incidence and prevalence, are used to describe epidemiological findings. Although these terms are interrelated, they are not synonomous; they are used interchangeably but often erroneously in the literature (Hansen, Belmont, & Stein, 1980).

Incidence

Incidence refers to the occurrence of new cases of a condition in a population over a period of time. For example, the incidence of mental retardation is estimated at about 125,000 births per year. Incidence figures serve as a barometer to measure society's efforts to prevent mental retardation. Lower incidence figures for mental retardation would indicate fewer occurrences of the condition over a given period of time.

Prevalence

Prevalence refers to the actual number of individuals identified as having a particular condition at a given point in time. For example, the number of children classified as EMR in a school system on a particular date represents a prevalence figure. It is prevalence figures that are used to project the type and amount of services needed for a particular population.

It is not always the case that high incidence figures will result in higher prevalence rates. For example, while the incidence of low birth weight babies might increase, higher infant mortality rates (particularly among the poor) may reduce the prevalence of children in the population who were born with low birth weights. Similarly, a reduction in incidence does not necessarily mean lower prevalence. While prenatal diagnosis may have decreased the incidence of Down syndrome births, prevalence figures have increased, owing to medical science's ability to prolong the life of an increasing number of these individuals. Prevalence estimates are sensitive both to how mental retardation is defined and to the methodological approaches used in data collection.

Definitional influences. We have already seen how changing the cutoff points used to define mental retardation can significantly influence its prevalence. Although according to the theoretical normal distribution of IQ scores, approximately 2.3 percent of the population would have an IQ lower than 70, the 3 percent figure is often used because of the discrepancy between empirical findings and the normal curve estimate. Dingman and Tarjan's 1960 study of individuals actually identified as mentally retarded illustrates some striking differences (see Table 1-3). The actual study (adjusted for a population of 210 million) estimated 6,323,106 persons with an IQ between 50 and 70, whereas the normal curve estimates 6,269,106. At the lower IQ levels the variance becomes increasingly large. Thus, the study estimates 420,000 mentally retarded persons with an IQ between 20 and 50, whereas the normal curve estimates only 186,635 (125 percent excess). There are 104,935 persons with an IQ under 20, whereas the normal curve estimates but 57 persons (185,500 percent excess). (Dingman & Tarjan, 1960).

It should be obvious that prevalence cannot accurately be estimated on the basis of the normal distribution of IQ, especially at the lower end of the distribution curve. While the normal curve is a reasonable description of the distribution of intelligence within the normal range, the farther a given IQ is from the average, the less well the normal curve predicts. That is, many more individuals in the moderate, severe, and profound ranges of mental retardation exist than would be predicted from the normal curve. One widely accepted explanation for this is the high incidence of severe mental retardation due to organic defects. Thus, this "bump of pathology" will result in a skewed number of persons with extremely low intelligence (Dingman & Tarjan, 1960).

Mercer (1973b) estimates that only 1 percent of the population is mentally retarded at any given time. She attributes higher prevalence estimates to psychometric definitions (i.e., IQ scores only) that do not consider measures of adaptive behavior, resulting in an excessive number of minority group children being classified as mildly retarded. It has been estimated that the effect of considering adaptive behavior is to reduce the prevalence of mild retardation from about 2.3 percent to not more than 0.5 percent (Reschly, 1981; Baroff, 1982). Commenting on the debate over 3 percent versus 1 percent prevalence, Ramey and Finkelstein (1981) conclude:

> More refined epidemiological data are necessary to determine whether the 1% or 3% prevalence is the most correct estimate. Based on the literature to date, it is likely that the correct estimate will be between the two figures. (p. 75)

TABLE 1-3   Mental Retardation and the Normal Distribution Curve

IQ RANGE	NUMBER CALCULATED FROM NORMAL CURVE	ESTIMATED ACTUAL PREVALENCE	"EXCESS"	PERCENT "EXCESS"
0–20	57	104,935	104,878	185,400
20–50	186,635	420,000	233,365	125
50–70	6,269,106	6,332,106	63,000	1
Total	6,455,798	6,857,041	401,243	6

Adapted from Dingman and Tarjan, *The American Journal of Mental Deficiency,* Vol. 64, p. 993, 1960. Copyright, 1960, The American Association on Mental Deficiency. (Adjusted to a general population estimate of 210 million.)

Grossman (1983) adds:

> The issue of whether 1 percent or 3 percent, or some figure in between, of the general population is mentally retarded has obvious implications for national planning and allocation of needed resources. At the operational level of service delivery, however, such estimates have limited application. For example, anywhere from 10 to 30 percent of school-age populations of poor rural communities and urban ghettos are reported to be functioning in the retarded range. By contrast, in affluent communities most retardation is of biological origin, with a far lower prevalence rate. Such marked variations in prevalence between communities highlight the inadequacy of national estimates in determining the extent of the problem at local levels, distributions by age and severity of handicap, and the nature of services required. (p. 77)

Methodological influences. Two major methodologies are used to determine the prevalence of mental retardation. One is to take a random or stratified sample of a population, asking people to identify mentally retarded persons in their households and in the community. The other approach is to cull all the records of the community's social service agencies (e.g., schools, clinics) that serve mentally retarded persons. Sampling techniques usually yield higher prevalence rates than the use of agency information (Reschly & Jipson, 1976). However, if a community offers a wide range of services for mentally retarded persons, prevalence rates might be closer to the random sampling rates. Another factor that may contribute to misleading information about the number of mentally retarded persons is the system of multiple coding used by service providers. For example, an individual's mental retardation may be coded as a secondary disability and not be recorded in data collection.

Demographic Influences and Trends

A number of variables affect data on the prevalence of mental retardation. These variables include chronological age, sex, socioeconomic status, and geographical location (i.e., urban or rural).

Age. The prevalence of mental retardation varies across age groups. The lowest prevalence of mental retardation is found in children from birth to 4 years of age. Because the diagnostic instruments for identifying all but the most severely retarded children have questionable validity, the prevalence figures for preschool age remain relatively low. Mild to moderate mental retardation generally displays its highest prevalence during the school-age years, particularly during adolescence (B. Farber, 1959a; Lemkau & Imre, 1969; Levinson, 1962; Scheerenberger, 1966). As academic tasks increase in difficulty, an increasing number of children begin to display learning problems. Thus, more children are identified as retarded during adolescence, since more of the school-related tasks require the ability to think and reason abstractly. However, many of these children come from lower socioeconomic backgrounds and return home from school to find themselves totally adjusted and able to function quite well in their neighborhood environments. Consequently, as the President's Committee on Mental Retardation (1969) has pointed out, these children are retarded only during school hours and, therefore, represent what is called the "6-hour retarded child."

In adulthood the identifiable prevalence of mental retardation decreases. The reason for this is that many mildly retarded persons are able to make their way successfully in society, albeit sometimes marginally (Edgerton & Bercovici, 1976; Koegel & Edgerton, 1982).

Trends. The recent emphasis on early diagnosis and the provisions for preschool programs for retarded children from birth to 4 years of age may result in higher prevalence figures for this age group. (Prevalence rates will also be influenced by the incidence of infants born with birth defects.) A decrease in the school-age population of mildly retarded children will be affected by the overall drop in school enrollments and the practice of classifying fewer children as educable mentally retarded. On the other hand, an increase in the prevalence of severely retarded children of school age can be anticipated as they gain increased access to public school programs. The "graying" of the general population will be accompanied by the aging of the mentally retarded population. Furthermore, improved medical care is increasing the life expectancy of older, more severely retarded persons.

Sex. Like almost all conditions associated with developmental disabilities, mental retardation tends to be more prevalent among males than females. Sex differences have been attributed to (1) the higher probability of adversive biological factors affecting male children, thereby increasing the incidence of mental retardation (Singer, Westphal, & Niswander, 1968); (2) the greater role expectations placed on males (Kurtz, 1977); and (3) the greater likelihood of aggressive behavior among males, leading to their labeling as mentally retarded (Ingalls, 1978).

Trends. It is speculative that societal changes in the role expectations of females (i.e., greater cognitive demands, pursuit of professional careers) may contribute to a change in the sex patterns of those labeled mentally retarded.

Socioeconomic status. While some have argued that differences in IQ are attributable primarily to heredity differences among ethnic and racial groups (e.g., Jensen, 1969), economic and social class differences remain significant variables in accounting for lower IQ scores among minority groups. Higher prevalence rates for mild mental retardation are found primarily among low-income families, whereas moderate, severe, and profound retardation cuts across all income groups, with only a slight overrepresentation among low-income families (Maloney & Ward, 1979; Ingalls, 1978). As cited earlier, Mercer (1973a) attributes this finding to intelligence tests that are culturally biased in favor of the white middle class American child. Children from black, Spanish-speaking, and American Indian backgrounds experience a vastly different social and cultural milieu than do children in the white middle-class culture. Consequently, their scores on IQ tests tend to be lower.

Trends. Safeguards to ensure the nondiscriminatory testing of culturally different children will further reduce the prevalence of those classified as mildly retarded. While social welfare programs have reduced the prevalence of poverty in the United States and its consequences (e.g., mental retardation), any substantial reductions in these programs will result in more poverty and thereby increase the risks for true mental retardation. Conversely, an improvement in social and economic conditions for the poor would reduce retardation. See Chapter 6 for further discussion of the relationship between poverty and mental retardation.

Geographical location. Community and regional variables can affect the prevalence of mental retardation. For example, urban areas tend to report higher prevalence rates for mental retardation than do rural areas. MacMillan (1977) suggests that this trend may be due to the relative sophistication of most urban districts in identification and diagnostic services. At the same time, cultural influences may dictate different social standards by which mental retardation is defined in urban and rural settings.

Trends.   The increasing complexities of living in both renewed urban environments and industrialized rural environments may result in more people being labeled mentally retarded. This argument is in keeping with the relative nature of mental retardation discussed earlier (Kanner, 1948).

SUMMARY

The epidemiology of mental retardation is influenced by a number of factors (1) how mental retardation is defined; (2) advances in medical and educational diagnosis and treatment; and (3) the cognitive demands of a specific social setting. Demographic trends indicate an increase in the prevalence of mental retardation among preschool children and older adults, while the prevalence among school-age children will continue to decrease. Epidemiological researchers need to conduct studies that relate social and medical risk in an analytic etiological framework.

CHAPTER TWO
DEINSTITUTIONALIZATION

DEINSTITUTIONALIZATION DEFINED

Since the end of World War II, the United States has made major strides toward the formulation of social policy designed to improve the care and education of mentally retarded persons. Policy represents the "broad plans, general principles, and priorities from which programs stem" (Cronbach et. al., 1981, p. 101). In recent decades, terms such as "deinstitutionalization," "normalization" and "mainstreaming" have signified an ideological shift in mental retardation policy. According to Zigler and Meunchow (1979), these terms have become the policy slogan for treating mentally and physically impaired children. In Chapters 2 and 3, the origin and meaning of these terms will be examined as well as the policies they advocate. Also to be considered is the progress that has been made and the obstacles that still remain in policy implementation.

Deinstitutionalization is a sociopolitical movement that has both physical and psychosocial connotations. Physically (as well as by word derivation) *deinstitutionalization* means the relocation of retarded persons from large public institutions and their placement in smaller community-based residential facilities (Stedman, 1977). The underlying assumption behind this movement is that community care will improve the quality of life of mentally retarded persons. Psychosocially, deinstitutionalization is a process of countering institutionalization to reduce or eliminate those forces that compromise the interests or the integrity of the developmentally disabled (Thiele, Paul, & Neufield, 1977). That is, programmatic efforts are made to counter the dehumanization and mortification that characterize the lives of mentally retarded persons in total institutions (Goffman, 1961; Vail, 1966). The most widely referred to definition of deinstitutionalization is that formulated by the National Association of Superintendents of Public Residential Facilities for the Mentally Retarded. This three-prong definition requires the concurrent implementation of the following practices:

1. The prevention of admission to the institution by finding and developing alternative community methods of care and training
2. The return to the community of all residents who have been prepared through programs of habilitation and training to function adequately in appropriate local settings
3. The establishment and maintenance of a responsive residential environment which protects human and civil rights and which contributes to the expeditious return of the individual to normal community living, whenever possible. (1974, p. 5)

In short, *deinstitutionalization* means more than the mere "depopulation" of mentally retarded persons from large institutions. If the ultimate goals of deinstitutionalization are to enhance the independent functioning and social participation of mentally retarded people, then high-quality services must be provided for *both* the increasing number of retarded persons living in the community and the decreasing number of retarded persons preparing to leave the institution (Stuckey & Newbrough, 1981).

Before a discussion of the confluence of social forces that have provided an impetus to the present-day deinstitutionalization movement, the history of the treatment of mentally retarded persons in the United States will be briefly reviewed. This historical sketch will attempt to put the movement within historical context.

HISTORICAL PRECURSORS

In order to understand the rationales underlying deinstitutionalization, it is necessary to examine the evolution of social systems in the United States for the care of mentally retarded persons. It has been maintained that societal responses to retardation were not specific, but were part of a more generalized pattern of response to deviance (Wolfensberger, 1976; Lerman, 1982).

During the colonial period, the care of mentally retarded persons was considered the responsibility of the family. The expectation was that members of the nuclear and extended family would, if necessary, provide for the lifelong needs of their retarded member. "Placing-out" programs established by the towns provided financial assistance for individuals or families to care for retarded persons. Later, state and local governments provided "outdoor relief" (i.e., financial support) to families and relatives to enable them to provide home care. Some retarded persons were cared for by their neighbors (Scheerenberger, 1983a).

The rapid growth in population and commerce in the colonial towns was accompanied by public concern about the increasing numbers of dependent and deviant individuals in the community (Begab, 1975). Moreover, the changing social and economic demands on the family made it increasingly more difficult (and stigmatizing) to care for a retarded member at home. These developments led to the creation of publicly supported institutional configurations to care for the dependent and deviant. The beginning of the 19th century saw the indiscriminate placement of retarded persons in almshouses for the poor, asylums for the mentally ill, and penal institutions for criminals (Deutsch, 1949; Rothman, 1971). Deutsch (1949) summed up the predicament of mentally retarded persons during this period:

> Whether they were maintained at home or in general pauper and penal institutions, or left to wander abroad, their treatment was usually characterized by neglect, ignorance, confusion and cruelty. (p. 340)

It was not until the middle of the 1800s that the needs of retarded persons were differentiated from those of other dependent and deviant groups and reforms were undertaken to improve their care.

On February 28, 1848, Dr. Samuel Howe chaired a commission to inquire into the condition of idiots in the Commonwealth of Massachusetts. In his report to the legislature, he pleaded:

> Massachusetts admits the right of all her citizens to share in the blessings of education; she provides it liberally for all her more favored children; if some are blind or deaf, she still continues to furnish them with special instructions at great cost; and will she longer neglect the poor idiots—the most wretched of all who are borne by her—those who are usually abandoned by their fellows, who can never, of themselves, step upon the platform of humanity—will she leave them to their dreadful fate, to a life of brutishness, without an effort on their behalf? (Kanner, 1964, p. 41)

Persuaded by Howe's plea, the Massachusetts legislature appropriated public funds to establish the first state institution for mentally retarded persons in the United States. By today's standards, Howe's "experimental school" would be considered "normalizing." Fernald (1883) has provided us with a description of the facility:

> It was a school—organized in the family plan. The pupils sat at the same table with the principal, and were constantly under the supervision of some members of the family in the hours of recreation and rest as well as training. It was the belief of the managers that a relatively small number of inmates could be successfully cared for in one institution. It was deemed unwise to congregate a large number of persons suffering fron any common infirmity. (p. 206)

Howe, a humanitarian and social reformer, was influenced by the promising work of the French educators Itard and Seguin. It was his conviction that the application of their educational techniques (i.e., moral treatment and the physiological method) would result in short-term habilitation of mentally retarded persons and their successful "reintegration" into society.

For two decades following the establishment of the Massachusetts school, the education of mentally retarded persons was emphasized. During this educational period two principles gained importance: the principle of capacity for change, and the principle of separation and diffusion. Howe recognized that, though the school "has not changed the nature of any born idiot and given him common sense," it "has rescued some children of merely feeble minds from the imbecility into which they might have fallen . . . given speech to some who were dumb . . . and trained many in habits of industry" (cited in President's Committee on Mental Retardation, 1977, p. 5). Furthermore, Howe sounded an early warning against the establishment of large, isolated institutions:

> Now the danger of misdirection in this pious and benevolent work is, that two false principles may be incorporated with the projected institutions which will be as rotten piles in the foundations and make the future establishments deplorably defective and mischievous. These are: first, close congregation; and, second, the life-long association of a large number of idiots; whereas, the true, sound principles are: separation of idiots from each other; and then diffusion among the normal population . . . For these and other reasons it is unwise to organize establishments for teaching and training idiotic children, upon such principles as will tend to make them become asylums for life (Howe, 1847, cited in President's Committee on Mental Retardation, 1977, p. 5)

To the disappointment of Howe and his followers, reports on the adjustment of mentally retarded persons returning to the community were discouraging. Many retarded persons joined the ranks of the poor, some engaged in criminal activity, and others regressed upon community placement; many could not return to community life for lack of a place to live. These events were incompatible with society's expectation of complete and quick cure of mental retardation (Wolfensberger, 1976). Consequently, instead of educating or treating mentally retarded persons, society shifted to a belief that these dependents must be sheltered from society through custodial institutional care. Accordingly, from 1870 to 1880 the emphasis in institutional programs shifted from education to the protection of the retarded person.

By the turn of the century, mental retardation began to be viewed as a social problem and a threat to the welfare of the community (Rhodes, 1972). Rather than protecting mentally retarded persons from society, institutions now functioned to control mental retardation in order to protect the community. These changing attitudes were brought about by three developments. First, standardized tests of intelligence were developed that revealed that there were more mentally retarded persons in society than had been previously recognized (Menolascino, 1977; Wolfensberger, 1976). Second, studies of family histories suggested that mental retardation might be inherited (Dugdale, 1910; Goddard, 1912; Fernald, 1912). There was a fear that the rate of reproduction of mentally retarded persons was greater than that of the normal persons. Third, mental retardation came to be associated with juvenile delinquency, crime, and other social evils (Wolfensberger, 1976). Kanner (1964) describes the change in societal attitudes:

> The mentally defectives were viewed as a menace to civilization, incorrigible at home, a burden to the school, sexually promiscuous, breeders of feeble-minded offspring, victims and spreaders of poverty, degeneracy, crime and disease. Consequently, there was a cry for the segregation of all mental defectives with the aim of purifying society, of erecting a solid wall between it and its contaminators (pp. 85–86).

By 1920, though the social-menace view of mental retardation was no longer widely accepted, the number of public institutions in the United States had multiplied , and these organizations had become firmly entrenched in our social system. There were significant increases in the number of institutionalized mildly retarded persons who were "put away" in "mysterious, unknown places," where for decades they remained "out of sight, out of mind" (Goldberg & Lippman, 1974). These institutional placements were now considered long-term; little more than custodial care was provided to control and prevent retardation. Within a short period of time, public neglect resulted in a deterioration in many institutions that would go unchecked for several decades.

Historical analyses conducted by Davies (1959) and Lakin, Bruininks, and Sigford (1981) reveal that even during the institutional epoch, a parallel system of community care was being established in the United States. The impetus for this *"first wave"* of the deinstitutionalization movement came from new scientific evidence that refuted earlier claims regarding the application of Mendelian laws to the inheritance of mental retardation and from early follow-up studies that showed that mentally retarded persons could make a successful adjustment to community living (Fernald, 1919). Alternatives to institutional care were sought because of the intolerable overcrowding in institutions and because of the increasing costs anticipated in the maintenance and expansion of the institutional system. Thus, concurrent with the growth of the institutional system, there appeared the "colony" and "parole" plans, designed to reduce the institutional population. The colony plan placed retarded persons off the institutional grounds in small residential settings where men typically engaged in farm labor and women in domestic employment in the community. The income they earned helped to defray the costs for their care. According to Davies (1959), the colony plan served as "a safe midway station between the institution and community life where some may remain indefinitely on a more or less self-supporting basis, and from which others, carefully selected, may be permitted to pass to the larger social responsibility of parole, and perhaps, eventually discharged" (p. 292). Lakin (1979) reports that nationally between 1910 and 1927 the total number of discharges from public institutions grew fourfold, from 1,009 to 4,165. Efforts to return mentally retarded persons to the community continued in the following decades and became the dominant force in the third quarter of the 20th century. In a sense, today's momentum to return a larger number of mentally retarded persons to the community constitutes the *second wave* of the deinstitutionalization movement. In the following section, recent social forces that have given an impetus to this movement will be considered.

IMPETUS FOR DEINSTITUTIONALIZATION

During the 1960s and 1970s, six interrelated social forces provided the impetus for the accelerated rate of deinstitutionalization of mentally retarded persons in the United States. These social forces included: (1) the indictment against public institutions; (2) the acceptance of the normalization principle; (3) parent advocacy; (4) judicial activism; (5) legislative action; and (6) the costs of care.

Institutional Indictment

Research findings. During the 1960s the federal government supported mental retardation research that focused on the effects of institutionalization. Although some of the research has been criticized for its methodological weaknesses and for the tendency to generalize findings to all institutions (McCormack, Balla, & Zigler, 1975; Edgerton, Eyman, & Silverstein, 1975), these findings could not be totally ignored:

1. Intellectual functioning among retarded persons was negatively affected by institutionalization (Centerwall & Centerwall, 1960; Stedman & Eichorn, 1964; Butterfield, 1967; Sternlicht & Siegle, 1968).
2. Institutionalization disrupted the social and personality development of mentally retarded persons, as evidenced in frequently occurring maladaptive and stereotyped behaviors (Kauffman, 1966; Francis, 1970).
3. Mortality rates among institutionalized retarded persons were high, particularly among infants and children (Forssman & Akesson, 1970).

Reports on the conditions within public institutions revealed a number of inadequacies. A national study of 134 public institutions between 1966 and 1969, conducted by the American Association on Mental Deficiency (AAMD) (Helsel, 1971), found:

1. Sixty percent of the institutions were overcrowded.
2. Fifty percent of the institutions rated below minimum safety standards.
3. Eighty-nine percent of the institutions did not meet acceptable attendant/resident ratios, and 83 percent did not meet professional staffing requirements.

Sixty percent of the institutions provided insufficient space for programming (e.g., education, recreation).

3. Sixty-four percent of the institutions used residents to maintain the institution, and only 23 percent compensated residents.

The results of these investigations came as no surprise to mental retardation professionals. Yet little was done to improve institutional conditions. It was not until the general public became aware of the hellish conditions underlying these reports that something was to be done (Rothman, 1981).

Public exposés. Following Senator Robert Kennedy's 1965 televised tour and his shocked reaction to the "snakepit conditions" in Willowbrook State School, a New York institution for mentally retarded persons, Blatt and Kaplan (1966), and later Rivera (1972), captured pictorially for the public eye Willowbrook's dehumanizing conditions. Their exposés showed residents contained by fences, barbed wire, cells, ropes, and chains. Residents were shown poorly fed and clothed, walking aimlessly around gloomy and sterile recreation areas. Their environment was devoid of any stimulation except for smells of urine and feces. In this "purgatory" the residents cried from lack of attention and from physical abuse. The exposés produced a public outcry for improvement in institutional care. After visiting mental retardation institutions in the United States, Nirje (1969) commented:

> Such conditions are shocking denials of human dignity. They force the retarded to function far below their levels of developmental possibilities. The large institutions where such conditions occur are not schools for proper training, nor are they hospitals for care and betterment, as they really increase mental retardation by producing further handicapping conditions for the mentally retarded. They represent a self-defeating system with shocking dehumanizing effects. Here, hunger for experience is left unstilled; here, poverty in life conditions is sustained; here, a cultural deprivation is created—with the taxpayer's money, with the concurrence of the medical profession, by the decision of the responsible political bodies of society. (p. 56)

It was Nirje who was to recommend an alternative pattern of human service delivery for mentally retarded persons in the United States based on the *normalization principle.*[1]

The Normalization Principle

According to Nirje (1976), the normalization principle is based on a value system or ideology that advocates making "available to the mentally retarded patterns and conditions of life which are as close as possible to the norms and

[1] Neils E. Bank-Mikkelsen of Denmark is credited as the originator of the normalization principle, which he defined as letting the mentally retarded obtain an existence as close to the normal as possible. Recently, Wolfensberger (1984) coined a new phrase to replace normalization—social role valorization. This term may prove inane, if not more confusing.

patterns of society." Wolfensberger (1972) reformulated the normalization principle to read, "the utilization of means which are as culturally normative as possible, in order to establish and/or maintain personal behavior and characteristics which are as culturally normative as possible" (p. 28). As distinguished from Nirje's definition, which emphasizes normalization as a means, the Wolfensberger definition emphasizes both means and goals. In Wolfensberger's reformulation, the goals of normalization are twofold: (1) to increase the functional independence of retarded persons so that they may be more easily assimilated into the community; and (2) to modify environmental structures in order that the individual differences among retarded persons can be accommodated in the community. Bjaanes, Butler, and Kelly (1981) have referred to the first goal as *client normalization* and the second goal as *environmental normalization*.

The interpretation that the *means* used to attain these goals be limited to normative means has been a point of misunderstanding among professionals. The use of nonnormative, specialized procedures (e.g., functional analysis of behavior) to teach adaptive skills to retarded persons is not inconsistent with the normalization principle (Zahara, 1975; Throne, 1975; Roos, 1972; Tennant, Hattersby, & Cullen, 1978). Similarly, extraordinary approaches (e.g., zoning variances) may be required to modify environmental structures to accommodate retarded persons. Humane care, developmental expectations, and integration are essential correlaries of the normalization principle.

Humane care. The normalization principle is antithetical to the dehumanizing conditions often characteristic of total institutions (Goffman, 1961). In practice, for *all* retarded persons the normalization principle means opportunities:

1. To have a normal rhythm of the day (e.g., awakening, eating, and retiring at regular times)
2. To experience a normal routine of life (e.g., living in one place, working, attending school, and playing in other places)
3. To experience the normal rhythm of the year (e.g., holidays, special family days)
4. To undergo the normal developmental experiences of the life cycle (e.g., family living, schooling, employment)
5. To express one's choices, wishes, and desires
6. To experience respect and heterosexual relationships
7. To live under decent economic and environmental standards (Nirje, 1976)

In short, *normalization* refers to services, interactions, and attitudes that enhance the welfare of mentally retarded persons.

Developmental expectations. While *normalization* does not mean "making retarded persons normal, " this concept emphasizes the importance of adopting the *developmental model* to enhance higher levels of adaptive behavior. McCord (1983) explains:

> The emphasis is not on services which treat disabled people as normal by ignoring or glossing over their impairments, but as forms of assistance which help them to achieve patterns of life which meaningfully challenge their abilities and which also stimulate positive perception among non-disabled persons. (p. 249)

Despite this acknowledgement, a number of writers have mistakenly criticized the normalization principle for overlooking real differences between retarded and non-retarded persons that are important to program development (Smoskoski, 1971; Throne, 1975; Mesibov, 1976; Schwartz, 1977; Rhoades & Browning, 1977; Aanes & Haagensen, 1978; Hendrix, 1981).

The normalization principle requires that we have a higher expectation of the capabilities of mentally retarded persons. As long as we perceive retarded persons as helpless, passive, and dependent, they are likely to exhibit these behaviors. As expectations become more positive, gains in adaptive behavior can be expected, thereby increasing the persons' chances for more normalized living. Of course, if the normalization principle is erroneously applied, it can lead to unrealistic expectations and even harmful consequences for mentally retarded persons. But higher expectations for growth among retarded persons does require responsible *risk-taking* by parents, professionals, and retarded persons themselves (Perske, 1972). Such risk-taking may challenge currently accepted protective-care practices. In programming considerations for retarded persons, it will be necessary to balance the degree of protection against the degree of risk (both physical and emotional) to further the individual's growth, independence, and sense of dignity.

Integration. The normalization principle is integrative in that retarded persons belong in the community (Gilhool, 1976). Nirje (1969) captures the essence of normalization when he states:

> When residential facilities for the mentally retarded are constructed, located, operated and integrated as homes for children; when special schools for the mentally retarded are integrated into regular schools for children and youth; and when group homes for the adult are looked upon mainly as homes for the adult; then such direct and normal experiences will result in normalization of society's attitudes toward the retarded. (p. 187)

Normalization requires not only the expansion of opportunities for retarded persons, but also the sharing of generic community services (O'Brien, 1980). Such integration is dependent on community acceptance and involvement, as well as on interaction among retarded and nonretarded persons. Both social and physical integration are necessary for the successful implementation of the normalization principle. While physical presence increases the likelihood of community participation and service utilization, it does not guarantee the social integration of mentally retarded persons (Glenn, 1976). If social interaction is restrictive and needed services are unavailable, then the effects of the community placement on retarded persons can be more detrimental than institutionalization.

In summary, the normalization principle serves as the philosophical under-pinning for the deinstitutionalization movement. It reminds us that disabled citi-zens are entitled to those legal and human rights afforded to other citizens. In order for this ideology to be translated into social change, the actions of a number of advocacy groups were required. These groups included parents, attorneys, and legislators.

Parent Advocacy

In 1950, parents of mentally retarded persons formed the National Associa-tion of Parents and Friends of Mentally Retarded Children. Now called the As-sociation for Retarded Citizens (ARC) of the United States, it represents the largest advocacy group for mentally retarded people in the United States, with some 1,700 state and local units and a membership of approximately 200,000 persons. Many local units of the ARC provide community services for retarded persons and their families, including preschool classes, sheltered workshops, and citizen-advocacy programs. During the 1970s local ARCs began to rely more heavily on public funding for the support and expansion of their programs. There has been considerable debate within the organization over the philosophical issue of "obtain versus provide." Officially, the ARC posture favors an advocacy stance to obtain resources through public and private agencies.

The ARC group has lobbied at the local, state, and federal levels of govern-ment for increased expenditures for community programs. In 1976, an ARC policy statement declared:

> It is the right of handicapped persons to live their lives as normally as possible within the community. Every state and community must give precedence to the establishment of a variety of living arrangements and the necessary support and program services within the community.

Recently, local ARC organizations have operated group homes as well as other residential settings in communities throughout the United States. In addition, they have waged campaigns to educate the public about mental retardation. When they have been unable to obtain or improve services for their children through administrative or legislative channels, militant parents have taken their grievances to the courts. In the 1970s parents, on behalf of their retarded sons and daughters, filed suits to improve institutional services and to secure for their children a right to habilitation in less restrictive community settings.

Judicial Activism

The 1970s marked the beginning of the civil rights movement for physically and mentally disabled people. Litigation was perhaps the most significant social force contributing to the rapid rate of deinstitutionalization of mentally retarded persons. One commentator has referred to public-interest attorneys as "the heroes of the mentally retarded" (Blatt, 1972). Litigation was brought to obtain for retarded persons a right to habilitation in the least restrictive setting.

Right to habilitation. In the landmark right-to-habilitation case, *Wyatt* v. *Stickney* (1972), judicial fact finding and expert testimony found Partlow State School and Hospital in Alabama to be a "warehousing institution incapable of furnishing habilitation to the mentally retarded and conducive only to the deterioration and debilitation of the residents." Judge Frank Johnson held that a mentally retarded person committed involuntarily to a public institution possessed "an inviolable constitutional right to habilitation." Habilitation was defined as including programs of "formal structural education and treatment" and designed to equip a retarded person with "life skills which enable him to cope more effectively with the demands of his own person and of his environment and to raise the level of his physical, mental, and social efficiency." The right to a *"minimally adequate habilitation"* is further defined by 49 standards enumerated under the following broad areas: (1) a humane physical and psychological environment; (2) an individual habilitation plan for each resident; (3) an improvement in the quantity and quality of staff; and (4) habilitation in the least restrictive alternative (Halpern, 1976). Subsequent cases argued that custodial programs in institutions resulted not only in nonhabilitation (*Welsch* v. *Likins*, 1974), but also in conditions that were psychologically and physically harmful to the residents (*New York State Association for Retarded Children, Inc.* v. *Rockefeller (Carey)*, 1975). (Commonly referred to as the *Willowbrook* case.) More than 50 witnesses reported harmful conditions in Willowbrook State School, such as "bruised and beaten children, maggot infested wounds, assembly-line bathing, inadequate medical care, cruel and inappropriate use of restraints and insufficient provisions of clothing" (Friedman, 1976). As in the *Wyatt* decision, the consent decree in the *Willowbrook* case promulgated standards to ensure the residents *protection from harm.* Protections included safeguards to prevent institutional abuses in the areas of human experimentation, involuntary sterilization, resident peonage, and the use of medications. Subsequent court orders called for the phasing out of Willowbrook and the placement of all but 250 residents into community settings.

The initial thrust of the *first generation* of right-to-habilitation cases (*Wyatt, Likins, Willowbrook*) was on institutional reform, with the courts ordering massive changes in the delivery of services *within* the institution at great public expense. Halpern (1976) regarded these developments as tragic and misguided, in that the courts failed to focus on the suitability of the institutional system itself as a locus of habilitation. In his analysis of the *Wyatt* case, Burt (1976) concluded:

> Approaching the Partlow problem by means of a constitutional right to habilitation is misleading. The approach permitted the court and parties to address the institutional habilitation resources in isolation without forcing them to justify the very existence of the institutional habilitation modality. Neither the court nor the parties were ignorant of the inherent shortcomings of residential care. Rather, they either failed to perceive or were unwilling to use a legal principle that would have brought this problem into higher visibility and relevance it properly deserved. (p. 424)

The legal principle referred to by Burt is the *least restrictive alternative*, which is the legal correlate to the normalization principle. It was this principle that was argued more forcibly in the *second generation* of right-to-habilitation cases.

The least restrictive alternative. The principle of the least restrictive alternative establishes the rule that in any legitimate state intervention that limits an individual's freedom, consideration must be given to means that are "least restrictive to the individual's liberty and most appropriate to his care, treatment, and development" (Coval, Gilhool, & Laski, 1977). Thus, the institutionalization of mentally retarded persons without having considered any less restrictive community placements is a violation of this rule. Not only does institutional placement severely restrict one's liberty, but it also is doubtful whether such placement is beneficial. Mason and Menolascino claim (1976):

> The logic of normalization and the developmental model . . . suggests full implementation of habilitation can only be achieved in a non-institutional setting. Institutions, by their very structure—a closed and segregated society founded on obsolete custodial models—can rarely normalize and habilitate the mentally retarded citizen to the extent of community programs created and modeled upon the normalization and developmental approach components of habilitation. (p. 156)

The second generation of anti-institution litigation sought to close down public institutions and to order states to develop a system of community care for mentally retarded persons (Ferleger & Boyd, 1979). In the landmark case *Halderman* v. *Pennhurst State School and Hospital* (1977), a federal district court found conditions within a Pennsylvania institution so "abominable" so as to be "inappropriate and inadequate for the habilitation of the retarded" and "not conducive to normalization." Furthermore, the court declared that Pennhurst should be closed, since "it could never provide adequate habilitation because of its very status as a large institution." The court concluded that "the confinement and isolation in the institution called Pennhurst is segregation in a facility that clearly is separate and not equal," in violation of the equal-protection clause of the Fourteenth Amendment of the United States Constitution. The court ruled that it was the duty of the state to provide community-based programs for all retarded persons in Pennsylvania, including the 1,200 residents at Pennhurst. On appeal, the Third Circuit Court of Appeals (1979) affirmed in part the decision of the federal district court. It ruled that under the Developmentally Disabled Assistance and Bill of Rights Act of 1975 (called the DD Act), there was a "clear preference" for a legal right to habilitation in the least restrictive alternative (e.g., the community); however, it reversed the lower court's ruling that placement in the institution was *per se* unconstitutional.

> Whatever the Constitution requires by way of least restrictive alternatives, it does not preclude resort to institutionalization of patients for whom life in an institution has been found to be the least restrictive environment in which they can survive. (p. 115)

The Third Circuit Court's decision, while retreating from the "abolisionists" position regarding institutions, affirmed the "preference" to habilitate mentally retarded persons in the community as a matter of legal right. A more up-to-date account of the Pennhurst decision will be given later in this chapter. What should be recognized here is that these court decisions had a significant impact on the deinstitutionalization of mentally retarded persons.

Zoning. During the 1970s, deinstitutionalization efforts were also accelerated by a number of successful legal challenges to local zoning ordinances; these ordinances were designed to prohibit the establishment of group homes for retarded persons in a single-family zone (*Driscoll* v. *Goldberg,* 1970; *City of White Plains* v. *Ferraioli,* 1974; *Little Neck Community Association* v. *Working Organization for Retarded Children,* 1976). In all of these cases, the courts ruled that a group home for mentally retarded persons constitutes "a single family residence" within the definition of the local zoning ordinance. Subsequently, in at least 17 states legislation was adopted that prohibited restrictive zoning ordinances that barred the development of a group home for mentally retarded persons. More recent developments in this area will be discussed later.

Not only was there a considerable amount of activity in the courts to further the deinstitutionalization of retarded persons, but also a number of pieces of federal and state legislation were promulgated to further this policy shift. Both federal and state legislation were crucial to the diversion of resources away from large, segregated institutions toward smaller, community-based facilities. The following discussion will describe the key pieces of federal legislation.

Legislative Action

Federal legislation intended to stimulate community-based residential and day services for mentally retarded persons was intiated by presidential proclamations in the 1960s and 1970s. In 1963 President Kennedy urged the Congress to pass legislation to create services for mentally retarded persons as close to the community as possible. The Congress responded by passing the Mental Retardation Facilities and Community Mental Health Centers Construction Act of 1963 (P.L. 88-164). Eight years later President Nixon set as a national goal the return to the community of one-third of the more than 200,000 retarded persons in public institutions. Throughout the 1970s Congress passed additional legislation to further both institutional reform and the community placement of mentally retarded persons.

Social Security Act provisions. Several provisions under the Social Security Act further the deinstitutionalization of mentally retarded persons. In 1971, Title XIX (Grants to States for Medical Assistance Program) was amended (P.L. 92-233) to authorize Medicaid funds to be used by states to ensure that institutions provide a range of adequate services to help residents develop maximum independent capabilities and to return to the community at the earliest possible time. Eligibility for federal funds is contingent on institutions' compliance with a set of standards that include (1) active treatment; (2) recognition of residents' rights; (3) preparation of an individualized habilitation plan; (4) improvements in staffing; (5) adherence to fire and safety regulations; and (6) specifications for minimum space in programming areas and maximum occupancies in sleeping areas. [Institutions meeting these standards are designated as intermediate-care facilities for the mentally retarded, or ICF/MR.] In order to meet these standards, states were required to decrease the rated bed capacities of their institutional facilities. A 1977 revision of the ICF/MR regulations enabled states to use Medicaid funds to develop small ICF/MR facilities (15 or fewer beds) in the community. Consequently, states began to develop community-based residential programs to relocate institutionalized mentally retarded persons.

Title XVI, Supplementary Security Income for the Aged, Blind, and Disabled (P.L. 92-603), became law in 1972. Commonly known as SSI (Supplemental Security Income), this program provides monthly income support for needy aged, blind, and disabled persons. Federal SSI benefits, which may be supplemented by the states, can be used by retarded persons to pay for community housing (e.g., apartment rent). The assistance is also available to low-income families who provide home care for their severely retarded son or daughter. In most states mentally retarded persons receiving SSI are also eligible for Medicaid (i.e., health services) and social services under Title XX.

Another important Social Security Act provision is Title XX, Social Service Amendment of 1974 (P.L. 92-603). This act provided federal reimbursements for up to 75 percent of a state's expenditures for social services for its needy citizens. Eligible retarded persons and families with a retarded child could receive protective services, day care, transportation, and other social and recreational services as enumerated in the state plan. A major goal of the Title XX program is to prevent inappropriate institutional care.

Additional legislation. A number of additional pieces of federal legislation support the policy to create a system of community services for the mentally retarded. The Developmentally Disabled Assistance and Bill of Rights Act of 1975 (P.L. 94-103) declared that it is in the national interest to strengthen programs that reduce or eliminate the need for institutional care. The act required that the states prepare a deinstitutionalization plan for mentally retarded persons and develop community housing and other vital services:

> The treatment, services, and habilitation for a person with developmental disabilities should be designed to maximize the developmental potential of the person and should be provided in the setting that is least restrictive of the person's personal liberty. (42 U.S.C 26010)

This legislation also required that protection and advocacy services become available for developmentally disabled persons in every state. The Health Planning and Resources Development Act (1979) requires states to develop community health services for retarded persons. The act prohibits the construction and renovation of unnecessary institutional health facilities. Section 8 of the Housing and Community Development Act of 1974 provides a rental subsidy for eligible retarded persons to assist them in the costs of renting an apartment or house. Under Section 202 of the same act, seed money is available to groups interested in developing housing for retarded people. The Community Development Block Grant Program (1981) also provides financial support to local governments to develop community housing and services for retarded persons. The Education for All Handicapped Children Act of 1975 (P.L. 94-142) and the Vocational Rehabilitation Act of 1973 (P.L. 93-112) provide state grants in aid for the creation of educational, employment, and independent-living services for retarded and other disabled persons in the community. More will be said about this legislation in other sections of this text.

Unquestionably, this patchwork of federal legislation provided financial support for the development of a community system of care for mentally retarded persons. Funding has always been an important prerequisite in the implementation of social policy, and this has been no less true during the present epoch.

Costs of Care

In the final analysis, it may not be the humanitarianism or the enlightenment expressed in the normalization principle or the moral imperatives of legal advocacy that resulted in the formulation of deinstitutionalization policy, but the simple fact that, in an inflationary period when budgets for social programs are being cut, it is considered cost-effective to care for retarded persons in the community rather than in institutions. According to Scull (1977), "anti-institutional movements only met with success when the economic burden of institutions was more than public officials and policy makers considered feasible" (p. 57).

In recent years institutional costs have increased exponentially, as a result of high inflation, the increasing costs of fuel, and the demand for higher wages by institutional employees. The improvements in institutional conditions mandated by litigation and legislation have added to these costs. Scheerenberger (1982) reported a 615 percent increase in the per diem rate of the cost of institutional care between fiscal year 1970-71 and fiscal year 1980-81. It is primarily the escalation in institutional costs that has driven 49 states to participate in the federal ICF/MR program, thereby shifting institutional costs from the state to the federal government.

A concurrent economic factor providing an impetus to deinstitutionalization emerged in early studies indicating that community care was more cost-effective than institutional care (Baker, Seltzer, & Seltzer, 1977; Murphy & Datel, 1976; Heal & Daniels, 1978; Intagliata, Willer, & Cooley, 1979). (The validity of these findings will be discussed later in this chapter.) These findings made bedfellows of fiscal conservatives and progressive reformers, resulting in increased momentum for deinstitutionalization of mentally retarded persons. In short, support for deinstitutionalization "allowed governments to save money while simultaneously giving their policy a humanitarian gloss" (Scull, 1977, p. 139).

In summary, each of the six social forces discussed above has interacted with the others over a 20-year period, producing the so-called *deinstitutionalization movement*. In the following sections, the impact of the implementation of deinstitutionalization policies will be discussed.

IMPACT OF DEINSTITUTIONALIZATION

Earlier in this chapter, deinstitutionalization was defined as: (1) the prevention of admission to public institutions; (2) the return to the community of residents in institutions; and (3) the improvement of conditions for residents remaining in the institutions. The following sections will consider the impact of deinstitutionalization policies in these three areas.

New Admissions

The implementation of deinstitutionalization policies has resulted in a dramatic decrease in the number of new admissions to public institutions for the mentally retarded. Whereas in 1970 it was estimated that there were 16,000 new admissions, in fiscal year 1980–81 there were an estimated 5,547 new admissions (Scheerenberger, 1982). This 66 percent decrease is attributed not only to the declining birth rate but also to more stringent civil commitment procedures and to efforts by mental retardation agencies to place more retarded persons in less restrictive community settings. (In some states, new admissions to institutions have been halted.) Interestingly, the mean chronological age for first admissions has increased from 13 years of age in 1967 to 18 years of age in 1977 (Lakin, Hill, Hauber, & Bruininks, 1982). This finding suggests that the availability of expanded community services may be delaying the family's need for institutional services. However, it is important to note that 15 percent of all new admissions to public institutions are less than 11 years old (Lakin, Bruininks, Doth, Hill & Hauber, 1982).

While a majority (64 percent) of new admissions are of severely and profoundly retarded persons, a significant percentage (36 percent) of new admissions continue to be of mildly and moderately retarded persons (Scheerenberger, 1982). Many of the less retarded have serious behavior problems (Hill & Bruininks, 1984). This reflects a shortage of suitable community alternatives for many higher-functioning retarded persons, as well as for those persons who are severely retarded.

Discharges

Fiscal year 1967–68 marked a downward trend in the average daily population of retarded persons in public residential facilities for the mentally retarded (PRFs/MR). As depicted in Figure 2-1 between fiscal 1970–71 and fiscal 1981–82 the average daily PRF/MR population decreased from 189,546 to 119,335 (Scheerenberger, 1983b). These figures represent a 37 percent decrease in the institutional population over an 11-year period. It is projected that by the mid-1980s, the number of retarded persons in public institutions will decrease to below

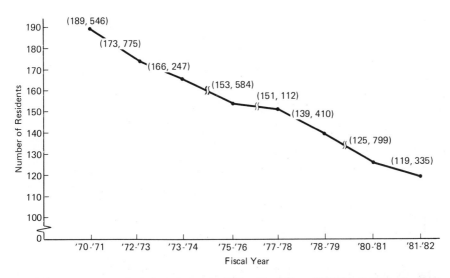

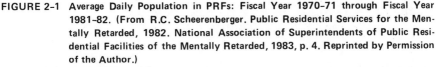

FIGURE 2-1   Average Daily Population in PRFs: Fiscal Year 1970-71 through Fiscal Year 1981-82. (From R.C. Scheerenberger. Public Residential Services for the Mentally Retarded, 1982. National Association of Superintendents of Public Residential Facilities of the Mentally Retarded, 1983, p. 4. Reprinted by Permission of the Author.)

100,000, or by approximately one-half of the institutional-population zenith of 1967 (Gettings & Mitchell, 1980). Thereafter, it is expected that the rate of deinstitutionalization will slow down because of the greater difficulty in developing community alternatives for severely and profoundly retarded persons.

Readmissions

Accurate data on institutional readmissions is unavailable. Estimates have ranged between one percent (Scheerenberger, 1982) and 30 percent (Conroy, 1977). Besides the methodological problems in defining what constitutes a readmission, there is considerable variance in readmission rates across the different types of residential settings (see Chapter 5).

Scheerenberger (1982) reported a total of 1,961 readmissions in 239 PRFs for the fiscal year 1981-82. This represented a 10 percent decrease from the 2,312 readmissions for fiscal 1980-81. Scheerenberger (1981) reported that 48 percent of the persons readmitted to institutions in fiscal 1980-81 were either moderately or mildly retarded. Maladaptive behavior that is unacceptable in the community is most frequently associated with readmission.

Community Based Services

The dramatic decrease in the institutional population has been paralleled by a significant increase in the number of community residential facilities (CRFs) and social services for mentally retarded persons. The Center for Residential and Community Services at the University of Minnesota (1983) reports that 243,669

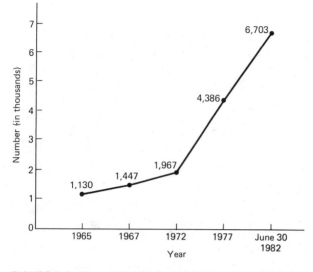

FIGURE 2-2 Year of Opening for 15,633 Community Residential Facilities (CRFs) Operating in the United
States in 1982.

retarded persons reside in 15,633 various types of residential facilities in the United States (see Figure 2-2).

Considerable variation exists among the states in the pattern of CRFs available to their mentally retarded population. Some states are moving toward developing a continuum of residential services that include placements in foster homes, group homes, boarding homes, and supervised and unsupervised apartments. Nationwide, placements in group homes and specialized group homes are increasing, while nursing home placements are decreasing. In addition, a substantial number of deinstitutionalized persons are returning to their natural families. In Chapter 5 a description of these settings will be provided, and data will be presented on the outcomes of the placement of mentally retarded persons.

In addition to the growth in community-based residential services, there has been an expansion of day programs. Severely and profoundly retarded persons between 5 and 21 years of age (in some states from birth to 21) now have access to free, publicly supported educational programs. There has also been an increase in the number of sheltered workshops and adult activity centers that serve lower-functioning adults. More will be said about these services in Chapter 5.

Institutional Reform

It may sound contradictory, but as the number of residents in the PRF/MR has decreased, the number of institutions has increased (Conroy, 1977; Scheerenberger, 1981). Whereas there were 190 PRFs in 1970, by fiscal 1980–81 there were 279 such facilities (Scheerenberger, 1982). Most of the institutions recently constructed are smaller and are designed to take care of fewer residents. In fiscal

1981-82, the median average daily population was 347; however, there were 27 institutions that each still served more than 1,000 residents (Scheerenberger, 1983b). Many retarded persons from larger and older institutions are being transferred to these smaller institutions in order to satisfy requirements for immediate-care facilities (ICFs/MR).

Scheerenberger (1983b) reported that for fiscal 1981-82, severely and profoundly retarded persons accounted for 81 percent of mentally retarded persons in institutions, whereas only 19 percent were moderatley and mildly retarded. Seventy-eight percent of the residents were over 22 years of age; a larger percentage (43 percent) had multiple handicaps (e.g., physical disorders and behavior disorders). The population of a given institution is likely to become more disabled as increased numbers of mildly and moderately retarded persons are released (Eyman & Borthwick, 1980). By 1985, it is predicted that 90 percent of institutional populations will be severely and profoundly retarded (Roos, 1978).

Despite increased expenditures to improve conditions within older institutions, substantial reform either has failed to occur or is occurring very slowly (Blatt, 1979). Braddock (1977) reported that 35 of 48 institutions surveyed between June 1973 and September 1977 failed to meet the accreditation standards of the Joint Commission on the Accreditation of Hospitals (JCAH). Substantial deficiencies were reported in the planning, documentation, and evaluation of resident programs. In the states in which the leading deinstitutionalization litigation has occurred, there have been repeated resistance to court orders. Judges have had to appoint special masters or review panels to ensure the implementation of their decrees (A. Hansen, 1977; Burda, 1977; "Note: Implementation Problems," 1977). Even the court's use of these compliance mechanisms has failed to result in full compliance with its legal mandates. More will be said about institutional reform in Chapter 5.

In summary, in the past 20 years there has been both a significant decrease in the number of retarded persons admitted to institutions and a significant increase in the number discharged and placed in community settings. This might lead to the conclusion that considerable progress is being made toward deinstitutionalization. However, readmissions, which can be attributed both to inadequate institutional programs that fail to prepare residents for community living and to inappropriate community placements, indicate that many problems still need to be overcome if deinstitutionalization policy is to prove successful. In the following sections, those counterforces that are impeding the deinstitutionalization of mentally retarded persons and threatening to create a backlash will be discussed.

DEINSTITUTIONALIZATION BACKLASH

Webster's (1975) defines *backlash* as "a sudden violent backward movement or reaction." Just as certain forces in the 1960s and early 1970s gave impetus to progressive reforms on behalf of mentally retarded persons, the conservative climate of the late 1970s and 1980s suddenly brought counterforces that may produce a regressive shift in social policy in the care of mentally retarded persons. Ironically, these counterforces are emanating from those parties that were the prime movers in the formulation of deinstitutionalization policy in the last two decades—the courts, parents, mental retardation professionals, and legislators.

Legal Retrenchment

Institutional litigation.   In two recent decisions the Supreme Court failed to recognize a mentally retarded person's constitutional right to habilitation in either an institution or a community residence. In reversing the decision of the United States Court of Appeals for the Third Circuit, the court ruled that, as a matter of law, the Developmentally Disabled Assistance and Bill of Rights Act of 1975 did *not* require Pennsylvania to provide appropriate treatment for mentally retarded persons in the least restrictive environment (*Halderman* v. *Pennhurst State School and Hospital,* 1981). While the Court interpreted the act to express a Congressional preference for certain kinds of treatment, the Court ruled that the act did not grant a legal right to treatment in smaller community centers rather than in large institutions. The Court remanded the case back to the Appeals Court for further consideration of the issues on the basis of Section 504 of the Rehabilitation Act of 1973, the Pennsylvania Mental Health/Mental Retardation Act of 1966, and the Fourteenth Amendment to the U.S. Constitution. On remand, the Third Circuit avoided addressing either the Federal Constitution or federal legislative grounds supporting the District Court's original decision; rather, it ruled that its earlier decision can be sustained solely on the basis of Pennsylvania's Mental Health/ Mental Retardation Act. Citing the Pennsylvania Supreme Court's interpretation of this state statute (*In re Schmidt,* 1981), the Third Circuit Court ruled that it is the state's responsibility under its state statute to provide habilitation for mentally retarded persons in the least restrictive environment (i.e., the community). On appeal, the U.S. Supreme Court held that the Eleventh Amendment's sovereign immunity principle prohibits a federal district court from ordering Pennsylvania officials to conform their conduct to the requirements of state law (*Pennhurst State School and Hospital* v. *Halderman,* 1984).

In 1982, the Supreme Court granted certiorari to another Pennsylvania case, *Youngberg* v. *Romeo.* For the first time, the Court considered the substantive constitutional rights of involuntarily committed mentally retarded persons. In an unanimous decision, the Court held that Nicholas Romeo, a 33-year-old institutionalized profoundly retarded man, had a constitutionally protected liberty interest under the Due Process Clause of the Fourteenth Amendment, which requires the state to provide minimally adequate or reasonable training to ensure safety and freedom from undue restraint.

If, as seems the case, respondent seeks only training related to safety and freedom from restraints, this case does not present the difficult question whether a mentally retarded person involuntarily committed to a state institution has some general constitutional right to training per se, even when no type of or amount of training would lead to freedom. (*Youngberg* v. *Romeo*, 1982, p. 2459)

The case was remanded to the Court of Appeals for the Third Circuit for a determination as to whether or not the procedures used to control Nicholas's self-injurious behavior and to ensure his safety were professionally reasonable. In a concurring opinion, three judges expanded the definition of minimally adequate habilitation to include interventions "to preserve those basic self-care skills possessed when he first entered Pennhurst—for example, the ability to dress himself and care for his personal hygiene." Conversely, Chief Justice Burger would hold that there is "no constitutional right to training, or habilitation, *per se*," and that the circumstances of this case requires that the state has no further duty than to assure for Nicholas "provision of food, shelter, medical care, and living conditions as safe as the inherent nature of the institutional environment reasonably allows." In short, the Court constructed a narrow opinion addressing the particular facts of the *Romeo* case and, unlike federal courts in a number of earlier decisions, was reluctant to establish whether institutionalized mentally retarded persons have a broad-based constitutional right to habilitation.

The Court also noted that professionals in the habilitation of the mentally-retarded persons disagree strongly on the question of whether effective training of all severely and profoundly retarded individuals is even possible. The court was undoubtedly referring to the motions made by the defendants in the *Wyatt* case. In this ongoing litigation, the defendants claimed, supported by expert opinion, that many of the retarded residents at Partlow (350 to 700 of a total of 1,100) were "essentially untrainable" and could not benefit from formal programs of habilitation; it would be more compassionate to provide "enrichment programs" for these individuals. Furthermore, it was argued that the deinstitutionalization of most of the residents at Partlow is "an unrealistic and unachievable goal" (Ellis, 1981). These views have been challenged by a number of mental retardation professionals (Roos, 1979; Menolascino & McGee, 1981). While the *Wyatt* court refused to accept any modifications regarding habilitation programs for *all* residents, it did permit the modification of the deinstitutionalization standard by allowing those residents with severe handicaps (medical and/or behavioral) to remain in the institution. In a related case, *Connecticut Association for Retarded Citizens, Inc.* v. *Mansfield Training School* (1978), several groups have intervened, raising the same claims as the defendants in the *Wyatt* case—that severely and profoundly retarded persons are incapable of profiting from habilitation and community placement. Similar opposition to deinstitutionalization has arisen in two other cases, *Washington Association for Retarded Citizens* v. *Thomas* (1979) and *Kentucky Association for Retarded Citizens* v. *Conn* (1980). The Kentucky court was the first to be influenced by these arguments, refusing to halt the construction of a new, isolated institution, while showing reluctance to order the state to create community programs for mentally retarded persons. (Kentucky later reversed itself on policy grounds and committed itself to the development of community programs.)

On the question of which groups of retarded persons are entitled to a right to habilitation and placement in least restrictive community settings, these recent judicial developments reflect a dissolution of consensus among parents and mental retardation professionals (Roos, 1979; Frohboese & Sales, 1980; Cavalier & McCarver, 1981; Menolascino & McGee, 1981). Whereas the federal courts in *Wyatt* and *Pennhurst* (and their progeny) decisions extended these rights to all retarded persons, there now appears to be a movement among some to categorically deny these rights to some groups of mentally retarded persons. Nevertheless, the courts in Illinois and Florida have overseen plans to close institutions and place all retarded persons in community programs. In Pennsylvania and New York, the legislative and executive branches have called for the phasing out of its largest public institutions.

Zoning cases. Despite growing legislation in a number of states curtailing the power of municipalities to use zoning laws to exclude group homes, community groups in many parts of the country continue to challenge these zoning laws in order to prevent the use and construction of community residences for mentally retarded persons (Lippincott, 1979; Gardner, 1981). In *Garcia* v. *Siffrin Residential Association* (1980), the Ohio Supreme Court ruled that group homes for mentally retarded people are not considered a "family unit," and that the state's special statute barring the exclusion of group homes did not override the local zoning law. On appeal, this case was denied certiorari by the United States Supreme Court. This decision is atypical, however, and state zoning statutes in support of group homes for mentally retarded persons continue to be upheld (*Brandon Township* v. *North Oakland Residential Services*, 1981). To date, courts have also resisted the attempts to use private restrictive deed covenants to prevent the establishment of group homes (*J. T. Hobby & Son, Inc.* v. *Family Homes of Wake County, Inc.*, 1981; *Hopkins* v. *Zoning Board*, 1980; *People of State of New York* v. *Cornwell Co.*, 1981; *Crane Neck Association, Inc., et al.* v. *NYC/Long Island County Services Group, et al.*, 1983).

While the *Garcia* decision may be atypical, it is now law throughout Ohio; the restrictive covenant cases may preclude group homes from being established (*Cain* v. *Delaware Securities Investments Inc.* and *Piendak* v. *Delaware Securities Investments, Inc.*, 1983). Furthermore, these cases are representative of the continuing harassment aimed at preventing the opening of community residences for mentally retarded persons. In New York legislation has been adopted (and proposed in New Jersey) which requires that prospective providers give communities *prior notification* and a voice in the *site selection* of a group home. Such measures can lead to delay, heightened community opposition and the legalized veto of proposed residences by neighborhoods (Herr, 1983; Seltzer, 1983). It is unknown how many providers are intimidated in the establishment of a group home and give up their efforts because of the long delays and legal costs, but these are undoubtedly significant factors.

Reports indicate that one-quarter to one-half of group home providers have encountered some form of community resistance (Gardner, 1981). Underlying the opposition to community housing for retarded persons are neighborhood concerns that property values will decrease (despite evidence to the contrary; Wolpert, 1978; Berkiansky & Parker, 1977), community misconceptions that retarded persons are a dangerous threat to the welfare and safety of the community, and assertions that "the character of the neighborhood needs to be preserved."

Economic Realities

The shift in the political-economic policies of the 1980s presents a formidable obstacle to the successful deinstitutionalization of mentally retarded persons. Congress has approved cutbacks in the federal financing of social programs (e.g., Title XX; DD Act) that assist mentally retarded persons living in the community. Further reductions may be forthcoming. Moreover, the block-grant funding scheme leaves to the states wide discretion to determine which disadvantaged groups will benefit from whatever funds are available. According to Braddock (1981):

> Because of federal cuts the state budget process will dictate a more ruthless politics of choice between institutional and community priorities among other social objectives. (p. 17)

Although, under the funding provisions of Title XIX (ICF/MR) large sums of federal dollars have been allocated to construct and maintain public institutions, relatively small sums have been invested in the development of alternative community residences (Gettings & Mitchell, 1980; Taylor, Brown, McCord, Giambetti, Searl, Mlinarcik, Atkinson, Lichter, 1981). Recently, Senator Chafee proposed changes in Medicaid financing that would shift reimbursements from institutional to community systems of care (S2053, the Community and Family Living Amendments of 1983). However, proposed caps on Medicaid funds threaten to reduce even further the funds available for community living arrangements. There is a danger that state legislators may be persuaded by parents and institutional employees (Santiestevan, 1975) who oppose deinstitutionalization, to improve institutional conditions rather than to expand community programs (Bradley, 1978; Menolascino, 1977). Moreover, legislators concerned about governmental spending are unlikely to support community programs where aggregate costs (i.e., for residential plus community services) have not shown the programs to be cost-effective (Braddock, 1981; Mayeda & Wai, 1975). In short, quality community care is not cheap and, for particular types of clients, it may be more costly (Jones, Conroy, Feinstein & Lemanowicz, 1983; New York State Commission on Quality Care for the Mentally Disabled, 1982).

Another factor that has consequences for public support of alternative mental retardation policies is the economic well-being of society. It is surely not surprising that when personal income was rising in the 1960s, there was a general consensus toward improving the entire package of social welfare programs. In the 1970s, real incomes failed to match the growth of the previous decade. The change in sentiment toward public spending for disadvantaged groups can be attributed, in part, to the reduction in national economic growth. Thus, the future willingness to support an expansion of the mental retardation service system will require the control of inflation and improvements in productivity.

President Reagan's "new federalism" proposals and his support for a constitutional amendment to balance the federal budget will place an even heavier burden on the states to provide adequate services for mentally retarded persons and other disadvantaged groups. The absence of a federal role in the support of mental retardation services will result in wider disparities among the states in the care of mentally retarded people. Consequently, further progress toward deinstitutionalization will depend on a state's affluence and commitment to social reform (Sigelman, Roeder, & Sigelman, 1981).

Research Evidence

To date, there is an absence of a convincing data base to support the assumption that community care improves the quality of life of mentally retarded persons (S. J. Vitello, 1977). (Some of this data will be reviewed in Chapter 5.) In too many cases, expedient deinstitutionalization decisions have resulted in the "dumping" of mentally retarded persons into communities that are unprepared to provide adequate services (Sofrenko & Macy, 1978; Scheerenberger, 1978). The ghettoization of placements and lack of state monitoring of community programs have brought highly publicized neighborhood protests. Instances of financial and physical exploitation of mentally retarded persons living in the community have caused many parents to reconsider their support of deinstitutionalization policies.

A number of professionals predicted the failure of community placement because no empirical base is available for judging the most adequate settings for various retarded persons; these professionals have suggested a moratorium on deinstitutionalization until more research is conducted (Zigler & Balla, 1977; Edgerton, Eyman, Silverstein, 1975). In opposition to this view, Biklen (1979) argues that deinstitutionalization need *not* await the accumulation of supportive research findings. The presumption is that mentally retarded persons belong in the community, and that alternative placements (e.g., the institution) should be considered only if it can be demonstrated that these result in better care. Biklen points out that this has not been the case.

Bradley (1980) argues that the future commitment to deinstitutionalization policy in the United States needs not be determined by conflicting and always inconclusive research evidence on the efficacy and/or cost-effectiveness of community care. Although positive findings would make for a stronger argument by the proponents of deinstitutionalization, contrary findings should not dissuade us from our "moral imperative" to integrate mentally retarded persons into American society. The institutionalization of mentally retarded persons is "immoral and wrong given what we know of its consequences" (Bradley, 1980). Bradley observes:

> What remains clear to me as I view this field is that we cannot allow our pity and remorse over the unfortunate side effects of deinstitutionalization to deter us from continuing to seek and perfect change. Self-doubt may slow the momentum for reform. The resulting inertia could truncate our ideas and leave us with nothing more than a modern-day notion of the asylum. What is required is to work with mentally disabled persons in the creation of mechanisms that will allow such individuals maximum autonomy and freedom from the tyranny of our good will. (p. 87)

In historical time, the second wave of the deinstitutionalization movement in the United States has run about 20 years. This movement must reverse nearly 100 years of social policy that has segregated mentally retarded persons. History teaches us that social movements designed to bring about equality in religion, race, and sex are incremental, as opposed to revolutionary. Attempts to provide greater equality to retarded persons by integrating them into society must be guided by a moral vision that is not overcome by early failure to achieve the totality of the ideal (Bradley, 1980).

CHAPTER THREE
MAINSTREAMING

MAINSTREAMING DEFINED

What deinstitutionalization is to community living, mainstreaming is to public schooling for mentally retarded persons. Simply defined, mainstreaming reflects a policy that is opposed to removing children from regular classrooms and segregating them in special classes (Sarason & Doris, 1979). Kauffman, Gottlieb, Agard, and Kukic (1975) provided a more comprehensive definition of *mainstreaming*:

> Mainstreaming refers to the temporal, instructional, and social integration of eligible exceptional children with normal peers based on an ongoing, individually determined, educational planning programming process, and requires clarification of responsibility among regular and special education administrative, instructional, and supportive personnel. (p. 35)

Gottlieb (1981) refers to the above as the *idealized definition* of mainstreaming. The definition stresses the preference of providing appropriate educational programs for handicapped children in regular integrated settings. Educational programs should be developed and delivered cooperatively by both regular and special-education personnel. The idealized definition is contrasted with the *practical definition* of mainstreaming, which is defined administratively as placing a handicapped child in a regular setting for an arbitrary, fixed minimum amount of time.

Mainstreaming is usually discussed in reference to alternative educational placements (e.g., regular classes, resource rooms) for mildly retarded children who are enrolled in segregated special classes; however, the term will be used more broadly in the following sections, to refer to the integration of *all* retarded children (including the severely retarded) into public school programs.

HISTORICAL PRECURSORS

Whereas the term *mainstreaming* today is used in reference to integrating handicapped children into public school programs, in the past this term could have applied to efforts to provide an equal educational opportunity for children from America's ethnic and racial minority groups. Then, as today, legislation had a significant impact on policies to integrate these diverse groups of children into the American common schools. The passage of compulsory-education laws in the late 19th century meant that European immigrant children "who because of intellect, temperament, motivation, physical traits, and cultural heritage, would previously have been forced out of the social context of the school system were being kept within the system" (Sarason & Doris, 1979). The presence of "these children" in increasing numbers presented a problem for the schools because, unlike other children, immigrant children were unable to progress through the lockstep system of class-graded instruction. Regular classroom teachers complained not only that these children were difficult to manage but also that they impeded the educational progress of other students. The solution to this problem was the creation of ungraded special classes, which quickly became the dumping ground for truants, discipline problems, backward children, and non-English-speaking children. In addition, auxiliary schools or centers were built to house a number of ungraded special classes. An inspection of those enrolled in these early undifferentiated special classes and schools revealed high percentages of immigrant children of Italian, Irish, German, and Jewish descent. In short course, one school system had now become two systems—one for the regular pupils and another for the "specials" (Sarason & Doris, 1979).

In 1898, the first special class for "backward" children was formed in the public schools of Providence, Rhode Island. Thereafter, special classes were created in communities throughout the United States for the primary purpose of reducing the number of children on waiting lists for institutional placement and relieving overcrowded institutional conditions. The invention of intelligence tests in the early 1900s resulted in a dramatic increase in the number of immigrant children labeled as *morons* and assigned to "fool classes" in the public schools (Davies, 1959). The number of school-age children in special classes for the educable mentally retarded (EMR) rose from 23,252 in 1922 to 936,000 in 1970 (Wiegerink & Simeonsson, 1975). In time, to be labeled EMR meant to be placed in a self-contained special class. In the latter half of the 20th century, the composition of minority children enrolled in these classes was to change from primarily Eastern European to primarily black, and Hispanic.

Although there had been some earlier efforts to educate more severely retarded children, not until the 1950s did the public schools assume the responsibility for providing educational programs for moderately retarded children—a result of legislative pressures brought by parent organizations and by professional advocates (Goldberg & Cruickshank, 1958). By 1968, 55,000 children were enrolled in special classes for the trainable mentally retarded (TMR), whereas in 1948 the number was only 4,509 (Dunn, 1973). Still excluded from the schools were children classified as profoundly and severely retarded. They either remained at home or were committed to public or private institutions. It would not be until the 1970s that severely and profoundly retarded children would obtain *access* to free public school programs. Also during this decade, minority-group parents would protest the labeling of their children as EMR and their placement in segregated, ineffective special classes. An increasing number of parents of both mildly and severely retarded children would demand that their children be "mainstreamed" into regular public school programs to the maximum extent possible. In the next section, we will examine some recent social forces that have contributed to the so-called revolution in schooling for handicapped children, with particular attention to mentally retarded children.

IMPETUS FOR MAINSTREAMING

The major social forces providing the impetus to the mainstreaming movement were (1) research evidence on the ineffectiveness of special classes for EMR children; (2) research on the educability of severely retarded children; (3) parent and professional advocacy; (4) judicial activism; (5) legislative action; and (6) the costs of education.

EMR Special Class Indictment

Throughout the 1950s and 1960s, a number of empirical studies were conducted that compared the educational progress of EMR children in special classes with comparable groups of EMR children who remained in the regular classes (Kauffman & Alberto, 1976). These *efficacy studies* failed to demonstrate that any significant benefit was obtained, either academically or socially, from special-class placement (Strain & Kerr, 1981). Conversely, such placement proved detrimental to children. The educational programs were typically inappropriate, teacher expectations for pupils were low, and the stigmatization of being labeled EMR contributed to the child's poor self-concept (Mercer, 1971). Moreover, these negative efforts were most harmful to a disproportionate number of impoverished and minority-group children, for whom placement in inferior EMR classes became permanent (Gallagher, 1972). These findings led educators to question the "justifiability" of special, self-contained classes for the EMR (Dunn, 1968). In their place, alternative educational placements were recommended, with the preference for regular class placement (Bruininks & Rynders, 1971).

Educability of Severely
Retarded Children

One basis for the exclusion of severely and profoundly retarded children from the public schools was the claim that they could not benefit from instruction. They were described as unteachable, uneducable, and noneducable. During the 1960s and 1970s, advances in educational technology (i.e., applied behavioral analysis) made possible the development of instructional interventions that resulted in positive behavior changes among members of this class of children. Research studies employing the techniques of applied behavioral analysis reported increases in functional levels in the motor, cognitive, social, and vocational areas (Landesman-Dwyer & Sackett, 1978; Luckey & Addison, 1974). These results demonstrated that, not unlike other children, severely and profoundly retarded children could benefit from appropriate instructional programs and, therefore, that they should also have access to free, publicly supported educational programs.

The convincing research findings on the ineffectiveness of special-class placement for mildly retarded children and the studies demonstrating the educability of severely and profoundly retarded children provided advocates with the evidence needed to argue for changes in educational policy.

Parent and Professional Advocacy

As mentioned earlier, during the 1970s parents of retarded children became increasingly disenchanted with school practices that resulted in poor-quality instruction or the total denial of instruction. Minority-group parents viewed the labeling and segregation of their children in special classes as another instance of racial discrimination in the United States and a reestablishment of "separate but unequal" education. For parents of severely and profoundly retarded children, the total exclusion from the public schools was considered a denial of a constitutional right to which parents believed their children were entitled.

Often excluded from the educational decision-making process, parents of mentally retarded children joined with other parent groups (e.g., Society for Autistic Children) at the local, state, and national levels to express their grievances with a louder voice, and to demand a significant role in public decisions concerning the education of their children. The parent movement progressed in several directions. First, it stimulated public awareness of the inadequate educational treatment of mentally retarded and other handicapped children. Secondly, parents began to exercise political power in order to influence educational policies at all levels of government. Finally, where political approaches proved unsuccessful, groups of militant parents secured the services of attorneys to force changes in school practices that were denying their children an equal educational opportunity.

After years of parent activism and protracted litigation over equal educational opportunity for handicapped children, special-education professional organizations (e.g., Council for Exceptional Children, American Association of Mental Deficiency) asserted a more active role. Recognizing that for many years they had been an impediment to securing educational rights for handicapped children, a number of national education organizations (e.g., National School Boards Association, The Council of Chief State School Officers, and National Education Association) gave their support to providing educational programs for all handicapped children. While committed to obtaining equal educational opportunity for handicapped children, these organizations were also interested in securing increased federal financial assistance to enable state and local schools to meet the increasing demands for special education. In all, this coalition of parent and professional groups presented a formidable interest group that lobbied for educational reform on behalf of handicapped children.

Judicial Activism

In the 1970s, litigation was brought on two fronts: (1) to obtain a right to education for those severely retarded children excluded from school; and (2) to reverse the alleged discriminatory testing practices that resulted in the placement of a disproportionate number of minority-group children in EMR classes.

Right to education.   The first *right-to-education* case to challenge a school's exclusionary practices was *Wolf* v. *Legislature of the State of Utah* (1969). The case involved the denial of admission to the public schools of two trainable mentally retarded children. In ordering the admission of the children, the court relied on the ruling in *Brown* v. *Board of Education* (1954), which recognized that education, once provided by the state to some children, is a right to which all school-age children are entitled. *Pennsylvania Association for Retarded Children (P.A.R.C.)* v. *Commonwealth of Pennsylvania* (1972) was the first federal, statewide, class-action lawsuit brought on behalf of mentally retarded children. In this seminal case, the plaintiffs presented convincing evidence that *all retarded children,* including profoundly and severely retarded children, could benefit from instruction. Therefore, by excluding some retarded children from schooling, the state was in violation of both state and federal constitutions, which entitled all children to equal protection of the law. In reaching a consent agreement, the parties affirmed:

> The Commonwealth of Pennsylvania has undertaken to provide a free public education for all its children between the ages of six and twenty-one years. It is the Commonwealth's obligation to place each mentally retarded child in a free, public program of education and training appropriate to the child's capacity. (p. 306)

Mills v. *Board of Education of the District of Columbia* (1972) can be regarded as the landmark case recognizing a right to education for *all handicapped children.*

Unlike *P.A.R.C.,* this case resulted in a judicial opinion that carries precedential authority for future litigation in this area. The *Mills* court declared:

> The District of Columbia shall provide to each child of school age a free and suitable publicly supported education regardless of the degree of the child's mental health, physical, or emotional disability or impairment. (878)

Mills proceeded to refute the argument that education should be denied the handicapped on the basis of prohibitive costs. The court held that "available funds must be expended equally in such a manner that no child is entirely excluded from a publicly supported education and furthermore insufficient funding cannot be permitted to bear more heavily on exceptional or handicapped children than on the normal child." Both *P.A.R.C.* and *Mills* require that not only handicapped children have access to publicly supported educational programs, but also that these programs be *appropriate* to their needs. The failure to provide an appropriate education is equivalent to a child's functional exclusion from school. The cases also established the legal principle that retarded children should be placed in the *least restrictive educational setting.* The presumption should be that the *preferred* educational placement for the retarded child is in the regular class with his non-retarded peer. More restrictive alternatives (e.g., special classes) would be considered only after it was determined that an appropriate educational program could not be provided in the regular class. In order to protect a retarded child's right to an appropriate education, the courts required that parents be provided *procedural due process,* which entitles them to notice and a hearing before administrative decisions are made.

Discriminatory testing. As mentioned earlier, studies of the composition of children in EMR classes during the late 1960s and early 1970s revealed a disproportionate enrollment of minority-group children. The use of standardized intelligence tests (e.g., Stanford-Binet and WISC) as the primary determinant of the EMR classification and the subsequent placement of the child in a segregated special class brought loud protests from civil rights groups. In short course, litigation challenged the alleged discriminatory overlabeling of minority group children, which was attributed to the biases of intelligence testing.

Diana v. *State Board of Education* (1970) was the first case to challenge the use of the individualized intelligence test in the educational classification of minority group children. In a class-action suit, nine named Mexican-American elementary school students complained about their overrepresentation in EMR classes in the California public schools. They contended that the use of standardized intelligence tests discriminated *linguistically,* in that many of the verbal items were derived from the experiences of native-English-speaking American children. Furthermore, the testing was unfair in that Spanish-speaking children were tested solely in English by a non-Spanish-speaking examiner. Evidence was presented showing that when a bilingual school psychologist readministered the intelligence test in Spanish, seven of the nine Mexican-American children gained an average of 15 IQ points and scored above the cutoff set for EMR placement (Tractenberg & Jacoby, 1977). In the face of this evidence, California signed a consent decree that included the following stipulations: (1) All intelligence tests administered for the purpose of placement in EMR programs should be given in the language in which the child is most fluent. (2) No child should be placed in an EMR class unless the child has been given a comprehensive evaluation by a properly certified school psychologist, inlcuding not only an intelligence test, but also data from a developmental history, and measures of educational and social attainment.

In going a step beyond the *Diana* decision, *Larry P.* v. *Riles* (1972) challenged the use of intelligence tests for the classification of black children, no matter what the form of the test. *Larry P.* v. *Riles* was a class-action suit brought by six black children in the San Francisco public schools (amended later to include all black children in California), who claimed that they were misclassified and placed in harmful EMR special classes. It was argued that the *racially* and *culturally* discriminating intelligence test was the primary basis for their misclassification and misplacement. As in *Diana,* evidence was presented showing that on retesting by a black school psychologist, all six plaintiffs scored above the 75 IQ cutoff point for EMR placement. The court, in holding that the school system's practices were in violation of the equal protection clause, concluded that "the defendants failed to sustain their burden of demonstrating that IQ tests are rationally related to the purpose of segregating students according to their ability to learn in regular classes, at least insofar as those tests are applied to Black students." A preliminary injunction was granted that enjoined the future placement of black children in EMR classes if the placement was based primarily on a score from an IQ test. In October 1979, the court permanently enjoined the defendants "from utilizing, permitting the use of, or approving the use of any standardized tests . . . for the identification of Black EMR children or their placement in EMR classes, without receiving prior approval of this court." In effect, IQ tests could no longer be used to test black children in California, and alternative assessment procedures would need to be developed. This decision was upheld by the 9th Circuit Court of Appeals and may go to the Supreme Court.

In summary, a right to education embodies five essential elements: (1) free access to publicly supported programs of education, (2) proper testing and classification of children, (3) appropriate educational programming, (4) placement in the least restrictive educational alternative, and (5) parental procedural due process. Prior to 1975, a right to education for all handicapped children had been affirmed in over 46 court cases filed throughout the United States. The culmination of this flood of judicial activity was the passage of federal legislation that required state and local governments to assume "a national minimum floor of responsibility for the education of handicapped children" (Zettel & Ballard, 1982).

Legislative Action

The Education for All Handicapped Children Act of 1975 (P.L. 94-142) is a federal mandate to state educational agencies to develop a plan to provide "a

full educational opportunity to all school age handicapped children." The preamble
of the Act reads:

> It is the purpose of the Act to assure that all handicapped children have
> available to them a free appropriate public education which emphasizes
> special education and related services designed to meet their unique needs,
> to assure that the rights of handicapped children and their parents or guard-
> ians are protected, to assist State and localities to provide for the education
> of all handicapped children, and to assess and assure the effectiveness of
> efforts to educate handicapped children. (Sec. 601)

A state's failure to provide educational programs for all handicapped children may
result in the federal government withholding all federal support for education.

P.L. 94-142 requires that certain standards be followed in the administration
of psychological tests. States are to follow these standards to ensure that testing
devices are nondiscriminatory—racially, culturally, and linguistically. Several of
the guidelines developed in the *Diana* case are incorporated into the federal law.
All assessments are to be comprehensive and multifaceted. Tests cannot be used
that are "merely designed to provide a single general intelligence quotient," nor
can one single procedure be "used as the sole criterion for determining an appropriate educational program for a child."

In order to ensure an appropriate education for every handicapped child,
P.L. 94-142 requires that an individualized educational program (IEP) be prepared.
The Act contains a definition specifying the components of an IEP:

> . . . a written statement for each handicapped child developed in any meeting
> by a representative of the local educational agency or an intermediate educa-
> tional unit who shall be qualified to provide, or supervise the provision of,
> specially designed instruction to meet the unique needs of handicapped
> children, the teacher, the parents or guardian of such child, and, whenever
> appropriate, such child, which statement shall include (A) a statement of the
> present levels of educational performance of such child, (B) a statement of
> annual goals, including short-term instructional objectives, (C) a statement of
> the specific educational services to be provided to such child, and the extent
> to which such child will be able to participate in regular educational pro-
> grams, (D) the projected date for initiation and anticipated duration of such
> services, and (E) appropriate objective criteria and evaluation procedures
> and schedules for determining, on at least an annual basis, whether instruc-
> tional objectives are being achieved. (Sec. 602)

The IEP must also include those related services that will assist the child in benefiting from educational programs.

Placement of the handicapped child in the least restrictive educational alternative is also mandated. States must establish "procedures to assure that to the
maximum extent appropriate, handicapped children, including children in public
or private institutions or other care facilities, are educated with children who are
not handicapped, and that special classes, separate schooling, or other removal of
handicapped children from their regular educational environment occurs only when

the nature or severity of the handicap is such that education in regular classes with the use of supplementary aids and services cannot be achieved satisfactorily." (Sec. 612)

P.L. 94-142 defines the due process to which parents of handicapped children are entitled. It is required that parents (1) receive written notification before the evaluation, classification, or placement of their child; (2) have a right to an impartial hearing to challenge administrative decisions; (3) have access to all relevant records; and (4) obtain an independent evaluation of their child, if necessary.

The Rehabilitation Act of 1973 (P.L. 93-112) was an earlier piece of federal legislation that forbade programs receiving federal funds to discriminate against handicapped persons. P.L. 93-112 has been referred to as the "civil rights act for handicapped persons." Section 504 of the Act reads:

> No otherwise handicapped individual in the United States . . . shall, solely by reasons of his handicap, be excluded from participation in, be denied the benefits of, or be subjected to discrimination under any program or activity receiving Federal financial assistance. (Sec. 504)

Since public school systems receive federal funds, they cannot exclude handicapped persons. While designed primarily to address employment discrimination, this Act includes provisions consistent with P.L. 94-142 regarding the testing and placement of handicapped children and their placement in the least restrictive educational settings. Unlike P.L. 94-142, however, the Act provides no funds for implementation, but the states are required to adhere to its provisions. Unquestionably, both these landmark pieces of federal legislation brought about a revolution in educational programs for handicapped children and a significant increase in federal funds appropriated to support these programs.

Costs of Education

Some argue that the increasing costs for educating an increasing number of handicapped children in special classes provided a major impetus for the mainstreaming movement. Lilly (1979) observed: "Mainstreaming has been used as a professional excuse for cutting special education costs by reassigning children to regular classrooms without special help or supportive services." This observation is supported by some cost-comparison data indicating that the costs for educating a handicapped child in a less restrictive setting are substantially less than the costs for special class placement (Conley, 1973; Marinelli, 1975; Wiegerink & Pelosi, 1979). It is not clear what type of handicapped children are in these alternative settings and whether they are receiving needed services.

As mentioned earlier, state and local educational agencies viewed the passage of P.L. 94-142 as an opportunity to obtain federal assistance needed to alleviate the increasing demand for special-education services, particularly for those severely handicapped children who required costly private school placements.

The six social forces discussed above provided the major impetus to the mainstreaming movement. In the following sections we will discuss the impact of mainstreaming.

IMPACT OF MAINSTREAMING

School Access

P.L. 94-142 was implemented during the 1976-77 school year. Each state was mandated to provide by September 1, 1978, a free, appropriate public education for all handicapped children aged 6 through 17. (In 1983, 41 states had special education laws that met the federal standards.) First priority was to be given to providing education to handicapped children who were unserved; the second priority was to be given severely handicapped children who were inadequately served. Child-find procedures were instituted to locate handicapped children needing special-education services. Preschool programs for handicapped children aged 3 to 5, as well as programs for children 18 to 21 years old were to be made available by September 1, 1980 (unless such provisions were inconsistent with state law). Prior to this date, the legislation provided Pre-School Incentive Grants ($300.00 per pupil) to local school districts to assist them in developing preschool programs for handicapped children.

State education agencies reported serving 4,189,478 handicapped children (between 3 and 21 years of age) under P.L. 94-142 and P.L. 89-313 during the 1980-81 school year (U.S. Department of Education, 1982). (P.L. 89-313 provides federal funds for the education of mentally retarded persons in public institutions.) Since 1976, an additional 480,890 handicapped children have been served; this figure represents a 13 percent increase over a five-year period. In 1976-77 approximately 900,000 mentally retarded children were served; in 1980-81 the number dropped to 844,180, or 20 percent of the total handicapped population. This represents a substantial decrease in the percentage of children classified as mentally retarded. Significant increases in educational services occurred for preschoolers (3 to 5 years of age) and for students aged 18 through 21. Given that there are an estimated 5.8 million handicapped children between 3 and 21, many mentally retarded children still remain unserved or underserved (General Accounting Office, 1981a).

Some states have failed to comply with the federal mandate, and this failure has limited many handicapped children's access to educational programs (*Mills* v. *Board of Education of the District of Columbia*, 1980; *Mattie T.* v. *Holladay*, 1979; *Jose P.* v. *Ambach*, 1979; *New Mexico Association for Retarded Citizens* v. *State of New Mexico*, 1980). In *Mills*, the court held the school district in contempt of court for its failure to implement its right-to-education decision. It was reported that children waited 1 to 2 years to be evaluated. There were instances of overcrowded and understaffed classes, lack of teaching materials, and a number of children who received either no education or less than 1 hour of education a day.

The federal courts have ruled in the *Mattie T.* and *New Mexico* cases that the states are required to provide all handicapped children educational services under Section 504 of the 1973 Rehabilitation Act, despite the state's refusal to comply with P.L. 94-142. However, an appellate court recently reversed the decision of the New Mexico lower court, on the grounds that Section 504 prohibits discrimination but does not mandate affirmative relief upon the receipt of federal financial assistance. The case was remanded to the lower court for a determination whether the state, in fact, discriminated against handicapped children. This litigation is now moot since the New Mexico state legislature has voted to bring the state in compliance with P.L. 94-142.

Classification

P.L. 94-142 requires that multiple, nondiscriminatory assessment criteria be used before a determination is made that a child be classified as mentally retarded. Forty states have changed their laws and/or regulations to meet the requirements of P.L. 94-142 (U.S. Department of Education, 1980). Adherence to federal law and court decisions has resulted in the "declassification" of thousands of children enrolled in EMR classes and their assignment to regular classes. In a number of cases, EMR children have been "reclassified" as learning-disabled to avoid allegations of discriminatory practices (Tucker, 1980; Polloway & Smith, 1983). Whether or not declassified and reclassified EMR children are receiving appropriate educational programs is open to question (Gottlieb, Gottlieb, Schmelkin & Curci, in press).

Although some states have adopted alternative educational evaluation procedures (e.g., Louisiana has adopted SOMPA) and others are giving increased emphasis to measures of adaptive behavior (Patrick & Reschly, 1982), reports indicate that the IQ test continues to be used as the predominant instrument in the initial classification of children as mentally retarded (Huberty, Koller, & Ten Brink, 1980). Consequently, a large number of children from different racial and ethnic backgrounds still continue to be misclassified and placed in segregated special classes. Recent studies indicate that black children in elementary and secondary schools continue to be placed in EMR programs at more than three times the rate of white children (Edelman, 1980; Education Advocates Coalition, 1980).

Contrary to the *Larry P.* case, the continued use of IQ tests to assess minority-group children was upheld in a recent federal court decision. In *Parents in Action on Special Education (PASE)* v. *Hannon* (1980) the court ruled that standardized intelligence (IQ) tests are *not* culturally unfair when used in conjunction with other "substantive criterion" in the decision to place black children in EMR classes. It remains to be seen whether the *Larry P.* and *PASE* decisions, which require multiple measures of a child's ability, will have a significant impact on the assessment and placement of minority-group children in special classes.

Appropriate Education

Individualized educational plan (IEP). In order to ensure that all handicapped children receive an appropriate education, P.L. 94-142 requires the development of an IEP that specifies short-term objectives and long-term goals of a child's instructional program. Also, the IEP should indicate any related services (e.g., speech correction, transportation) that the child needs. Evaluation studies on the implementation of this requirement present a mixed picture. In its first report to the Congress, the then Bureau of the Education of the Handicapped (U.S. Department of Education, 1979) found wide variations in the preparation of IEPs. In some cases, the IEPs were incomplete, the objectives and goals were not clearly stated, and related services were not included. However, in a second report (Research Triangle Institute, 1980), considerable improvement was noted in the preparation of IEPs. Over 90 percent of the IEPs for public school children included mandated information such as present levels of education performance, annual goals, and short-term objectives. The need for improvement was noted in the following areas: (1) information as to the extent of participation in regular education programs; (2) proposed evaluation criteria for determining the extent to which short-term objectives are being achieved; and (3) specification of related services to be provided, particularly physical education and vocational education services. In contrast, a report by the General Accounting Office (1981a) found that 84 percent of the IEPs reviewed lacked one or more of the required items of information. Parents or other required participants had not attended IEP conferences, and needed services were not indicated when they were not available. A lack of parent participation in the development of their child's IEP was also reported in studies conducted by the National Committee for Citizens in Education (1979) and the Stanford Research Institute International (1980a). Simons and Dwyer (1978) reported that school personnel view the IEP as a monitoring tool and a clerical task unrelated to instruction. Consequently, the IEP tends not to be absorbed into the teaching process.

Some positive outcomes have emerged from the implementation of the IEP requirement. Despite the amount of time involved in the preparation of the IEP, regular and special educators report that they have learned more about the educational needs of handicapped children and have appreciated the opportunity to participate with other professionals in educational planning (Education Turnkey Systems, 1978; Simons & Dwyer, 1978). Teacher-parent communication has increased as more parents are becoming involved in the planning of their child's program, according to a study by S. Goldstein, Strickland, Turnbull, and Curry (1980). However, this study too found that parent participation in the actual decision making is very limited. Turnbull and Turnbull (1982) have challenged an assumption underlying P.L. 94-142 that all parents want to be involved as decision makers in the development of their child's IEP. They argue that most parents perceive the special educator not as an enemy but as an ally and wish to defer to the professional educator decisions pertaining to their child's educational program. The Turnbulls recommend the following:

> Rather than mandating that all parents be equal participants with the school personnel to make decisions jointly, public policy should tolerate a range of parent involvement choices and options, matched to the needs and interest of the parents. (p. 120)

Related services. The Educational Advocates Coalition (1980) report confirms the Research Triangle Institute (1980) finding that handicapped children are being denied needed related services (e.g., physical therapy, occupational therapy, health resources, and transportation). There has been a controversy over the scope of services Congress intended the school to provide under P.L. 94-142. Among related services that have been frequently disputed are catheterization and psychotherapy. School districts argue that these are *medical services* that do not come under the rubric of special-education services. However, a number of recent court decisions have ruled that catheterization (*Tatro* v. *State of Texas,* 1980; *Tokarcik* v. *Forest Hills School District,* 1981) and psychotherapy (*In re "A" Family,* 1979; *Gary B.* v. *Cronin,* 1980; *Papacoda* v. *State of Connecticut,* 1981) are related services that must be provided by the schools to ensure to handicapped children the benefit of an education. (The *Tatro* case has been appealed to the Supreme Court.) Nevertheless, the controversy continues over what related services are obligatory for school districts to provide. Consequently, service gaps exist in many handicapped children's IEPs, owing to the vague and open-ended definition of *related services,* the pressures for cost containment, the lack of trained staff, and the lack of coordination and communication among social service agencies (Thomas & Reese, 1982).

Extended school year. Parents and special educators have argued that for some handicapped children (usually the more severely impaired), an appropriate education requires that they receive educational services beyond the normal 180-day school year. Eligibility for an extended school year would be based on evidence showing that a severely handicapped child had a regression/recoupment problem. That is, evidence must show that over the summer months the child would undergo regression in skill acquisition (i.e., self-help skills) significant enough to necessitate the recoupment of lost skills before new skills can be attained. *Scanlon* v. *Battle* (1981) upheld the landmark *Armstrong* v. *Kline* (1980) decision on the basis of P.L. 94-142, noting that the inflexibility of the 180-day rule "imposes with rigid certainty a program restriction which may be wholly inappropriate to the child's educational objectives." A number of recent rulings have followed the Armstrong decision (*Georgia Association for Retarded Citizens* v. *McDaniel,* 1980; *In re Anderson,* 1980; *Fetzer* v. *Mandau Public School District,* 1980; *Crawford* v. *Pittman,* 1983). (The Georgia case was recently upheld by the 11th Circuit Court of Appeals.) Larsen, Goodman, and Glean (1981) reported that during the summer of 1980, 2,089 handicapped children in Pennsylvania were found eligible for extended school-year programs, with a statewide cost of $2.6 million. Nationwide, however, many handicapped children who could benefit from an extended school year are not provided this service (Education Advocates Coalition, 1980). Research is needed to determine the efficacy of extended school year programs.

Education in institutions. One recurring problem is the provision of a free appropriate public education for mentally retarded children residing in state institutions. Typically, the local educational agency where the parents reside refuses to pay for educational services, arguing that the child is not served in its district; the local educational agency in which the institution is located refuses to pay on the grounds that the child's parents have legal residence outside of its school district. In *Association of Retarded Citizens in Colorado* v. *Frazier* (1981), a federal district court ruled that the receipt of federal special-education funds under P.L. 94-142 required that the *state educational agency* provide a free appropriate public education to all handicapped children, including those children in state institutions. Also, at issue in institutional placements is the distinction between the child's educational and noneducational needs and whose responsibility it is to pay for these services (*North* v. *District of Columbia Board of Ed.*, 1978; *Guempel* v. *State*, 1980; *Kruelle* v. *New Castle County School District*, 1981).

Least Restrictive Alternative

The U.S. Department of Education (1982) reported that in the 1979-80 school year, 68 percent of the handicapped children in public schools were educated in regular classroom settings; 25 percent were educated in separate classes within regular school buildings. Between 1976 and 1980 the porportion of mentally retarded children in regular classes declined from approximately 37 percent to 34 percent, while placements in special classes increased from approximately 51 percent to 58 percent. The decrease in regular class placements can be attributed to an increased number of mildly retarded children being fully integrated into regular classes and no longer being counted among children receiving special-education services. According to MacMillan and Borthwick (1980), fewer EMR children are being placed in regular classes because this population is "a more patently disabled group" than earlier groups of EMR students. The increase in special classes can be attributed to the increasing number of severely and profoundly retarded children receiving services in the special classes in regular schools.

Due Process

One of the major strengths of P.L. 94-142 is the due-process framework it established to protect the educational rights of handicapped children and their families. All the states have made efforts to modify their statutes and regulations to meet the due-process requirement (U.S. Department of Education, 1980). The result has been greater involvement by parents in conferences to discuss diagnostic findings, program planning, and pupil placement. The following issues have been identified as the focus of due-process hearings: (1) private school versus public school placements; (2) appropriateness of evaluation and eligibility for special education; (3) appropriateness of programs and services; (4) the length of the school day and/or year (especially for severely handicapped children); and (5) transportation arrangements (National Association of State Directors of Special Education, 1980; Stanford Research Institute, 1980b; Kuriloff, Kirp, & Buss, 1979).

A number of reports have shown that parents of higher socioeconomic status benefit more from the availability of due-process procedures than do parents of low socioeconomic status (Kuriloff, et al., 1979; Weatherly & Lipsky, 1977; Budoff & Orenstein, 1981; Stanford Research Institute International, 1980b). School systems are more likely to respond to the appeals of parents of higher socioeconomic status and to consent to their demands for private school placement. Parents of lower socioeconomic status are often unaware of their due-process rights (McClung, 1975). They are uninformed about alternative placements and the type of instruction their child needs (Goldstein, Strickland, Turnbull, & Curry, 1980). Given these circumstances, parents are often intimidated by school personnel and give their signatures willingly to documents that indicate little understanding of the recommendations for their child (Simons & Dwyer, 1978). Commenting on the differential impact that the due-process procedure has on parents, Sabatino (1981) states:

> In response to the law, parents who are well informed and who have always engaged in the education of their handicapped child are now in a team relationship with special educators. But parents from rural, poverty-stricken areas, parents with little education and often beset by family breakdowns, suffer more confusion than anything from the call to participate. (p. 18)

Parents or school personnel request a formal, impartial due-process hearing when they are unable to resolve their differences through negotiation. Typically, the school district obtains the services of a hearing officer, who cannot be an employee of the local or state educational agency. In *East Brunswick Board of Education* v. *New Jersey State Board of Education* (1982), a district court held that the state's due-process hearing regulations violated the "impartiality" requirement under P.L. 94-142. In this case a hearing officer was employed by the state education agency. (Due process hearings are now heard by administrative law judges in New Jersey.)

Greater efforts by both parties to reach an agreement at the negotiation stage can prevent the development of an adversarial relationship, which often occurs at the hearing stage. Moreover, the considerable costs, both psychic and economic, would be spared for all the parties involved. Kirp and Jensen, 1983 observe that "Due process hearings cannot assure good education or even consistent outcomes; instead, they degenerate into law-ridden affairs that often upset the participants, and thanks to the federal bureaucrats' interpretation of the law, undermine the possibility of fruitful discussion" (p. 89). Several states (e.g., Massachusetts, Pennsylvania, New Jersey and Connecticut) have prescribed a mediation process to resolve differences between local education agencies and parents.

MAINSTREAMING BACKLASH

Legal Retrenchment

As noted earlier, there is no doubt that P.L. 94-142 and Section 504 of the Rehabilitation Act of 1973 have triggered a revolutionary change in the delivery of special-education services for mentally retarded children. But just as with the deinstitutionalization movement, some are beginning to question and resist educational reforms that would provide a free, publicly supported education for *all* retarded children (Kauffman & Krause, 1981). The issue has again risen, over the nature and meaning of *education,* and over which children are entitled to this service at public expense. For those for whom there is such an entitlement, a related issue focuses on the question, How much education should a retarded person receive?

Right-to-education litigation.   In an early right-to-education case, *Cuyahoga County Association for Retarded Children and Adults* v. *Essex* (1976), a federal court in Ohio seriously questioned the *right* of mentally retarded children to receive services within the public school system. The court held that the classification system by which some retarded children were excluded from the public schools was constitutionally permissable. The statutory basis for disqualification of a particular retarded child was the determination that the child was "incapable of profiting substantially from further education." The court reasoned that only children who can derive an actual benefit from the education system need be provided instruction. This court's view that some mentally retarded children are not entitled to an education was a disparate decision among a number of earlier decisions upholding the right of all children to a free, publicly supported education. Recently, however, in two consolidated cases, *Levine* v. *State Department of Institutions and Agencies* (1980) and *Guempel* v. *State* (1980), the New Jersey Supreme Court issued an opinion that revived the view that some mentally retarded children may not be judged eligible for public education. The court ruled that under the state's constitution, a free, publicly supported education need *not* be provided to institutionalized profoundly retarded children. Since profoundly retarded children cannot "function politically, economically, or socially in a democratic society . . . the constitutional mandate for a free public education simply does not apply to these unfortunate children." The court explained that this "subtrainable" group are not capable either of receiving or of benefitting from any additional instruction or education as such. Consequently, the residential care that they require for their day-to-day well being, including the minimal incidental instruction involved, does not qualify as "education" within the meaning of the education clause of the New Jersey Constitution.

Contrary to opinion in a number of right-to-education cases, the court concluded "there is a category of mentally disabled children so severely impaired as to be unable to absorb or benefit from education." Similar decisions in the future may undercut the right of more severely retarded children to have access to free, publicly supported educational programs, just as attempts have been made to deny more severely retarded persons a right to habilitation.

In *Board of Education of Hendrick Hudson Central School District* v. *Rowley* (1982), the Supreme Court for the first time ruled on the Congressional intent of P.L. 94-142. The case involved a bright 7-year-old deaf girl whose parents sued the local school district for its refusal to provide their child an appropriate education, which, they argued, required the services of a sign-language interpreter. In reversing the decisions of two lower courts, the Supreme Court held that an appropriate education under P.L. 94-142 did not require the school district, given the facts of the case, to provide Amy Rowley with an interpreter. Justice Rehnquist concluded that the requirement of a free, appropriate education "is satisfied when the State provides personalized instruction with sufficient supportive services to permit the handicapped child to benefit educationally from that instruction." Since the educational benefit indicated for the deaf child was progress from grade to grade (which was being accomplished), those services (e.g., tutoring, use of a FM hearing aid) provided by the school district were judged *sufficient* to meet this goal. Justice Rehnquist rejected those interpretations of *appropriate education* that would require schools to provide handicapped children educational services that would enable them to achieve their full potential or their "full potential commensurate with the opportunity provided other children." Instead, an appropriate education under P.L. 94-142 requires that handicapped children receive some benefit from instruction, to enable them to develop some potential with the least amount of related services—that is, sufficient related services. The Supreme Court decision gives the professional educator considerable discretion in determining what *some benefit* means and what related services are "sufficient" in the development of a handicapped child's IEP. The danger is that, given economic constraints, what is judged as beneficial and sufficient may in fact constitute an inappropriate education, particularly for those severely handicapped children whose programs are more costly (Anthony, 1982).

The reasoning of the court in *Rowley* could lead to other adverse results for handicapped children. For example, in a number of recent cases the courts have held that school districts need not provide private school placements for severely handicapped children (*Harrell* v. *Wilson County Schools*, 1982; *Lang* v. *Braintree*, 1982). Where the local public schools are providing an equally "adequate" or "appropriate" program, they are not obligated to provide a private school placement that may offer the "best possible" or "most appropriate" program. On the other hand, when tied to the mainstreaming requirements of the Education for All Handicapped Children Act, the results may be beneficial to a handicapped child. Thus, in *Springdale School District* v. *Grace* (1981) a federal court of appeals upheld the contention of the parents, the Arkansas Department of Education, and the trial court that an 11-year-old girl who was profoundly and prelingually deaf should be educated within her local school district. The court found that she would receive an appropriate education within the local school district. The local school district had argued that the child should be sent to the distant Arkansas residential school for the deaf, since it would provide the best education for her. The court concluded that when balanced with mainstreaming requirements, the law requires the provision of an "appropriate" and not the "best" possible education.

Future litigation is likely to continue to address the degree of appropriateness of educational programs pupil placements, and the financing of special services.

Economic Realities

Costs are the major barrier to providing all handicapped children access to schooling (Stark, 1983). A Rand Corporation study (Kakalik, Furry, Thomas, & Carney, 1982) found that a handicapped child's education costs on the average 1.98 times that of a nonhandicapped child's education at the elementary level, and 2.48 times more at the secondary level. The average educational costs at that time for an educable child, a trainable child, and a severely retarded child were $3,795, $5,519, and $5,926 per year, respectively. (These figures are considerably higher today.) In addition, special class placements are more costly than placements in less restrictive alternatives (e.g., regular classes, resource rooms).

Under P.L. 94-142, the federal government is to assist local school districts to pay the excess costs for a handicapped child's special education. Over a 5-year period, for each handicapped child the federal government was to reimburse local districts an increasing percentage of the national average expenditure per pupil—5 percent (fiscal year 1977-78), 10 percent (fiscal 1978-79), 20 percent (fiscal 1979-80), 30 percent (fiscal 1980-81), and 40 percent (fiscal 1981-82). From fiscal 1981-82 on, the federal contribution would remain at 40 percent. However, during the 1979-80 fiscal year the federal government authorized payment of only 12 percent of the costs. The economic policies of the Reagan administration have resulted in a reduction to 10 percent of costs in the 1981-82 fiscal year. Although educational funds for handicapped children have been exempted from the block-grant scheme, cuts as great as 25 percent have been projected in the federal special-education budget.

While financial assistance to the states and local school districts is being reduced, regulations and court decisions requiring due process hearings, payment of related services, summer schooling, and the placement of severely handicapped children in private schools have resulted in the escalation of special-education costs (Kakalik et al., 1982). Furthermore, these services are being provided for a larger number of children over a longer school career; an increasing number of states are providing special education from birth to 21 years of age. The failure of the federal government to allocate the amount of money promised has placed a heavy fiscal burden on state and local budgets, particularly school districts in poor urban and rural areas (Pittenger & Kuriloff, 1982). According to Breslin (1980):

> Special education, combined with inflation, taxpayer reluctance to increase education taxes (local education taxes are among the few left that are controlled by voters), and a steady rise in the number of disabled children seeking services, have left local school districts short of money and, according to educators, made compliance almost impossible. (p. 353)

In many local districts, monies are being diverted from other parts of the budget to pay for special-education services. Such actions are bringing loud protests from school administrators, school boards, and parents of nonhandicapped children who are concerned about the poor quality of public education as evidenced by declines in SAT scores and other measures of school achievement (Budoff, 1975). On the other hand, limited financial resources present the danger that handicapped children in regular classes will not be identified or, if identified, that they will remain on waiting lists in order to relieve fiscal pressures (Cole & Dunn, 1977; Weatherly & Lipsky, 1977; Rebell, 1981). As noted earlier, these economic realities make it unlikely that many handicapped children in regular and special classes will get the needed services to enable them to benefit from schooling (Thomas & Reese, 1982; Wright, Cooperstein, Renneker, & Padilla, 1982). A further consequence of limited funds will be for school districts to establish priorities regarding which handicapped children will be served—the mentally retarded, the emotionally disturbed, or the learning-disabled. Equity and cost-benefit arguments will be used to determine which children will be served, with decisions based upon the severity of their handicapping condition (Wright, Padilla, & Cooperstein, 1981). These unintended consequences would violate the spirit of P.L. 94-142, which was enacted to provide *all* handicapped children an appropriate education.

In an effort to reduce the skyrocketing costs of special education and return more authority to the states in the operation of their schools, the Reagan administration has proposed to deregulate a number of the provisions under P.L. 94-142. On August 4, 1982, the administration proposed the following major modifications:

1. Eliminate the requirement that parents give written consent prior to an evaluation to determine if their child needs special education.
2. Eliminate the requirement that a multidisciplinary approach be used in evaluating all handicapped children, and that multifaceted evaluations be conducted.
3. Eliminate the requirement that parents participate in the actual writing of their child's IEP.
4. Eliminate the requirement for reevaluations of students at least every three years.
5. Allow schools to limit the kind or amount of related services. Provisions for school health review, social work services, and parent counseling and training would be deleted from the existing regulations. Most medical services would not have to be provided.
6. Allow school officials to determine how disruptive it would be to place a handicapped child in a regular educational setting and permit them to refuse to make such a placement if it would disrupt other students.

The proposed regulations caused a "firestorm of protest" from parents and advocacy groups throughout the country as well as from the Congress. On September 29, 1982, the administration withdrew its proposals and has recently decided to keep the 1975 law intact, at least for now. Whereas the administration's new-federalism initiatives may lead to further efforts to give the states and local school districts more flexibility in the formulation of public policy for educating handicapped children, recent recommendations from a report prepared by the

National Commission on Excellence in Education (1983) recognized the primary responsibility of the federal government to fund and support efforts to achieve equal educational opportunity for handicapped children.

Professional and Public Opinion

Edward Martin, former Assistant Secretary of Special Education and Rehabilitation Services, predicted that the implementation of P.L. 94-142 would become problematic. The law, he said, "hopes to achieve a higher level of responsiveness to parents and handicapped children than the system has ever provided to anyone." (Martin, 1979, p. 1)

School districts are experiencing negative reactions from several groups as they attempt to mainstream handicapped children (Orelove, 1978). As mentioned above, parents of the nonhandicapped are concerned that both the design and the expense of programs for the handicapped will further diminish the quality of instruction for their children (Budoff, 1975; Cole & Dunn, 1977; Simons & Dwyer, 1978). Many parents perceive mainstreaming as a further threat to their children and give this as another reason to seek private schooling. In short, it is argued that the growth in programs for handicapped children has resulted in greater inequality of educational opportunity for other children and has contributed to "the rising tide of mediocrity" in the public schools (National Commission on Excellence in Education, 1983). This claim is supported in the rhetoric of Secretary of Education Terrell Bell, who in his public statements has called for a halt to the "leveling" that characterized public education in the 1960s and 1970s—that is, educational policy designed to bring up academically those children at the bottom (i.e., the disadvantaged, the bilingual, and the handicapped) at the cost of bringing down academically those children who are average and above average children. Today, there is increasing public support to do more for the top quartile of students in our public schools, who, it is argued, have been neglected. Investments in human capital are being directed to the average and above-average student in the interest of national defense and economic competition. Thus, we see education budgets increasing allocations for the development of mathematics and science programs, computer literacy, and leadership training. The emphasis is on efficiency, merit, and productivity; there is less concern about equality, need, and the learning potential of all children.

These developments present an interesting paradox. Whereas there is a trend to impose a limitation on the educational benefits and services for handicapped children, school programs for the nonhandicapped are moving toward expanding and maximizing educational opportunities. A number of states are reconsidering *minimum* competency testing requirements and recommending educational programs designed to *maximize* educational outcomes. This sudden shift in national priorities and values increases the vulnerability of handicapped children by decreasing the likelihood that they will receive appropriate educational programs.

Parents of handicapped children also fear that mainstreaming will result in their children not receiving the type of program they require (U.S. Department of

Education, 1979; Gliedman & Roth, 1980). The limited number of trained personnel, the unavailability of related services, and the lack of acceptance of their children justify these parental concerns (Orelove, 1978). Further justification for these parental concerns can be found in several recent professional reports. In a recent review of the research on mainstreaming, Gottlieb (1981) concluded:

> There is little evidence that children's social adjustment is superior in mainstreamed settings, or that children achieve more in mainstreamed classes. EMR children continue to be socially rejected by their peers, they continue to be educated in socially segregated classrooms, at least in those school systems having large numbers of minority children, and the daily quality of instruction in regular classrooms does not appear radically different from the quality of instruction offered in self-contained classes. (p. 16)

Gottlieb predicted little improvement in the quality of education programs for mildly retarded students as long as educators focus on placement issues rather than instructional issues. Similar results and conclusions were reported in a review of the literature conducted by Madden and Slavin (1982) and Leinhardt and Palley (1982). John Goodlad (1983) recently published a report that raises serious questions regarding the mainstreaming of mildly retarded children into regular classrooms. In a study of 1,000 elementary and secondary classrooms throughout the United States, they reported the following major findings:

1. The predominant mode of teaching was total, large-group instruction; individualized instruction and small-group instruction were rarely observed.
2. Teacher behavior constituted primarily of giving instruction and monitoring seatwork; teachers asked mostly closed factual questions and did little to encourage concept formation and problem solving.
3. Teachers provided little corrective feedback and offered no guidance in their interactions with students.
4. The classroom environments were described as affectless.

Goodlad found regular classroom settings that can be described as restrictive, both academically and socially, for average learners. One has to wonder about the appropriateness of placing children with learning and behavior problems in such environments.

Negative reactions are expressed by teachers as well as parents. Regular classroom teachers may be unwilling to teach handicapped children or, if willing, they feel unprepared to do so without in-service training and a reduction in class size (Mosher, Hastings, & Wagoner, 1979; Flynn, Gacka, & Sundea, 1978; Rauth, 1981). On the other hand, many special-class teachers are reluctant to recommend that a handicapped child be mainstreamed into a setting that will provide an inappropriate program. Special educators fear a diminished need for their services if too many of their children are mainstreamed. School personnel are increasingly being caught in the position of weighing job security against their advocacy for a handicapped child (Frith, 1981; Craig, 1981; *Forrest* v. *Ambach,* 1982).

A major complaint by both regular and special-education teachers is the increased workload required to meet the requirements of P.L. 94-142 (U.S. Department of Education, 1979; Mosher et al, 1979; Simons & Dwyer, 1978; Price & Goodman, 1980). It is argued that the law is too prescriptive. The preparation of IEPs and the participation in professional and parent meetings reduce the amount of instructional time for children. Some teachers perceive the IEP as a binding contract and fear that they will be held accountable for not obtaining stated objectives (Simons & Dwyer, 1978; Mosher et al, 1979). Teachers' unions view these demands and pressures as contributing to increased burnout among their members and to the high rate of teacher turnover in recent years.

To recapitulate, some unintended consequences have resulted from the implementation of mainstreaming policies. Conservative legal and economic forces may restrict or even eliminate educational services for many retarded children. Parental concerns about the potential negative outcome of placing retarded children in regular classes may further impede the mainstreaming movement.

SUMMARY

The deinstitutionalization and mainstreaming movements paralleled each other during the 1970s. While each has its history, its own supports and rationales, and its own landmark legislation and litigation, the two movements are to a great extent interdependent.

For deinstitutionalization and mainstreaming, the same principles serve as underpinnings. Normalization, the developmental model, and the least restrictive alternative are all principles that have provided a common impetus to both movements. Mainstreaming without deinstitutionalization would be an empty concept, since many mentally retarded people would be deprived of those social and educational benefits that would come from integrated housing. Deinstitutionalization without mainstreaming and appropriate special-education services would likewise be nothing more than an irresponsible dumping of mentally retarded people into the community.

The availability of special-education services for all mentally retarded children is a necessary prerequisite to preventing institutionalization and to continuing the deinstitutionalization of mentally retarded persons. One of the basic causes of institutionalization is an inability to cope with a child in the home or in the community. Without appropriate educational developmental services, the burden on the family can become intolerable. With the availability of free, publicly supported school programs, parents now expect some respite from the full-time burden of care. The child will be in school during the school term and, in some cases, beyond the school term. This will enable the child to receive needed services to further his development and independence and, thus, will improve the chances for community living. In the future, the demand for educational resources will increase as more retarded persons live in the community. Therefore, the necessity for the advancement of public policy in both areas, mainstreaming and deinstitutionalization, is essential to the long-term welfare of mentally retarded persons.

CHAPTER FOUR
FAMILIES

Despite changes in the family's structure and function, it remains a vital social institution and essential mediator between the child and society. Sarason and Doris (1979) remind us that when we talk about a retarded child, we must never forget that the child is in a particular family in a particular society at a particular time. It is estimated that one in ten Americans has direct contact with mental retardation within his immediate family (National Association for Retarded Citizens, 1976). Mental retardation strikes all types of families—black and white, rich as well as poor.

Without a consideration of the question, What's happening to the American family? one cannot begin to understand the difficulties that families with a retarded child encounter (Levitan & Belous, 1981). While a thorough analysis of the status of American families is beyond the scope of this chapter, several observations are worth noting. Modern living places a number of stresses on family life that threaten its resiliency. Cyclic inflation, unemployment and job insecurity, changing gender roles, alternative lifestyles, and the negative influences of television, peer groups, and schools are some of the factors contributing to family stress. As a consequence, national concern has focused on the increase in family dysfunction, a condition that is manifested in high rates of divorce, domestic violence, drug use, teenage pregnancy, adolescent suicides, incest, runaway children, and juvenile delinquency. Unable to cope with the demands of work and family life, many families are seeking assistance in the rearing of their children. According to Keniston (1977), the idea of the American family as being "self-sufficient" and "independent" is fast becoming a myth. Yet the majority of families are left to going it alone in our "unresponsive society" (Kamerman, 1980).

Families with mentally retarded children are particularly vulnerable to the stresses of daily living, and they run a higher risk of family dysfunction (Gath, 1977; Friedrich & Friedrich, 1981). In addition to the general family stresses mentioned above, there are specific stresses associated with having a retarded child. These stresses include the stigma of negative community attitudes, the frustration in obtaining needed services, and the struggle to cope with the excessive human and financial demands that result from their child's disability (Turnbull & Turnbull, 1979; Featherstone, 1980). For these families there is a critical need for understanding and assistance beyond that of ordinary families. This need was recognized in the final report of the White House Conference on Families (1980), which highly recommended that social policies be developed to provide supportive services for families with disabled persons. The failure to provide these needed services may lead many families to experience not only stress but also a family crisis. In the following sections, the potential crisis periods for families with mentally retarded children will be described. A crisis may occur at the time of diagnosis, during the period when the family provides home care, or when the family decide to have their child cared for outside the home.

DIAGNOSIS

In American society, great expectation accompanies the birth of a child. We expect the infant to be born healthy, attractive, and bright. In short, we expect to have the perfect "Gerber baby" or, in the current vernacular, a "superbaby" ("Bringing Up Superbaby," 1983). Prior to birth, parents plan how they will rear the child, where the child will go to school, and even what career they would like the child to pursue after growing up. Moreover, parents and our society "hurry children" through these development stages (Elkind, 1981). These expectations and aspirations are shattered when the family learns that their child is severely mentally retarded. Farber (1979) contends that the family's disappointment and sense of failure is magnified by "exaggerated expectations" in American life.

> In refusing to consider disappointment and tragedy as normal modes of existence (as concomitants of achievement) we magnify frustration and suffering for families with disabled children. We blame them for failing to achieve the Modern Dream. (p. 36)

Nevertheless, few would disagree that the birth of a severely retarded child is a tragic event whose consequences can be catastrophic for a family. While no two families react to the birth of a retarded child in the same manner, reactions tend to be understandably disheartening and potentially destructive to family cohesion.

Prenatal Period

In the past, the diagnosis of severe forms of mental retardation occurred at birth or shortly thereafter. Recent advances in medical technology (e.g., amniocentesis, fetoscopy) now make possible the prenatal diagnosis of a defective fetus. (More about this technology will be presented in Chapter 6.) Amniocentesis is usually performed in those pregnancies in which there is a risk of having a retarded child. In those cases where there are positive signs of a defective fetus, parents must confront the diagnosis of mental retardation at an earlier point in time. Parents must make the difficult and agonizing decision either to continue the pregnancy (and care for the infant) or to elect a therapeutic abortion of the unwanted pregnancy. For a given family, a number of factors (e.g., economics, religion) will be weighed in reaching a decision. In some families increased family stress and conflict will result from a lack of unanimity in the decision. Ultimately, no matter what decision is made, adverse effects are likely to occur even among the strongest of families.

The parents' decision to abort a defective fetus is influenced by the values expressed by the larger society. The 1973 Supreme Court decision (*Roe* v. *Wade*) legalizing abortions has made it easier to abort an unwanted pregnancy. A number of public opinion polls have showed high levels of support for legalized abortion, particularly in these cases where there is a serious fetal defect (Jaffe, Lindheim, & Lee, 1981). In a recent survey by Yankelovich, Skelly, and Wright (1981), 87 percent of those polled agreed that a woman should be permitted to obtain a legal abortion if there is evidence of a severe genetic defect. It is estimated that 1500, or one-tenth of one percent, of all abortions in the United States in 1982 were attributed to the prenatal diagnosis of a defective fetus. Allen and Allen (1979) suggest that the values expressed by society can pressure ambivalent parents to consent to the abortion of a defective fetus. Obtaining an abortion is considered the "right" thing to do, not only because it avoids a life of suffering for the child and family, but also because it saves society the high cost of care for a mentally retarded person. In short, the parents are made to feel that they have a moral obligation to abort their defective fetus (Fletcher, 1975). Some fear that the abortion of a defective fetus may be accepted as a cure for mental retardation.

A case reported in the *New England Journal of Medicine* has raised a number of legal and moral questions regarding the abortion of defective fetuses (Kerenyi & Chitkara, 1981). Parents elected to abort a fraternal twin diagnosed as having Down syndrome, while allowing the normal fetus to survive. This was made possible by a high-risk procedure of puncturing the heart of the Down syndrome fetus at 20 weeks' gestation. The parents did not want a retarded child, because of "the burden of caring for an abnormal child for the rest of her life," and because of the "unhealthy experience" the retarded child would present to their normal child. This case arises at a time when there is a wave of antiabortion sentiment in the United States. Pro-life advocates are arguing that life begins at conception and that the fetus's right to life overrides the woman's right to control of her body. Federal legislation (Senate Bill 158) has been proposed that would reverse the 1973 Supreme Court decision by placing restrictions on the circumstances under which an abortion could be legally performed. On June 28, 1983, the Senate decisively rejected a proposed constitutional amendment that would have given states and Congress the right to restrict abortion. However, attempts such as this, which will undoubtedly be made again in the future, raise a number of important questions. Could abortions continue to be performed where there was evidence of fetal defects? Would this apply to all types of fetal defects? Who would decide those cases in which a defective fetus has a right to live? What criteria would be used in making these decisions? If laws are enacted that prohibit abortions even in cases of severe mental retardation, what purpose would prenatal diagnosis serve? What would be the consequences of denying the biological mother the choice of aborting an unwanted retarded child? What obligation does society have, if any, to provide assistance in the care and treatment of severely impaired newborns? The resolution to these questions will have a profound impact on parents who conceive a retarded child.

Postnatal Period

While most severely and profoundly retarded children are diagnosed early in life, children with moderate and mild retardation may not be diagnosed until they reach school age. Parents who might suspect that their child is "slow" or "developmentally delayed" are unprepared for the diagnosis of mental retardation. Oftentimes parents do not perceive their son or daughter as handicapped and consider the child a normal member of the family. This perception is confirmed by the child's normal progress in the early years of schooling. Thus, when their child is judged to be mentally retarded and assigned to a special class, parents are often confused and express anger and dismay with school officials (Marion, 1980). As mentioned earlier, school districts have been sued by militant parents from culturally diverse backgrounds who allege that discriminatory testing practices have led to the misclassification and miseducation of their children.

When informed that they have given birth to a severely retarded child, parents experience considerable distress and sorrow. Frequently, the parents' anxieties and fears are heightened by the insensitive manner in which medical personnel inform them of their child's condition. Sarason and Doris (1979) attribute this situation to the failure of the physician, the communicator of the diagnosis, to view the birth of a retarded child within a "social-interpersonal context." While physicians are able to provide clinical information about the child's conditions, many are unable by training and temperament to provide support to help the family cope with the diagnosis of mental retardation. Instead, what the physician communicates to the family is the occurrence of a tragic event. The physician's reaction can have a considerable influence on the emotional reactions of parents and on the decision they eventually make about their retarded child's future (Lavelle & Keogh, 1980; G. L. Adams, 1982).

After the initial shock and despair of having a retarded child subsides, most parents decide to take their child home. In time, they come to a realistic acceptance of their child's retardation and provide loving care (Darling, 1979). In some cases the presence of the retarded child in the home brings family members closer together and enriches the meaning of their lives (Perske, 1973; Cleveland & Miller, 1977). For other families, however, adjustments are not as easy, nor are outcomes as satisfying. The normal emotional reactions that parents have to the birth of a retarded child may become maladaptive, threatening everyday family transactions. Feelings of grief, sadness, and disappointment may progress to chronic sorrow and depression (Olshansky, 1966). Parents may regard their child's condition as "hopeless" and may do little to obtain services to enhance the child's development. Denial of the child's retardation may have similar consequences. Initial feeling of shame and embarrassment may lead to social withdrawal and isolation (Reid, 1971; Birenbaum, 1968). Withdrawal not only affects the mental health of family members, but it also deprives the retarded child of those normalizing human interactions outside the home that are critical to social development. Feelings of guilt may be manifested in compulsive self-sacrificing and overprotective behavior, thus damaging marital relationships and inhibiting the growth of the retarded child. Parental fears can lead to obsessive concern about the future. When these maladaptive reactions fail to enable the family to cope with their retarded child, a crisis may ensue. In some cases, it may become necessary to seek alternatives to home care to prevent further individual and family deterioration.

As noted above, most families eventually accept their child's condition and provide care without a breakdown. While they do experience stress, most families do not experience pathology (Wikler, 1981). Yet there is a tendency to categorize all parents of retarded children as guilt-ridden, anxious, insecure, and emotionally traumatized persons (Begab, 1963). Darling (1979) attributes this perception to a psychoanalytic orientation in the literature on parents with retarded children. This literature often concludes that "something must be wrong" with parents who have a retarded child. Therefore, it is believed that the emotional reactions mentioned above will remain with the parents forever, exerting a long-term deleterious effect on the family. Several writers have refuted this deficit model of families with retarded children (Dunlap & Hollingsworth, 1977; Wikler, Wasaw & Hatfield, 1983). Roos (1978) expresses a concern about professionals who perceive parents with a "negative assumption"; that is, about professionals who see these parents as prime candidates for counseling and psychotherapy. Parents who need and want information about available services and the cause of their child's retardation encounter professionals "eager to unravel their intrapsychic conflicts." In short, parents are treated as patients (Roos, 1978; Darling, 1979; Gliedman & Roth, 1980). Parents' common emotional reactions to these professional encounters are frustration, irritation, anger, and distrust. Ironically, these reactions are also misunderstood by professionals as "emotional maladjustments" to having a retarded child.

In some cases, there is total rejection of the retarded child at birth. Parents may refuse to see the child and may be unwilling to take the infant home from the hospital. If an alternative community placement cannot be arranged, early institutionalization may occur. Parents may never visit their child and may decide to give up legal guardianship. Cases in which parents refuse to give their consent to medical treatment to save or prolong the life of a retarded child may be another manifestation of parental rejection.

Perhaps because they are the easiest to identify at birth, many reported cases dealing with the withholding of medical care from retarded newborns have involved Down syndrome infants. Gustafson (1973), in his discussion of the "Johns Hopkins case," described the circumstances that characterize many of these cases. A Down syndrome infant was born with the added complication of an intestinal blockage (i.e., duodenal atresia). For the child to survive, an operation was required to correct the intestinal obstruction. Despite counseling from the physician that the degree of retardation is not typically severe among Down syndrome children, the parents refused to give their consent for the operation. Consequently, the infant died of starvation within 15 days. The death of this infant was not an isolated incident. Duff and Campbell (1973) reported 43 similar deaths in a New England hospital over a 2-year period. The decision to withhold treatment and, consequently, to deny the infant's right to life, is typically made by parents (with the concurrence of their physician) on the basis of a quality-of-life ethic. In essence, the parents conclude that there is no hope that the retarded infant will ever have a "meaningful life." Moreover, it is argued that it is cruel to permit a retarded child to live a life of great physical and emotional pain. The social and economic costs to the family and society are additional justifications given for the nontreatment of retarded infants.

As with the abortion issue, the practice of passive euthanasia among defective newborns has raised a number of legal and moral questions (Soskin & Vitello, 1979). Do parents decide what is in the best interest of the child, or instead, what is in their own best interests? Are parents or physicians qualified to judge what constitutes a "meaningful life" for a mentally retarded person? When a conflict of rights exists between parental autonomy and the right to life of the mentally retarded infant, is deference always given to the parents' wishes? While parental wishes seem to determine the outcome in a number of hospitals where passive euthanasia is common practice, until recently, the opposite result usually occurred where the case reached the courts. In *Maine Medical Center* v. *Houle* (1974), parents refused to give their consent to surgery for a blocked esophagus, because the child was born severely handicapped. In rejecting any consideration of the quality of life involved, the court ordered that the surgery be performed. The court ruled that parents have "no right to withhold such treatment and to do so constitutes neglect in the legal sense." In a number of similar cases, the courts have ordered that medical treatment be given to save the life of a severely impaired infant (*In re Baby Girl Obernauer*, 1970; *In re Cicero*, 1979). However, *In the Matter of Treatment and Care of Infant Doe* (1982), an Indiana state court ruled that parents of a Down syndrome child with duodenal atresia could refuse to consent to surgery. The infant died within a week. A loud public outcry followed the disclosure of this case, and as a result the state prosecutor threatened to bring criminal action against the parents. The threat was never realized, however, and a subsequent appeal of the state court's decision to the U.S. Supreme Court was dismissed as moot, since the baby was no longer alive.

Following the *Baby Doe* decision, the Reagan administration issued a regulation under Section 504 of the Rehabilitation Act of 1973, which states that no handicapped person shall be excluded from a federally supported program solely by reason of his handicap. Some 6,400 hospitals were instructed to post a notice in delivery rooms that read: "Discriminatory failure to feed and care for handicapped infants in this facility is prohibited by Federal Law." Individuals knowledgeable about this violation were instructed to call HHS officials on a toll-free 24-hour hot line. The regulation was supported by pro-life groups (e.g., National Right to Life Committee) and a number of disability organizations (e.g., Association for Retarded Citizens, Down Syndrome Congress), but opposed by members of the medical profession (e.g., American Academy of Pediatrics, American Medical Association), who filed a suit against the Department of Health and Human Services. Physicians argued that the regulation interfered with the family-physician relationship and that to prolong the lives of some severely handicapped infants would be inhumane. Judge Gerhard Gesell ruled that the federal regulation was invalid because it violated the Administrative Procedure Act, which requires federal agencies to give the public the opportunity to comment on proposed rules before they are adopted. Judge Gesell added, "As even the most cursory investigation by the Secretary would have revealed *there is no customary standard of care* for the treatment of severely defective infants. The regulation thus purports to set up an enforcement mechanism without defining the violation, and is virtually without meaning beyond its intrinsic *in terrorism* (threatening) effect" (*American Academy of Pediatrics* v. *Margaret M. Heckler,* 1983). The federal government's appeal was ruled moot by the Supreme Court because the infant had died. In the meantime, the administration promulgated revised regulations that encouraged hospitals to create infant care review committees to decide on the medical treatment of defective newborns.

In a 1983 case, *Baby Jane Doe,* the New York State Court of Appeals, in overruling a lower state court decision, permitted the parents of a spina bifida infant to withhold medical treatment that would have prolonged their child's life (*Weber* v. *Stony Brook Hospital,* 1983). Again, the federal government intervened on the grounds that the court's decision violated federal law that prohibits discrimination against handicapped infants in need of medical treatment ("A Legal Knot in Baby Case," 1983). The Supreme Court declined to hear the case letting stand the decision of the New York court. (The U.S. Congress, too, has responded to the Baby Doe case by including provisions in the reauthorization of the Child Abuse Prevention and Treatment and Reform Act that insures the proper treatment of infants at risk with life threatening impairments.) The federal government's request to examine the medical records of the severely handicapped infant was also denied by the federal courts. *United States* v. *University Hospital of State University of New York at Stony Brook,* No. CV-83-4818 (E.D.N.Y. Nov. 17, 1983).

Should the practice of passive euthanasia be prohibited in all cases of severe mental retardation? Are there cases in which it is in the best interests of the child to withhold treatment? E. S. MacMillan (1978) proposes that a medical feasibility standard be used to determine which infants would be left to die. According to MacMillan, medical feasibility is determined by a consideration of the infant's medical condition and the positive outcome of treatment. A treatment is unfeasible it if it cannot benefit the infant—that is, if the treatment (ordinary or extraordinary) will prove futile once administered, or if it will cause the infant's condition to deteriorate. These cases would include anencephaly, trisomy 13 and 18, hydrocephaly, Tay-Sachs disease, and Lesch-Nyhan syndrome (see Chapter 6). Under the MacMillan standard, parents would be the ultimate decision makers. A decision to withhold treatment, however, would be subject to judicial review. Similarly, the President's Commission for the Study of Ethical Problems in Medicine and Biomedical and Behavioral Research (1983) recommended that "a very strict standard" of medical judgment be exercised in determining the treatment or nontreatment of newborns with birth defects. Infants should receive all therapies that are clearly beneficial to them, but medical treatment can be discontinued in those cases of permanent handicaps so severe that continued existence would not be a net benefit to the infant.

In another celebrated case, *In re Phillip Becker* (1979), parents refused to give their consent to heart surgery that would have prolonged the life of their 12-year-old Down syndrome son. In the parents' view, Phillip's life was not a life worth living, and they believed that it would be best for everyone, including Phillip, if he were dead. The parents held this view despite the evidence that Phillip had attained a high level of cognitive and social development and a prognosis that he could attend a sheltered workshop following his schooling. The parents also argued that they did not want Phillip to outlive them, for fear that he would receive poor custodial care and become a burden to his brothers. In deferring to the parents' decision, the California trial and appellate courts agreed that the surgery was elective and not a life-saving emergency. Moreover, the surgery had some element of risk, and the court did not want to second-guess the "good faith" decision of the parents. In 1983, a California appeals court awarded the legal guardianship of Phillip to a surrogate family and reports indicate that Phillip is doing well (*Guardianship of Becker,* 1983). Subsequently, the needed surgery was performed.

This brief discussion of the medical, legal, and moral issues surrounding the prenatal diagnosis and neonatal/postnatal treatment of defective infants illustrates the nature of life-and-death decisions faced by parents with severely retarded children. Both in law and morality, there is a lack of social consensus to guide parental decisions. This ambiguity adds to their confusion and sense of guilt as to what is the "right" thing to do. Parents must often feel that no matter what decision is made, they will be damned if they do and damned if they don't.

HOME CARE

Two types of families care for their retarded child at home: (1) parents who have cared for their child since birth and who have never sought an alternative placement; and (2) parents who in the past had put their child in an alternative placement (e.g., an institution) and who are now assuming or reassuming the responsibility for their child's care. We will refer to the former as the "stay homes" and the latter as the "return homes."

Stay Homes

In most cases, the most ideal, normalizing, and least restrictive setting for the care of a retarded child is with his natural family (Stedman & Eichorn, 1964; Zipperlin, 1975). In fact, only a small percentage of mentally retarded children live outside their natural homes during their early years (Bruininks & Krantz, 1979)

It is estimated that 165,000 severely retarded children are cared for at home (Moroney, 1980). This figure represents two-thirds of the severely retarded children living in the community. Moreover, more children who are severely retarded are cared for at home than in institutions. Clearly, many families have assumed the total care of these retarded children, who impose the greatest financial, physical, and emotional burdens.

For these families who choose to care for their severely retarded child at home, there are alterations in the family life cycle. Horejsi (1979) has distinguished the *intensive* and *extensive* demands placed on the family. Extensively, parents of retarded childen may be burdened with a lifetime of care. Unlike parents of non-retarded children, they do not proceed through the normative pattern of giving birth, raising a child, sending the child to school, and eventually having the young adult leave home. In short, parents of severely retarded children will always have a family member who requires attention (Farber, 1975; Birenbaum, 1971). Furthermore, the longer lifespan of mentally retarded persons and their parents will result in an even longer period of care. A source of ambiguity is created in our society concerning parenting. On the one hand, our changing mores now encourage adults to seek self-actualization, while on the other hand we continue to hold parents responsible for the care of their young children (Yankelovich, 1981). Undoubtedly, this sense of ambiguity and frustration is felt more intensely by parents with severely retarded children.

Intensively, families have increased physical, emotional, and economic stresses that affect their lifestyle and quality of life (Mercer, 1966; Fotheringham & Creal, 1974; Fotheringham, Skelton, & Hoddinott, 1971; Moroney, 1981; Gallagher, Beckman & Cross, 1983). The daily grind of managing a retarded child is demanding both in terms of physical effort and time committed (Schonell & Watts, 1956; Holt, 1958). These demands become increasingly more difficult to meet as both the child and the parents become older. Research has indicated that the burden of care places particular emotional and physical stress on mothers, particularly single mothers, leading to maternal burnout (Mercer, 1966; Farber, 1959; Farber & Ryckman, 1965; Holt, 1975; Eheart & Ciccone, 1982; Beckman, 1983). The mother's burden is aggravated when other family members (i.e., husbands and siblings) are unwilling to assist in the care of the retarded family member and complain about lack of attention (F. K. Grossman, 1972; Fowle, 1968; Farber, 1960; Fotheringham et al., 1971). Some evidence suggests that these strained interpersonal relationships may contribute to family disharmony and eventual breakdown (McAllister, Butler, & Lei, 1973; Farber, 1975; Gath, 1977; Ornic, Friedrich & Greenberg, 1983). Social and recreational activities may be restricted both by the time demanded in caring for a severely retarded child and by the stigma attached to the family (Holt, 1958). Visits to the homes of relatives and friends, as well as participation in community activities, may be curtailed. Short- and longer-term vacations may become difficult, if not impossible, to plan (Farber & Ryckman, 1965). Thus, it is not surprising that many families who care for their retarded child express a feeling of social isolation and a need for some type of respite (Suelzle & Keenan, 1981; Eheart & Ciccone, 1982; Rubin & Quinn-Curran, 1983).

The costs of maintaining a severely retarded child at home may be a constant drain on the family's financial resources, resulting in downward social mobility and a reduced quality of life (Holt, 1958; Culver, 1967; Eheart & Ciccone, 1982). Costs involved may include expensive medical and educational services, as well as special equipment and transportation. Care-providing mothers who would like to pursue careers or who need to work to provide additional family income may find this option closed to them. Salkever (1982) found that households with a handicapped child at home earned substantially less than those families without handicapped children. This situation may necessitate the father's taking a second job to supplement his income, or relocating in order to earn more money. For many, in a period of high unemployment, job insecurity, and escalating housing costs, this option may be foreclosed. The economic effects on single-parent families with a handicapped child are particularly harsh.

Any one or a combination of the above burdens increases the risk of a crisis that may result in the family's decision to have the child cared for in an alternative setting. Farber (1975) has described the stages families go through as they attempt to care for a severely retarded child—an attempt that may be unsuccessful. His work is based on the *minimal adaptions assumption*. This assumption implies a temporal progression of adaptions from the simple to the complex, from the least disruptive to the most disruptive of family relationships. During the *normalization phase*, the family attempts to maintain its normal pattern of behavior. The child's retardation may be ignored, or his abilities overestimated. Family members continue to function in their usual roles as they carry off "the fiction of normality." In the *mobilization phase*, the family recognizes that adaptations must be made in existing role functions. The mother recognizes that more time needs to be given in the care of the child. Fathers and siblings are called upon to assist the mother.

Consequently, the participation of family members in social activities may be curtailed. Feelings of resentment due to an unfair division of labor or to a lack of attention may surface. Unable to maintain a semblance of normal family lifestyle, the family enters the *revisionist phase*. Despite the adaptions made in the previous phases, greater demands from each family member are required to care for the retarded child. It is recognized that such care demands all of the family resources. This brings increased tension among family members. It is during this phase that families consider seeking help outside the family. Conflict among family members arises during the *polarization phase*. The family is unable, and in some cases unwilling, to care for the child. Outside assistance is now sought. Family cohesion becomes little more than family coexistence. Social isolation begins to characterize the behavior of many family members. In order to return the family to normal functioning and to prevent further deterioration, the family may decide that the removal of the child (i.e., institutionalization) is the only solution. At this point the family has reached the *elimination phase*. If parents do not agree that this is the best solution, one parent may leave the household (i.e., separation or divorce). Farber points out that interventions can stabilize a family at a particular phase or can enable the family to return to an earlier stage where fewer adaptations are required.

It is important to emphasize that for most families, the care of a severely retarded child is difficult but not of crisis proportions (Dunlap & Hollingsworth, 1977). In these families the mother is willingly assisted by other family members in the care of the retarded child (Darling, 1979). Siblings make a positive adjustment to having a retarded brother or sister (Cleveland & Miller, 1977; F. K. Grossman, 1972). Support from grandparents and relatives enables the parents to develop more positive feelings toward their retarded child (Waisbern, 1980). The availability of respite services for retarded children can relieve families of the need to provide constant care and supervision. Financial supports such as Supplemental Security Income (SSI) and family subsidies provide economic relief. Where these supportive family and community networks exist, there is usually a positive family adjustment in caring for a retarded child at home (Schipper, 1959; Caldwell & Guze, 1960; Birenbaum, 1970; Schonell & Rorke, 1960).

Deinstitutionalization policies are now encouraging more parents to provide home care (Spakes, 1983). Yet, as in the past, relatively little support is being provided to families who choose this preferred option (Moroney, 1980). Bruininks, Williams, and Morreau (1978) reported that incentives (e.g., respite services) to care for retarded persons within the home received the lowest "adequate" rating from parents, policy makers, and agency personnel. These findings increase the risk of a family crisis, which may eventually lead to the retarded child's removal from the family. Thus, it is not surprising that 36 percent of those retarded persons admitted to public institutions in fiscal year 1981–82 came from their own homes (Scheerenberger, 1982).

In an analysis conducted by Morell (1979), it was revealed that while considerable resources have been allocated to provide residential and social services for retarded *adults* who have been deinstitutionalized, comparatively little has been allocated to assist families with young, severely retarded children living at home. She recommended that measures be taken to provide families relief from financial pressures (e.g., a federal income tax exemption or payment for medical expenses), increased access to general social services (e.g., adjustments in income eligibility levels for social services), and additional options for short-term care (e.g., respite care).

A number of states, in efforts to reduce institutional costs and support home care, are providing incentives in the form of a direct family subsidy (Zimmerman, 1979). For example, under Minnesota law parents who keep their mentally retarded child at home are eligible for a monthly subsidy of up to $250. The Adoption Assistance and Child Welfare Act of 1980 (P.L. 96-272) also provides a federal subsidy for natural and adoptive families with a handicapped child. The Home and Community Medicaid Waiver (P.L. 97-35) under Title XIX will enable states to provide services (e.g., respite care; counseling) to families who have retarded members "at risk of institutionalization." Braddock's review (1981) of a number of cost-comparison studies on community alternatives indicated that state subsidies to the natural family were the least expensive option for caring for mentally retarded persons. It can be predicted that in a period of economic constraints, other states, as they view the natural family as a less expensive "social service," will consider providing similar subsidies. Wolfensberger's statement (1971b) seems particularly timely today:

> The social-political climate is now such as to permit expansion of this option, and the formulation of some direct forms of subsidy. These forms should be applied not only merely to the poor, but also to those families who are apt to seek residential placement for their child because of conditions which might be alleviated by modest, perhaps even short-term, expenditures of money. I predict that the family subsidy option will become an accepted provision that will contribute to the lowered demand for removal of a child from the home. (p. 34)

Another approach to the subsidization of the natural family is through foster-family-care programs. This strategy has met with limited success in New York State. In 1975 the Department of Mental Hygiene expanded its subsidized foster-family-care program to include parents who were members of the plaintiff class in the Willowbrook suit. Parents whose sons and daughters (*18 years of age or older*) were formerly institutionalized and who now were providing home care were eligible for this assistance. Subsequently, class-member parents caring for deinstitutionalized retarded children *under 18 years* of age also became eligible. However, parents who had never sought institutionalization for their retarded sons and daughters (i.e., nonmembers of the class) were not eligible. These parents challenged the department's policy on the grounds that the state offered a bounty to parents who had institutionalized their child while denying similar assistance to parents who, at considerable emotional and material cost, had provided home care for equally disabled children. In *Sundheimer* v. *Kolb* (1979) the New York Supreme Court agreed with the non-class-member parents and ruled that equal protection of the law required that *all* parents were equally eligible for the assistance under the state's foster-family-care program. The New York Department of Mental Hygiene then proceeded to circumvent the court's decision by declaring all natural parents "equally ineligible" for support under the foster-family-care program. However, in a suit pursuant to the implementation of the ongoing Willowbrook consent decree (*New York State Association for Retarded Citizens* v. *(Carey) Rockefeller,* 1980), a federal district court ruled that eligibility for foster-family-care benefits must apply as part of the court decree to those natural parents who were plaintiffs in the case. In effect, those natural parents involved in the litigation receive a subsidy to care for their retarded family member, whereas parents not involved in the litigation and who never institutionalized their child continue to be denied this assistance. This is an instance where deinstitutionalization policy creates a "dual citizenry"; one group of families is provided an incentive to resume care for their retarded member at home, whereas another group of families receives what amounts to a disincentive to continue home care. It should be noted that New York (and other states) have initiated deinstitutionalization policies to narrow the gap between services delivered to class-member and non-class-member parents (Baken, Ziring, Steindorf, Tillow, & Howe, 1979). In Chapter 5 a description of these services will be outlined.

Return Homes

Deinstitutionalization policy is resulting in a large number of institutionalized retarded persons returning to their natural homes. Early national figures estimated that 40 percent of the residents discharged were returned to their natural families (Gollay, Freedman, Wyngaarden, & Kurtz, 1978). More recent estimates indicate that 18 percent of the residents return home (Schereenberger, 1983b). Compared to residents being placed in other community settings, those returning home have tended to be more severely retarded (Gollay et al. 1978; Willer & Intagliata, 1980). Willer (1981) claims that a higher percentage of retarded persons would return to their natural families if mental retardation professionals gave this placement serious consideration. He found that 70 percent of the families whose retarded members were placed in alternative community settings were never asked if they would consider having their relative return home. Willer attributes these practices to mental retardation professionals who (1) assume that placement with the natural family is an undesirable option; and (2) find it more convenient to place mentally retarded persons in a community alternative. Moreover, institutional practices that discourage, and in some cases restrict, family contact and involvement with a retarded relative contribute to the estrangement between family members and the retarded person. According to D. L. MacMillan (1977), the natural bind between the family and the retarded individual becomes eroded. Given this history, it is unlikely that many families would consent to having their retarded child return home, even if they were asked. It is interesting to hypothesize whether families would respond differently if institutional practices had encouraged and assisted family members to remain involved in their child's life following institutionalization.

Willer, Intagliata, and Atkinson (1981) studied the impact of deinstitution-alization on 43 families between 1973 and 1975 in New York State. In 15 cases the retarded relative returned to the family home and in 28 cases the relative was placed in an alternative community setting. A discussion of the results of those placements in an alternative setting will be deferred to the following section. For the 15 families who consented to have their relative return home, 8 reported that a crisis situation ensued. Crises were attributed (1) to the family's fears about their relative's destructive behavior and their inability to provide a secure and responsive environment; and (2) to the family's concerns about who would care for their relative when they could no longer do so. It was reported that services provided to families to prevent or alleviate a crisis situation were inadequate. Compared to other community placements, natural families received very little in terms of follow-up services. Parents were unaware of the availability of community services, and the needed services that the parents knew about proved too costly. The one-third reduction in a retarded person's SSI benefit (when cared for at home) added to the families' difficulty in obtaining services. In short, the investigators found that natural families are "on their own" when their retarded child is returned home.

The absence of family support has negative consequences both for family members and for the deinstitutionalized mentally retarded person. Many families express feelings of increased stress and decreased free time as a result of caring for their retarded son or daughter (Willer & Intagliata, 1980; Mercer, 1966). The care provided to retarded persons in their homes has been described as restrictive and overprotective (Benoit, 1973; Willer, 1981). Activities outside the family household are often limited, and as a consequence, little positive change in adaptive behavior occurs among retarded persons; instead, there may be regression. In what may be regarded as an effect detrimental to the interest of the retarded person, aging parents became overly dependent on their sons and daughters. Perhaps, placement in more adultlike settings (e.g., boarding homes, apartments), particularly for higher-functioning individuals, would be more normalizing and would be in the retarded persons' best interest.

The implications of the above findings are that, not unlike parents who have always provided home care for their retarded children, families having their child return home are in need of supportive services. The failure to provide these families with needed services undoubtedly leads to reinstitutionalization (Willer, 1981; Keys, Boroskin, & Ross, 1973).

In summary, while a presumption should favor the home care of mentally retarded persons, it is a rebuttable presumption (Boggs, 1979). Even with available family intervention and supportive services, there will be families who will be unwilling or unable to care for their retarded child, necessitating the availability of residential alternatives (Townsend & Flanagan, 1976; Ellis, Moore, Taylor, & Bostick, 1981). In Chapter 5 these residential alternatives will be examined in detail. In the next section, we will consider the reactions of families to alter-native community residential placements for their mentally retarded sons and daughters.

ALTERNATIVE PLACEMENT

In the past, families who were unable to cope with the burden of caring for their mentally retarded child sought the only residential alternative available—the institution. As discussed earlier, the deinstitutionalization movement has resulted in the creation of community living arrangements that provide parents with options in addition to family and institutional care. While some parents have filed and continue to file lawsuits seeking to have their retarded child placed in less restrictive community settings, other parents in an increasing number of cases have demanded that their retarded child remain in the institution (*Horacek* v. *Exon*, 1975; *Halderman* v. *Pennhurst State School and Hospital*, 1979; *Connecticut Association for Retarded Citizens, Inc.* v. *Mansfield Training School*, 1978; *Washington Association for Retarded Citizens* v. *Thomas*, 1979; *Kentucky Association for Retarded Citizens* v. *Conn*, 1980; *McEvoy* v. *Mitchell*, 1979). However, the majority of parents of mentally retarded children have not been parties to any litigation, and they remain confused and concerned by the changes in social policy. One parent confesses, "In the past, we were made to feel guilty when we did not institutionalize our children, and now, under the new normalization principle, we are made to feel guilty if we do" (Gorham, 1975). The implementation of deinstitutionalization policies may contribute to a family crisis, particularly among those families who institutionalized their child some years ago when it was considered the accepted and popular thing to do. Stedman (1977) observes:

> In most cases, deinstitutionalization probably involves a painful reversal and revisitation of this original decision and has the potential to serve as a major crisis for the family regardless of whether their handicapped family member returns home or is placed in an alternate care facility. (p. 81)

Deinstitutionalization policy that is more reflective of the retarded person's interests is likely to result in a conflict between the newly acquired rights of mentally retarded persons and the long-standing rights of their parents, thereby creating additional tension among parents, the retarded child, and the state. For example, litigation challenging the commitment of minors to institutions has led a number of states to tighten their commitment statutes, making it more difficult for parents to commit their retarded child (*Secretary of Public Welfare* v. *Institutionalized Juveniles*, 1975; *J.R.* v. *Parham*, 1976). Similarly, the courts have ruled that parents do not have "an absolute veto" in decisions to place their retarded son or daughter in a community living arrangement (*Halderman* v. *Pennhurst State School and Hospital*, 1982b; *Lelz* v. *Kavanagh*, 1983).

The failure of policy makers to anticipate the magnitude of the impact of deinstitutionalization policies on families has contributed to negative parental reactions that threaten further implementation (Colombatto Isett, Roszkowski, Spreat, Pignofrio & Alderfor, 1980; Frohboese & Sales, 1980). In a number of empirical studies on parent attitudes toward deinstitutionalization, an overwhelming percentage of parents expressed strong opposition to community placement

(Payne, 1976; Meyer, 1980; Keating, Conroy, & Walker, 1980; Vitello & Atthowe, 1982). It is interesting to note that while parents are opposed to deinstitutionaliza- tion of *their* child, they are supportive of the deinstitutionalization and normaliza- tion constructs in reference to other retarded children (Ferrara, 1979). If parents are not to become a major barrier in deinstitutionalization efforts, it is important for policy makers and program planners to understand the reasons parents give for their opposition to community placement. These reasons are both substantive and procedural in nature.

Preference for Institutional Care

Despite all the evidence on the debilitating effects of institutional placement, many families express not only their preference but also their satisfaction with institutional care for their children (Meyer, 1980; Keating et al., 1980; Vitello & Atthowe, 1982; Payne, 1976; Brockmeir, 1975). Klaber (1969) observed that parents are "convinced of the excellence of the facilities in which their children were placed" and that "the praise lavished on the institution was so extravagent as to suggest severe distortion in reality in this area." Parents appear to prefer inade- quate institutional care, basing this preference on a belief that conditions can be improved. Moreover, parents prefer that their child remain in the institution for a number of reasons.

First, many parents believe that their retarded child requires 24-hour care and the supervision that only the institution can provide (Meyer, 1980). Institutions are regarded as a "haven of security and permanence" (Keating et al., 1980). Parents are convinced that institutions are the tried and tested way of caring for mentally retarded persons and that they constitute the least restrictive alternative for their severely or profoundly retarded son or daughter. On the other hand, parents perceive community services as programmatically inadequate, financially unstable, and as little more than a "fad" (Keating et al., 1980; Vitello & Atthowe, 1982; Frohboese & Sales, 1980). They are suspicious about the motivation of private care-providers who may be "out to make money," leading to the dumping of retarded persons into the community (e.g., boarding homes). Many parents would prefer that limited resources be used to improve institutional conditions rather than expand the community system.

Second, many parents believe that their children are "better off with their own kind." They doubt the community's willingness to accept their children and express fear that harm will come to them. Parents believe that their children are happier and better adjusted in an institutional setting (Meyer, 1980; Vitello & Atthowe, 1982). Moreover, parents perceive their child as having reached his highest level of intellectual growth and see no value in community placement (Keating et al., 1980; Vitello & Atthowe, 1982).

Third, families express feelings of guilt and inadequacy when they are unable to care for their retarded child at home. These feelings are intensified when they must consent to the possibility that others can care for their child in a foster or group home (Willer, Intagliata, & Atkinson, 1979). Rather than accept this possibility, parents prefer that the institution be the permanent home for their child.

Recent follow-up studies on parental attitudes toward their deinstitutionalized mentally-retarded relatives reflect more positive findings. In a survey of 65 families who had relatives residing in community placement for a six-month period, Conroy and Latib (1982) reported (1) greater parent satisfaction with community living arrangements, (2) improvement in the parents's perception of their child's general happiness as well as their own, (3) increased expectations regarding the retarded person's development, and (4) positive feelings about the quality of services available in the community. But parents continue to be concerned about the future security and permanence of community arrangements.

Lack of Family Participation
in the Deinstitutionalization Process

Although it is widely accepted that parental involvement is vital to the successful deinstitutionalization of mentally retarded persons, their exclusion from the decision-making process is another factor contributing to growing opposition to community placement (Singer, Bossard, & Watkins, 1977; Schalock, Harper, & Genung, 1981; Frohboese & Sales, 1980). Title XIX and the Developmentally Disabled Assistance and Bill of Rights Act require the active involvement of the family in the deinstitutionalization process. According to Schodek, Liffiton-Chrostowski, Adams, Minahan, and Yanaguchi (1980):

> The policy of deinstitutionalization is intrinsically an argument for family involvement based on the view that it is most "normal" to receive support services through family and community. The family is seen as the best advocate for the developmentally disabled and the most likely to be aware of the needs of its members. However, no procedures were established to inform families officially of either the change in philosophy and policy regarding institutionalization and deinstitutionalization or the institution's changed expectations regarding family involvement. (p. 68)

Consequently, many families report that they have had little control regarding proposed changes for their child's future residential placement (Willer & Intagliata, 1980; Frohboese & Sales, 1980; Vitello & Atthowe, 1982). Moreover, families are often not invited to participate in placement decisions, have their opinions ignored when they do participate, and are denied the opportunity to visit community programs. In many instances, families are informed about the decision to deinstitutionalize their child after the fact.

Clearly, these research findings illustrate the need to give more attention to the needs of the entire family in the deinstitutionalization process (Morell, 1979; Schodek et al., 1980). Meyer (1980) suggests a two-prong family reeducation strategy. The first would be greater involvement by families in the deinstitutionalization process to help parents arrive at realistic expectations, fears, and motivation, as well as to provide a sense of control over their child's well-being. Secondly, professionals must recognize and understand the legitimacy of parent concerns regarding community care. Families must be perceived not as intruders and disrupters of the care-giving routine, but as a valuable resource in planning for the successful placement of their relatives in the community (Schodek et al., 1980).

FAMILY CARE: A SHIFT
IN SOCIAL POLICY

Whereas in the past in our society, families with mentally retarded members were provided substitutes or replacements for home care (e.g., institutions and, more recently, group homes), a shift in social policy is occurring, according to which families would be supported and strengthened as the primary care-providers for their disabled children. (Similarly, this shift in social policy is reflected in government interpretations of Medicaid regulations to mean that families of disabled parents would be required to pay an increased share of nursing-home costs.) Kamerman (1980) defined *family support systems* as "those programs, benefits, measures, or arrangements designed to have—or having—the effect of facilitating, enhancing, helping, or optimizing role enhancement of family members and the functioning of the family as a unit" (p. 14).

This shift in policy is gaining support by representatives at both ends of the political spectrum. Liberals who support the normalization principle advocate programs that support family care. Conservatives, who also voice pro-family sentiments, recognize the economic savings that can be recouped by reducing the costs of out-of-the home placements. As cautioned in this chapter, however, many families are ill-prepared—financially, educationally, and psychologically—to assume the primary responsibility of care for their retarded sons and daughters without some type of social support. Absent such support, the consequences of a radical shift of responsibility for the care of mentally retarded persons not only would have pernicious effects on these families involved but also would result in increased social costs. Moroney (1980) proposes a policy of *shared responsibility* between families and government:

> Policies might then be located on a continuum whose end points are extreme forms of substitution (the state becoming the family for the individual) and the lack of state involvement in family life. The needs of families and individuals vary in time and over time and ideally the state would respond to those variations with policies that support families when they need support and substitute for families when they are incapable of meeting the needs of members. (p. 19)

Similarly, Berger and Berger (1983) offer their "middle-ground" recommendation for family policy:

> Public policy with regard to the family should primarily be concerned with the family's capacity to take care of its children, its sick and handicapped and

its aged. The basic principle should be that, whenever possible, these needs are best taken care of *within* the family—*any* family (barring a very few families to whom one would not entrust those who are weak or in need), regardless of social or cultural type. This means that the overriding concern of public policy should be to provide support for the family to discharge these caring tasks, rather than to relieve the family of these tasks. The family should be recognized as the most stable and effective structure, not only for taking care of children but for meeting the needs of the sick and the handicapped and the aged. To be sure, there are families who are either unable or unwilling to perform these tasks. In such instances, which are remarkably few, other arrangements must, of course, be provided. But even here the evidence indicates that arrangements work best that resemble the family as much as possible. (pp. 208–209)

According to Dempsey (1981), whether such policies are a triumph or a tragedy depends on how well government holds up its end of the bargain. Not only must there be a shared responsibility between families and the government in assisting and strengthening families, particularly those with disabled members; but also, partnerships must be fostered among the private (i.e., corporate) and voluntary sectors of our society as well.

Such a shift in social policy will require better communication between families and professionals than presently exists. Family members must be perceived and treated as equal partners in the planning and implementation of programs for their retarded member. Professionals must reorient themselves to viewing the family, and not merely the retarded individual, as the unit of service. The family must be regarded as a valuable resource, and rather than professionals doing things *for* the family, they must begin doing things *with* the family. On the other hand, if parents are to be given or to assume more control over the welfare of their retarded son or daughter, they must do so responsibly. This will require that they take the initiative to obtain the information and assistance needed to make the appropriate choices among the service options available to them.

The emphasis in this chapter has been on the needs of families with severely mentally retarded members. However, there are an increasing number of families in need of support. They include families who have children with other types of handicapping conditions, as well as those single-parent and two-parent families with nonhandicapped children in which the adults are struggling to balance the competing demands of being a good parent against obtaining economic security for their children. This dilemma is exasperated by social policies that often put parents in a position where they are forced to make choices that may be detrimental to family welfare. Consequently, interventions became available only when families reach crisis levels, where the costs, both human and economic, outweigh any belated benefits. Instead, preventive policies are needed whose impact is designed to make the demands of parenting and work more reconcilable, thereby strengthening families.

FAMILIAL RIGHTS
OF MENTALLY
RETARDED PERSONS

Another class of families whose needs and rights must be recognized are those in which the parent(s) or potential parent(s) are mentally retarded. Despite the fact that they obtain jobs, marry, and raise children, our society continues to impose a number of legal and attitudinal barriers to deny retarded adults their familial rights (i.e., marriage, procreation, and parenting). If the normalization principle is to apply to the sexual and familial relationships among mentally retarded persons, it will be necessary to reconsider both these restrictive legal and social practices.

In a way, the lifestyle that has become available to many adult mentally retarded persons (although in many cases not by choice) is similar to that of non-retarded persons. Many adult retarded persons are living together with members of the same or opposite sex in various community arrangements (e.g., group and boarding homes). Attempts to normalize institutional settings by integrating the sexes into smaller living units is also occurring. While these environments are being designed to encourage heterosexual interactions and normal psychosexual development, at issue is the question regarding what degree of sexual freedom should be extended to retarded persons.

Mentally retarded persons are perceived as being at greater sexual risk in our society. Families with retarded relatives are concerned about the unfortunate consequences (e.g., sexual abuse and pregnancy) that may result from programmatic efforts to increase social interactions between retarded and nonretarded people. These legitimate concerns need to be balanced against the right of mentally retarded persons to express themselves sexually and to have a family life of their own. In acknowledging these rights, care-providers, including parents, will have to play as important an educative role as a protective role in order to enable mentally retarded persons to develop heterosexual and familial relationships to the degree to which they are responsible.

Marriage

Many people still marry for love, sex, social legitimacy, companionship, and/or economic stability. Mentally retarded persons, too, can benefit from any of these marital advantages; the argument can be made that marriage for mentally retarded persons is particularly beneficial, given the hostility and discrimination they often encounter in community living. It has been estimated that 50 percent of all mentally retarded persons do marry (Bass, 1973). Yet, over 80 percent of the states treat mentally retarded persons differently from nonretarded persons for the purpose of issuing a marriage license (Linn & Bowers, 1978). A review of the statutes revealed that 38 states and the District of Columbia either prohibit or restrict the right of mentally disabled persons to marry (Haavik & Menninger, 1981). Many of these statutes, however, remain dormant and unenforced by the states. Nevertheless, state statutes barring marriage continue to exist as an affront to the recognition of mentally retarded persons as full citizens. These statutes possess the potential, should they be enforced, to drastically curtail the mentally retarded person's fundamental right to marry.

Three presumptions underly these restrictive marriage statutes: (1) Retarded persons lack the mental capacity to understand the marriage contract; therefore, they cannot give their informed legal consent to marry. (2) Retarded persons will not make successful marriage partners. (3) Retarded persons will procreate retarded children or cause their normal children to become retarded by providing inadequate care. A discussion of presumptions 1 and 2 will follow; presumption 3 will be discussed in the following sections on procreation and raising children.

Informed consent is a legal term that embodies three elements: capacity, information, and voluntariness (Turnbull, 1977). Capacity involves the individual's ability to acquire or retain knowledge so that consent can be given. Capacity is determined by a consideration of a person's age, competence (i.e., intelligence), and the particular situation that requires the giving of consent. Information requires that the individual possess sufficient facts about the matter at hand in order to consent knowingly. What information is given an individual and how it is given are important factors. Finally, voluntariness means that the person is "so situated as to be able to exercise free power of choice without the intervening of any element of force, fraud, deceit, duress, overreaching or other ulterior form of constraint or coercion" (p. 10). All three of these elements of informed consent are important in determining the validity of a marriage contract engaged in by a mentally retarded person. It is presumed that all mentally retarded persons (as with nonretarded persons) who have not been declared legally incompetent are capable of giving their valid consent to a marriage contract. But even a legal judgment of incompetence *per se* should not necessarily prevent a retarded person from entering into a marriage contract. Some retarded persons may be capable, as a result of education and counseling, of understanding what the marriage contract entails. In these cases they would be able to give their informed consent, and they should not be prohibited the right to marry.

Another presumption restricting marriages is that mentally retarded persons do not make successful marriage partners. Research findings refute this presumption. Floor, Baxter, Rosen, and Zisfein (1973) surveyed the marital status of 80 formerly institutionalized retarded persons and concluded that they were capable of assuming the responsibilities of marriage and parenthood. Edgerton and Bercovici (1976), in their 12-year follow-up study of 30 deinstitutionalized retarded persons, found that over half maintained a successful marriage. McDevitt, Smith, Schmidt, and Rosen (1978) reported on four marriages between deinstitutionalized retarded people. They found all of the couples were functioning adequately, none were having serious marital problems, and all were happier than those in the study who had not married. Similar findings have been reported in the research studies conducted by Mattinson (1973) and Andron and Sturm (1973). These studies suggest that there may be little correlation between the level of an individual's mental functioning, as measured by IQ scores, and his or her performance as a marriage partner.

In a society where one out of two marriages ends in divorce, it would be preposterous to argue that mentally retarded persons are more prone to unsuccessful marriages. As with nonretarded persons, retarded persons may find marriage less than idyllic. Therefore, even if high rates of divorce were found among retarded persons, this should not be used as a justification to deny them the right to marry or remarry (Linn & Bowers, 1978). Unlike most nonretarded persons, retarded persons, who have been segregated from contact with the opposite sex and denied normative socialization processes, may be less prepared for marriage. Again, the remedy is not to deny these retarded persons the right to marry, but to create more normalizing environments with supportive family services (e.g., family-life education and counseling).

Bearing Children

Historically, prohibitive marriage laws were followed by the segregation and involuntary sterilization of institutionalized mentally retarded persons to prevent them from procreating. The presumption (and fear) was that retarded persons would bear retarded children and society would be swamped with incompetents. In *Buck* v. *Bell* (1927), which legalized the involuntary sterilization of institutionalized mentally retarded persons, Justice Oliver Wendell Holmes delcared that "three generations of imbeciles is enough." Shortly thereafter, the refutation of the scientific theories (e.g., Mendelian inheritance) underlying this decision, and the Supreme Court's recognition of a fundamental right to procreate (*Skinner* v. *Oklahoma,* 1942), led to a series of decisions requiring increased procedural safeguards and substantive justifications before a retarded person could be involuntarily sterilized (S. J. Vitello, 1978). As a result, the number of involuntary sterilizations of institutionalized mentally retarded persons has dropped sharply.

More recently, the courts have dealt with an increasing number of cases where parents of severely retarded daughters living at home have sought involuntary sterilizations. The courts have been reluctant to comply with these parental requests in the absence of a state statute authorizing the involuntary sterilization of noninstitutionalized mentally retarded persons. In several recent cases, however, the courts have defined their *parens patriae* powers to include the authorization of the sterilization of mentally retarded persons living in the community (Hinkle & Vitello, 1983). Moreover, these decisions have enumerated what standards should be followed in authorizing sterilizations. In *Ruby* v. *Massey* (1978), a Connecticut court ruled that a state statute that denied three incompetent, noninstitutionalized mentally retarded girls the right to be sterilized while making it available to institutionalized retarded persons violated the equal protection of the law. The court reasoned:

> This lawsuit is unmistakenly a poignant cry for help from these children uttered in their behalf by their parents. These children are what they are; they are unable to come to terms with reality sufficiently to make the decisions which are only theirs to make. That they are uncapable of comprehending the consequences of their action is clear beyond question. The fact that the demand for an "informed" decision from each of the children is an impossible one to meet makes imperative the need for an authoritative decision on their behalf. (p. 367)

The court ordered that the sterilization of mentally retarded persons living in the community should be governed by the state's institutional sterilization statute.

In a leading New Jersey case, *In re Lee Ann Grady* (1981), the court asked, "Should a person's right to choose between two fundamental rights—the right to bear children and the right not to bear children—be forfeited merely because a person is judged incompetent to decide the question for herself?" Thus, instead of characterizing the decision as one that terminates a right, the *Grady* court viewed the issue as how to give expression to the retarded person's right to choose (i.e., reproductive autonomy). Because of the sensitive nature of the sterilization decision and the potential conflict of rights between the parents and their 19-year-old severely retarded daughter, the court felt that judges and not family members must make the substituted judgment in the best interests of the child. In making the judgment the court must consider the following standards:

1. The possibility that the incompetent person can become pregnant. There need be no showing the pregnancy is likely. The court can presume fertility if the medical evidence indicates normal development of sexual organs and the evidence does not otherwise raise doubts about fertility.
2. The possibility that the incompetent person will experience trauma or psychological damage if she becomes pregnant or gives birth and, conversely, the possibility of trauma or psychological damage from the sterilization operation.
3. The likelihood that the individual will voluntarily engage in sexual activity or be exposed to situations where sexual intercourse is imposed upon her.
4. The inability of the incompetent person to understand reproduction or contraception and the likely permanence of that inability.
5. The feasibility and medical advisability of less drastic means of contraception, both at the present time and under foreseeable future circumstances.
6. The advisability of sterilization at the time of the application rather than in the future. While sterilization should not be postponed until unwanted pregnancy occurs, the court should be cautious not to authorize sterilization before it clearly has become an advisable procedure.
7. The ability of the incompetent person to care for a child, or the possibility that the incompetent may at some future date be able to marry and, with a spouse, care for a child.

8. Evidence that within the foreseeable future scientific or medical advances may occur that will make possible either improvement of the individual's condition or alternative and less drastic sterilization procedures.
9. A demonstration that the proponents of sterilization are seeking it in good faith and that their primary concern is for the best interests of the incompetent person rather than their own or the public's convenience.

These newly fashioned standards governing sterilization are for the most part untested. How they will be applied in future cases is yet to be determined. Undoubtedly, consideration must be given to their actual use in practice before they can be refined further. Quite obviously, no standard is perfect, and in the long run, what might prove to be more important is the attitude of judges applying the various standards to individual cases, rather than the standards themselves.

In summary, in the past several years the courts across the country have expanded their jurisdiction to confront the sterilization question, often placing themselves in the middle of disputes between parents and their child. It can be anticipated that as an increasing number of severely retarded persons are considered for community placement, the question of sterilization will arise. Some parents will be most accepting of community placement provided their son or daughter is sterilized. It is likely that the courts will continue to be called upon to determine whether parental decisions are in the best interests of their child. Interestingly, Wolf and Zarfas (1982) found that among 157 parents surveyed, 71 percent favored the involuntary sterilization of their son or daughter; 64 percent of the parents did not feel that a legally authorized third person or committee should be involved in the sterilization decision once they and their physician had decided what should be done.

Rearing Children

Whatever gains have been made in the rights of mentally retarded persons to marry and bear children, these gains may be offset by judicial decisions terminating their parental rights to keep and raise their children. The removal of the child and the termination of the parental rights of mentally retarded persons is based on two legal presumptions: (1) Mentally retarded persons are "inherently unfit" to provide "proper care" for their children; and (2) the children are likely to receive better treatment elsewhere. Both of these presumptions are rebuttable.

Fotheringham, Skelton, & Hoddinott (1971) found that parent intelligence is not necessarily correlated with childrearing ability; retarded parents can provide adequate child care. These parents are capable of giving their children love and affection (Brandon, 1957), performing housekeeping chores, attending to their child's physical needs (Mickelson, 1949), and stimulating the child intellectually (Skeels, 1966). All of these functions are associated with proper parenting. Furthermore, in those cases where mentally retarded parents have experienced difficulties in providing adequate child care, it has been demonstrated that intensive educational and social services can benefit parents in providing improved child care (Heber & Garber, 1975; Ramey, Farran, & Campbell, 1979; Haavik & Menninger, 1981). Other studies have shown an association between parental mental retardation and child maltreatment, but retardation *per se* is an insufficient ground to remove a child from the parents and to terminate their legal right to raise children (Shilling, Schinke, Blythe, & Barth, 1983). What should be shown is that the parent(s) have, in fact, been neglectful or abusive. Yet in a number of cases (*In re Green,* 1978; *In re Orlando F.,* 1976), newborns have been removed from their parents, absent such a finding, solely on the basis of the parent's mild mental retardation and the presumption that they are unfit to parent (Plamondon & Soskin, 1978). In some cases parental rights to rear their child have been eventually terminated (Katzman, 1981). However, a recent Supreme Court decision, requiring a standard of clear and convincing evidence for termination of parental rights, may be fairer to mentally retarded parents (*Santosky* v. *Kramer,* 1982).

The second legal presumption underlying termination is that children of mentally retarded parents can receive better treatment from someone else. This best-interest determination, however, should be made *after* it has been determined that the parent(s) are in neglect, not before. Moreover, less drastic alternatives (e.g., family assistance and temporary placement in a foster home) should be tried before termination occurs and an alternative placement is sought. Such procedures are seldom invoked, however, when the parent is classified as mentally retarded. In *Coffey* v. *Baltimore Dept. of Social Services* (1979), a Maryland court ignored serious allegations of systematic agency misconduct in ordering the termination of parental rights of a mentally retarded woman. This misconduct included the agency's consistent thwarting of the natural mother's attempts to maintain her relationship with her child. Clearly, these practices are contrary to the best interest of the child, if *best interest* is defined as maintaining children in their natural families whenever possible.

Goldstein, Freud, and Solnit (1973), argue for a policy of minimum state intervention in the parent-child relationship. They argue that the primary psychological ties between parent and child must be maintained and nurtured continuously, free from state intrusion or interference. As added justification, the authors assert that the state does not possess the capacity to supervise the fragile, complex interpersonal relationship between parents and children. Too often, state intrusion into the natural parent-child relationship results in worse outcomes (e.g., abuses in foster-home care). Applying the reasoning of these authors to the situation of families with mentally retarded parents can help overcome the discrimination practiced through the use of vague and undefined neglect and custody statutes. Limiting state intervention to situations involving "gross failures of parental care" (e.g., abandonment, physical or sexual abuse) would certainly prevent the state from breaking up families solely on the basis of measures of the parents' intellectual capacity.

In summary, the legal and policy arguments in support of the recognition of the familial rights of mentally retarded persons have been made. These arguments must, however, overcome years of unfounded presumptions and prejudices concerning the abilities of mentally retarded persons. As the principles of least restrictive alternative and normalization are put into operation in social policy and program practices, a consideration needs to be given not only to families with mentally retarded persons but to mentally retarded persons themselves during each stage of the life cycle.

CHAPTER FIVE
RESIDENTIAL, SOCIAL, AND ADVOCACY SERVICES

The success of deinstitutionalization policy will depend upon the development of a community-based system of services for mentally retarded persons (Scheerenberger, 1976; Gollay, Freedman, Wyngaarden, & Kurtz, 1978). Available and adequate services would eliminate the need for institutionalization and would result in the more rapid return of institutionalized mentally retarded persons to the community. Blatt, Bogdan, Biklen, and Taylor (1975) suggest that a "conversion plan" be developed cooperatively by mental retardation professionals who work in the institution and community. The plan would provide for an orderly transition from an institutional to a community-based system of services, with concomitant plans to transform existing physical facilities, staff resources, institutional ideologies, community attitudes, and agency policies to alternative, more humanized uses and postures. Regarding the implementation of deinstitutionalization and normalization principles, Bradley (1978) states:

> What must emerge from an acceptance of these guiding principles is a mechanism for achieving an efficient and effective transition from a system built around custodial institutions to one that is integrated into the community and that entails a rich array of service options to meet individual needs. (p. 51)

An array of community services is embodied in what is referred to as the *continuum of care*. According to the President's Panel on Mental Retardation (1962), a continuum of care

> . . . describes the selection, blending and use, in proper sequence and relationship, of the medical, educational, and social services required by a retarded person to minimize his disability at every point in his life span. Their "care" is used in its broadest sense and the word "continuum" underscores the many transitions and liaisons within and among various services and professions, by which the community attempts to secure for the retarded the kind and variety of help and accommodation he requires. A "continuum of care" permits fluidity of movement of the individual from one type of service to another while maintaining a sharp focus on his unique requirements. The ongoing process of assuring that an individual receives the services he needs when he needs them and in the amount and variety he requires is the essence of planning and coordination. (p. 75-76)

The continuum of care has both a horizontal and vertical dimension. The horizontal dimension refers to the availability of needed services from more than one agency in the community at any moment in time. Service integration is crucial to meeting the needs of mentally retarded persons. For example, educational services must be linked with vocational training programs to prepare retarded persons for employment. The vertical dimension refers to the potential need for specific services at each stage of development, from infancy through old age. Infants will require more medical services; adults will require more employment services (See Figure 5-1).

While expanded generic services should be provided for retarded persons, specialized services will still be needed where gaps occur. According to Sarason, Carroll, Maton, Cohen, and Lorentz (1977), a *social network* of special and generic community services that are coordinated, comprehensive, and accessible is needed to ensure the successful deinstitutionalization and habilitation of mentally retarded persons. Bradley (1978) recommends that a *client-management system* be instituted to assist retarded persons in obtaining needed community services. Specifically, the client manager or case manager would (1) ensure coordination and continuity among service providers, (2) assist in the development of linkages between the client and generic human services agencies, and (3) assess and document the gaps and obstacles in service delivery. In short, the case manager would be held accountable for the client's well-being.

RESIDENTIAL SERVICES

It is a misconception that most retarded persons are (or ever were) housed in large segregated public institutions. It has been estimated that less than 5 percent of all mentally retarded persons in the United States have ever resided in institutions; this

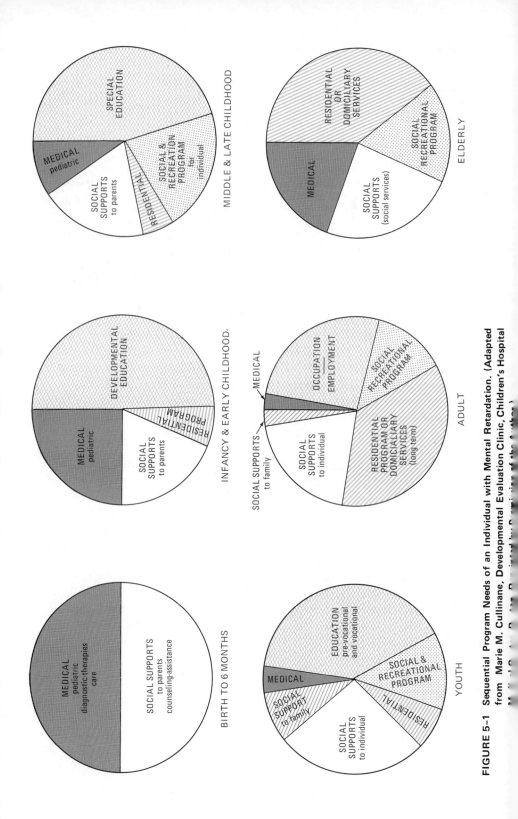

FIGURE 5-1 Sequential Program Needs of an Individual with Mental Retardation. (Adapted from Marie M. Cullinane, Developmental Evaluation Clinic, Children's Hospital

percentage has decreased with the implementation of deinstitutionalization policies. Like most nonretarded persons, the majority of retarded persons live in private single and two-family households or apartment buildings located in urban and rural communities. Earlier types of alternative community housing for retarded persons have included halfway houses, boarding homes, and family-care homes (Davies, 1959). As will be shown in the following sections, the present movement to place a greater number of retarded persons in community housing has resulted in variations in these earlier types of residential living.

Community residential services can be broadly classified into either individual or group arrangements (see Figure 5-2). Individual arrangements are family settings (e.g., adoptive and foster homes) that provide care for a small number (fewer than six) of retarded persons. Group arrangements are community residences (e.g., group homes) that provide care for a larger number (more than six) of retarded persons. A continuum of residential services is needed to meet the changing housing needs of retarded persons. Residential services should provide options that move retarded persons toward more independent and age-appropriate living arrangements. In the following section some of the more frequently used residential services for retarded persons will be described.

Individual Placements

Adoptive families. There is some disagreement among professionals on the question of what should be the recommended placement for a mentally retarded child who cannot be cared for by his natural family (Baroff, 1974; Adams, 1970). Those who prefer foster placement argue that a continuous effort should be made by welfare agencies to return the retarded child to the natural family, even if it takes years. Others argue that after repeated attempts to return the child to the natural family have failed, permanent placement with an adoptive family would be in the child's best interest. Adoptive placement would be "the least detrimental alternative" and provide the continuity necessary for the child's development (Goldstein, Freud, & Solnit, 1973).

Adoption of a retarded child entails a legal process whereby the biological parents relinquish their legal responsibility for the care of their child. Legal responsibility is assumed by the adoptive parents. Until recently, it was believed that retarded children were "unadoptable." Along with a better understanding of mental retardation, improved community attitudes, and the deinstitutionalization movement have come efforts to expand generic adoption services for retarded children (Krisheff, 1977). A less altruistic factor in the expansion of generic adoptive services is a scarcity of children who are easy to place (e.g., healthy white infants); social agencies are, therefore, pushing the placement of "hard-to-place" retarded children (J. A. Browder, 1975). Moreover, state agencies are giving increased attention to the placement of retarded children in adoptive homes as a component of their deinstitutionalization plans. Whatever the reasons for this change in policy,

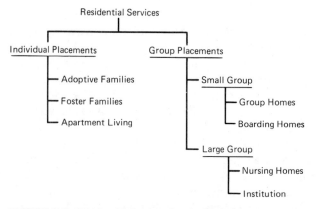

FIGURE 5-2   Residential Services for the Mentally Retarded Persons.

it is crucial that social agencies, in making such placements, give careful attention to the selection, training, and support of adoptive parents.

Hundreds of retarded children (including the more severely retarded) are being placed in adoptive homes through newspaper and television ads. Typically, an "A Child Is Waiting" column describes the child's history and needs. Interested parties are given an address to write or a telephone number to call if they wish to obtain additional information. One pioneering program to find adoptive families for mentally retarded children is operated by Spaulding for Children of New Jersey (President's Committee on Mental Retardation, undated). Spaulding accepts referrals nationwide from public and private welfare agencies that are unable to find adoptive homes for retarded children. The National Adoption Exchange has developed a system of "computer matches" to bring together children with special needs and prospective adoptive parents. The increase in the number of adoptions involving special-needs children can be attributed to these nationwide outreach efforts, and to the availability of state and federal subsidies (e.g., Adoption Assistance and Child Welfare Act of 1980, P.L. 96-272) to assist families in the care of a disabled child. Forty-six states now provide subsidies for adoptive families with special-needs children.

To date, very few data are available on the outcomes of retarded children placed with adoptive families. In a related study, Franklin and Massaril (1969) followed up 300 adopted children with major medical problems. Successful outcomes, measured in terms of long-term placement and positive parental attitudes, were found in more than three-quarters of the families. It has been reported that Down's syndrome children have benefited from placement in adoptive families (Wolfensberger, 1971b; "More Genetic-Defect Victims Adopted," 1979). If support for the present trend to place retarded children in adoptive families is to continue, data must be gathered to determine both the short-term and long-term benefits.

Foster families.   As early as 1930, foster families or foster-family-care homes for mentally retarded persons were a popular community alternative to institutionalization. Traditionally, generic foster-care services have not been provided for mentally retarded persons. Surveying 41 generic state agencies to determine their foster-care policies for retarded persons, J. A. Browder (1975) found that (1) only 10 states indicated any special policy for retarded persons; (2) payment for foster care was low, with no additional funds for special education, transportation, and respite care; (3) few programs emphasized experience and training in the selection of foster parents; and (4) evidence of child abuse necessitated the removal of retarded children from foster homes. In 1977, approximately 28,500 retarded children were in generic foster care homes (Lakin, Bruininks, Doth, Hill, & Hauber, 1982).

More recently, *specialized foster-care* services for retarded persons have been provided by public and private agencies. A specialized foster-family-care home is a family residence (home or apartment) owned or rented by one or more persons who provide care for six or fewer retarded persons. Foster-family homes are licensed by the state, with regulations specifying the physical size of the home, the number of children who can be cared for, and the age of the foster parents. Under a contract, foster parents are paid a monthly stipend for each child under their care. This stipend covers the costs of the child's food, clothing, and shelter. Whereas the foster parents are responsible for the daily care of the child, legal responsibility for the foster child remains with the child's natural parents or the social agency. Foster parents must accept and comply with any plans the agency makes for the child; this includes the removal of the child from the foster home if this is considered in the child's best interests (Mnookin, 1973).

A mentally retarded persons may be placed in a foster home for any of the following reasons: (1) to give the natural family time to accept their child's condition and plan for the child's care; (2) to provide respite care for the family; (3) to care for the child during a family crisis (e.g., poor health, divorce, death, unemployment); and (4) to remove the child from parents who may be neglectful or abusive. In all these situations, the goal of foster placement is short-term care and the return of the child to the natural family as soon as circumstances improve. Sometimes, this goal is unattainable for retarded children who present difficult management problems for the natural family or who come from chronically unstable homes. In these cases, foster care has served as a long-term placement to prevent institutionalization. For some of these retarded persons, foster care will be a transition placement for their movement into a less restrictive residential setting (e.g., apartment living).

Bruininks, Hauber, Hill, Lakin, Rotegard, and White (1983) reported that 40 states in 1982 licensed 6,587 specialized foster care homes that served 17,147 mentally retarded persons. Between 1970 and 1975, New York State placed two out of three deinstitutionalized retarded persons in family-foster-care homes (Willer & Intagliata, 1980). Foster care has become a preferred placement for deinstitutionalized retarded persons in California and New Jersey (Justice, Bradley, & O'Connor, 1971; New Jersey Department of Human Services, 1978). In Massachusetts (and some other states as well), couples or single persons who care for a retarded person in their homes not only are subsidized but also receive special training. Specialized Foster Family Services, a federally funded program operated by a Pennsylvania institution, has successfully placed severely and profoundly retarded children in foster homes (Bradley, 1978). Another noteworthy foster-care program is operated by the Retarded Infants Services (RIS) in New York City (O'Regan, 1974). This organization has established a foster-care committee of 30 participating statewide foster-care agencies to provide services for mentally retarded persons. A unique feature of this program is the placement of retarded children with families who have a retarded child of their own.

A number of investigations have been conducted on the efficacy of foster placement for retarded persons. These studies reveal wide variations in the quality of care in foster-family homes (Bjaanes & Butler, 1974; Willer & Intagliata, 1980). DeVizia (1974) and Soeffling (1975) provide descriptions of foster programs that have successfully placed retarded children. Nihira and Nihira (1975) studied the adaptive behavior of severely retarded persons placed in foster care homes. Interviews with caretakers indicated behavior gains in domestic skills (e.g., bed-making) and interpersonal relations (e.g., playing in the neighborhood). Positive changes in adaptive behavior have also been reported in a number of other studies (Eyman, Silverstein, McLain, & Miller, 1977; Freeman, 1978). However, Baker, Seltzer, and Seltzer (1977) and Willer and Intagliata (1980) found foster-care providers to be generally overprotective and doing little to encourage the development of community living skills. Bruininks, Hill, and Thorsheim (1980) conducted a comprehensive study of 2,609 specially licensed foster homes for mentally retarded persons. The following major findings were reported:

1. The mean number of mentally retarded residents per home was 2.5.
2. The average reimbursement per resident per day averaged $8.67.
3. While foster parents preferred residents with at least minimal self-help skills, 55 percent indicated that they did accept residents who were severely or profoundly retarded.
4. One-third of all residents were considered either severely or profoundly retarded, 38 percent moderately retarded, 21 percent mildly retarded, and 8.1 percent of borderline intelligence.
5. Sixty-nine percent of the residents in foster homes were over 21 years old.
6. Of all newly admitted residents, 42 percent came from public institutions, and 11 percent came from natural homes. A large proportion of new admissions (32 percent) were transferred from other foster homes.
7. Residents released from foster homes were placed in a variety of settings, including 7.3 percent who moved to their natural home, 22 percent who went to a different foster home, 31 percent who went to a group home, 20 percent who went to an institution, and 2.2 percent to a nursing home. Of the released residents, 8.2 percent went to more independent living arrangements, including supervised apartments, boarding homes, and independent living situations.
8. The following major problems were reproted by foster parents: inadequate funding (58 percent), lack of community support services (31 percent), and negative attitudes of the community toward residents (16 percent).

Several of these findings are noteworthy. Whereas foster care is usually thought of as a residential alternative for children, the majority of residents were over 21 years of age and more severely retarded. Willer and Intagliata (1980) reported similar findings in their study of foster-family care in New York State. It appears that retarded persons are frequently shifted from one foster home to another (J. A. Browder, 1975; Willer & Intagliata, 1980). Return rates to institutions have been reported as high as 30 percent (Gollay et al., 1978; Baker, Seltzer, & Seltzer, 1977). On the other hand, only 8.2 percent of those in foster care moved to more independent living arrangements. Inadequate funding, lack of services, and negative community attitude are problems reported in a number of studies on foster care for retarded persons (Justice et al., O'Connor, 1971; Sternlicht, 1978). A. Browder, Ellis, and Neal (1974) followed up 27 retarded children placed with foster families. These investigations found a need for substantial improvement in half the placements. Needed improvements included: (1) a more realistic acceptance among foster parents of the child's handicap; (2) an improvement in meeting the child's needs; (3) better selection of foster parents; (4) fewer placements in a given foster home; and (5) fewer changes in foster placements. Justice and colleagues (1971) reported that 70 percent of the care-providers in foster homes had problems in the care of a retarded child. Among those problems reported in a study by Willer and Intagliata (1980) were intensive supervision demands, lack of free time, and neglect of other family members. These studies indicate that considerable improvement is needed in foster-care services for mentally retarded persons. The available research indicates that what is needed most is better selection and training of foster parents and the availability of supportive services in the community.

Apartment Living.   For adult mentally retarded persons, supervised and unsupervised apartment living can provide a high level of normalization and self-sufficiency. This community alternative should be expanded to meet the needs of an increasing number of higher-functioning mentally retarded persons leaving family and group settings. Fritz, Wolfensberger, and Knowlton (1971) have delineated three types of apartment-living arrangements that offer varying degrees of supervision and integration. *Apartment clusters* are composed of several apartments in relative physical proximity, functioning in some extent as a unit. Mentally retarded persons are supervised by staff members who reside in one of the apartments. *Single co-residence* arrangements consist of one or two adult staff members (often college students) and two or three retarded persons living together as roommates. *Single maximum independence apartments* are occupied by two to four retarded adults, with all supervision and assistance supplied by a citizen advocate or a caseworker employed by the regional residential service agency. Retarded persons who are more capable could live in apartments with minimal supervision, either alone or with roommates. According to the Association for Retarded Citizens (1973):

> The ultimate goal of apartment living is to equip the resident with the skills to meet all of his needs, so that all depending ties to the residential services

system can be broken. This will require that the resident gradually begin to pay, from his own earnings, a greater and greater share of the cost of living in an apartment, until even financial dependence is eliminated if possible. (p. 19)

Fiorelli and Thurman (1979) followed up four deinstitutionalized retarded adults who were placed in apartments. In one apartment a counselor lived with three retarded adults. The fourth retarded person shared an apartment with another retarded person. The investigators reported generally positive behavioral changes among the four retarded adults. Successful adjustments to apartment living have been reported by Perske and Marguiss (1973) and Aninger and Bolinsky (1977). A follow-up study conducted by Schalock, Harper, and Garver (1981) indicates that an increasing number of high-functioning retarded persons are living independently in apartments and a number are purchasing their own homes.

Group Placements

Group homes. An earlier prototype of today's group-home and boarding-home placements were the colonies that were established to house retarded persons in the early 1900s (Davies, 1959; de Silva & Faflak, 1976). A group home, one type of community-based residential facility, operates 24 hours a day to provide services to a small group of mentally retarded persons who are presently or potentially capable of functioning in the community with some degree of independence (O'Conner & Sitkei, 1975). It is unfortunate that deinstitutionalization has become synonymous with the placement of a retarded person in a group home (Balla & Klein, 1981). Some retarded persons could be placed in a less restrictive alternative (e.g., apartments), whereas others may require a more protective placement (Baker, Seltzer, & Seltzer, 1977).

Group-home placements account for the largest percentage (approximately 30 percent) of retarded persons placed in the community (Scheerenberger, 1983b; Lakin, Bruininks, Doth, Hill, & Hauber, 1982). Janicki, Mayeda, and Epple (1983) found in a nationwide survey that approximately 57,494 retarded persons reside in 6,302 group homes. Absent a drastic cut in funding, it is anticipated that further growth in the number of group homes will continue.

Typically, small group homes are private, single-family dwellings that are purchased or rented (by public and private agencies) to provide residential services for 6 to 15 retarded persons. Live-in providers are responsible for the 24-hour care and supervision of the residents. The residents receive needed services (e.g., education, medical care) in the community. Retarded persons living in group homes include those placed from institutions as well as those from the community (i.e., natural families). The criteria used for group-home placement has been the potential for greater independence and social sufficiency (O'Connor, 1976). Consequently, those persons initially placed were mildly and moderately retarded (O'Connor, 1976; Gollay et al., 1978). More recently, the availability of ICF/MR funding under Title XIX has spurred efforts to create group homes for severely and profoundly retarded persons (Janicki et al., 1983; Vitello, Atthowe, & Cadwell, 1983). Available data have demonstrated that these placements can be successful (Close, 1977; Aanes & Moen, 1976; Schroeder & Henes, 1978; Polivka, Marvin, Brown & Polivka, 1979; Thompson & Cary, 1980; Landesman-Dwyer & Sulzbacher, 1981). For this population the group home may be a long-term placement, whereas for less retarded persons, movement to more independent living arrangements should be encouraged (Sitkei, 1980).

Reports indicate that the recidivism rate among group-home placements (about 15 percent) has been comparatively lower than among placements in foster-care homes (Moen, Bogen, & Aanes, 1975; Gollay et al., 1978; Willer & Intagliata, 1980). Follow-up studies on the quality of care provided by group homes have been favorable. Aanes and Moen (1976) took pre- and posttest adaptive behavior measures of 46 residents of group homes. Residents showed significant changes in levels of functioning in measures of independence (e.g., feeding), language development (e.g., speaking), and socialization (e.g., cooperativeness). A study by Schroeder and Henes (1978) reported similar findings, particularly in communication skills. Willer and Intagliata (1980) reported that group-home residents were involved in structured educational and recreational activities in the community. Residents were also more likely to learn new social skills related to community adjustment. A number of additional studies have found successful community adjustments for those placed in group homes (Scheerenberger & Felsenthal, 1976; Gollay, 1977; Eyman, Demaine, & Lei, 1979). However, Bercovici (1983), in her qualitative study of 24 group homes, found only four residences that provided a normalizing environment.

Boarding homes. As many as 30 older, higher-functioning residents may live in a boarding home. Boarding homes are licensed by the state, and care-providers are responsible for providing food and shelter for the residents as well as some supervision of daily living activities.

Studies on the efficacy of boarding-home care are also equivocal. While some investigators have reported positive findings (O'Connor, 1976; Bjaanes & Butler, 1974; Eyman, Silverstein, McLain, & Miller, 1977), the findings of others have not been as encouraging (Skarnulis, 1976; Birenbaum & Re, 1979; Edgerton, 1975). In his study of board-and-care facilities that housed between 30 and 40 residents, Edgerton (1975) reported:

> Some board and care facilities are "open settings" which provide more nearly normalized experiences than large institutions typically do. Most, however, are closed, ghetto-like places, whose residents are walled off from any access to community life. Such places frequently lack most medical, psychological, and recreational services and their amenities are few indeed. Perhaps most significant still, the residents of such facilities are given to understand, in no uncertain terms, that they can hope for nothing different in the future. (p. 131)

Edgerton concluded from this study that for most mentally retarded people in this system, the little institution where they now reside appears to be no better than the larger ones from which they came, and some are ·manifestly worse. Many boarding homes provide inadequate care and unsafe housing for both mentally retarded and mentally ill persons who have been released from institutions. The public is too familiar with newspaper reports of "boarding-home scandals."

Nursing homes.   Because they comply with standards that enable them to receive Medicaid funds, early deinstitutionalization efforts resulted in the dumping of large numbers of retarded persons into nursing homes (O'Connor, Justice, & Warren, 1970; Segal, 1977; General Accounting Office, 1977a; Butterfield, 1977). More recent studies indicate that this pattern has been reversed (Scheerenberger, 1983b; Lakin, Bruininks, Doth, Hill & Hauber, 1982). The quality of care provided by the nursing home is often inferior to that received in the institution. There is evidence that nursing homes are not "therapeutic communities" and that behavioral regression occurs among older profoundly retarded persons, eventually necessitating reinstitutionalization (Brown & Guard, 1979; Willer & Intagliata, 1980; Eyman, Silverstein, McLain, & Miller, 1976; Pagel & Whitling, 1978). However, an earlier study conducted by Lyon and Bland (1964) found a higher quality of care and higher levels of behavior in a group of 25 retarded persons placed in 14 nursing homes. For many elderly non retarded people requiring skilled care, nursing homes serve as a community-living alternative. The increasing number of elderly retarded persons should also have access to this residential option. For both groups, however, there is a need to upgrade the standards of care to provide a more humane environment (Vladeck, 1980).

Institutions.   The deinstitutionalization movement has brought acrimonious debate among mental retardation professionals on the future role of institutions. Some argue for the permanence of the institution as a component of the continuum of residential placements for mentally retarded persons. The National Association of Superintendents of Public Residential Facilities for the Mentally Retarded (1974) takes the position that the development of community programming should not be accomplished by sacrificing quality of services for retarded persons requiring residential care. It is not a question of residential or nonresidential programming. Both are essential and both, in reality, constitute community services.

While admitting there have been some institutions in which the conditions have been deplorable, it is argued there has been excessive generalizations to *all* institutions (Edgerton, Eyman, & Silverstein, 1973). As with community placements, the research indicates that there is considerable variability in the quality of care provided by institutions (Balla, Butterfield, & Zigler, 1974; Klaber, 1969). Kleinberg and Galligan (1983) argue that the assumption that institutionalization is, without qualification, detrimental to client growth is too simplistic. One cannot say that any place is better than an institution. Furthermore, it is claimed that institutional reform is possible and that habilitation programs can prepare residents for community placement (Raynes, Burnstead, & Pratt, 1974; Levy & McLeod, 1977; Witt, 1980; Kleinberg & Galligan, 1982). These proponents further argue that institutional care will always be needed to meet the needs of those retarded persons with severe behavioral and medical problems. To include this population in deinstitutionalization plans is to draw "too wide a swath" (Throne, 1979).

Another group of professionals argue for the "abolishment" of the institution and regard it as a nonviable alternative toward meeting the goals of deinstitutionalization and normalization (Dybwad, 1969; Wolfensberger, 1971a; Blatt et al., 1977; Biklen, 1979). Institutions are considered unreformable and unnatural environments, and it is felt that little can be done to overcome centuries of neglect and abuse inherent in these settings. Wolfensberger (1971b) concluded:

> On programmatic, ideological, and fiscal grounds, the present institutional system is essentially unsalvageable. Indeed, I believe that it is the duty of every institution's superintendent to do all he can to phase out his institution, and to encourage the new residential and service model (36).

Recent developments discussed in Chapters 2 and 4 make it unlikely that institutions will suddenly disappear. While deinstitutionalization efforts will result in the phasing out of many of our larger institutions over the next 20 years, there is a legal and moral responsibility to provide a higher quality of care for those retarded persons who have no other option but institutional placement.

Toward an Ecological Match

A continuum of residential services suggests that community placements vary along some relevant programmatic dimensions (e.g., degree of restrictiveness, types of services provided). In theory, a successful placement would occur by arranging an "optimal person-environment fit" (Butler & Bjaanes, 1977). That is, the needs and characteristics of a particular retarded person would be paired with the type of community services provided. As a retarded person's behavior changed, he would be moved along the continuum to a less (or more) restrictive setting. For example, an adult might move from a group home to an apartment. In practice, we have not yet developed a taxonomy of residential settings to increase the likelihood of appropriate matches (Crawford, Aiello, & Thompson, 1979; Sundberg, Snowden, & Reynolds, 1978; Mayeda & Sutter, 1981; Bjaanes, Butler, & Kelly, 1981). Consequently, mismatches between the retarded person and the recommended community placement may be the major reason for unsuccessful adjustments (Lakin, Bruininks, & Sigford, 1981; Landesman-Dwyer, 1981; Vitello, Atthowe, & Cadwell, 1983). According to Balla and Klein (1981):

> Our informal taxonomies of environments, judged by the extent to which they promote growth and development of retarded persons, have only the status of labels at this time. These labels have taken on great excess meaning. Many people assume that there is a great deal of firm evidence that family environments promote greater psychological growth than do all types of institutional environments, and that there is firm knowledge that the small

community-based institutions are more effective than large central institutions, but available evidence does not support this assumption. (p. 10)

Additional research is needed to determine what variables are associated with a successful community placement for a particular group of mentally retarded persons. Longitudinal studies designed to measure the determinants of client movement along the continuum of residential services are also needed.

Researchers have not adequately operationalized the constructs of "successful community placement" and "improved quality of life" by defining them in terms of the behaviors that these constructs involve. While most agree that a successful placement means more than simply not returning to the institution, there is a lack of consensus regarding what criteria should be used to measure success or quality of life (Edgerton, 1982). Some investigators have operationalized the terms by obtaining measures of changes in adaptive behavior, the degree of client participation in normalizing activities (e.g., use of community services, interaction with nonretarded persons), client self-satisfaction, and personal autonomy. While these multiple outcomes are dimensions of a quality-of-life construct, we must be cautious in our interpretations of their meaning—particularly when one outcome is judged more important than another. Are gains in adaptive behavior—the criteria used in most of the research studies cited in this chapter—more important in determining a successful placement for a severely retarded person than is living in a setting that provides more human care and quality services? Is a mildly retarded person living in an apartment considered a failure because he is unable to find and keep a job, yet is an active member of voluntary organizations in the community? Obviously, what we consider "success" or "quality of life" is a reflection of our own values and our own sense of what is important. In discussing the chimerical nature of "quality of life," Robert Edgerton has pointed out that the freedom to choose is, perhaps, of fundamental importance in determining one's quality of life. This consideration is extremely important in judgments regarding the success or quality of a mentally retarded person's life.

SOCIAL SERVICES

Nonretarded persons depend on social services to meet many of their human needs. The educational and recreational programs available in the community enable people to develop intellectually, socially, and physically. Medical and psychological services provide treatment for those with physical and mental disorders. More recently, these services have provided programs to prevent disabilities and to improve our physical and mental well-being. For example, community health fairs offer free diagnostic services, and the recent physical-fitness craze has stimulated the expansion of recreational programs.

In general, the social service needs of mentally retarded persons are not different from those of nonretarded persons (Fanning, 1973). Yet retarded persons and their families have been and continue to be denied access to generic community services. Unable to obtain community services, families have by necessity turned to the only source of assistance—the institution. According to McCord (1983):

> Human services have constructed a work paradigm of specialized settings and services which have had the effect of minimizing contact between disabled persons and the general population. Workers have learned to assess and respond to the needs of their clients within the confines of agency settings. This previously unchallenged "world view" is now engaged in a struggle with a new paradigm of thought which boldly asserts that unless physical and social integration are cornerstones of service delivery, people will not live valued lives. Normalization requires agency administrators to plan successful strategies for gaining community support for the integration of clients. It instructs human service workers to seek out generic community services which can appropriately replace specialized ones. It places a high priority on the ability of staff to develop relationships with diverse groups of people, such as neighbors of community residences, business people, and school personnel. In short, normalization requires human service workers to shift their energies from sequestering people to the markedly different task of integrating themselves and their clients into all aspects of community life. (p. 251)

In the following sections we will discuss those essential supportive, developmental advocacy services needed by mentally retarded persons and their care-providers.

Supportive Services

The term *supportive services* refers to the assistance provided retarded persons to enable them to benefit from developmental services. In addition, these services help family members or other care-providers in the acceptance and management of a retarded person. Supportive services include counseling, parent education, respite care, transportation, and community education. Financial assistance, another supportive service, will be discussed in Chapter 6.

Counseling. Both immediate and long-term counseling services should be available to retarded persons and their families. As discussed earlier, the birth of a severely retarded child presents a crisis to many families. Immediate emotional support and guidance are needed to help the family cope with this unexpected event. Upon learning that their newborn is retarded, parents want to know why it has happened and to find out what can be done. Obviously, physicians should be among the first to provide parents assistance with their inquiries. As cited earlier, many physicians often lack tact, truthfulness, empathy, and knowledge when counseling parents (Pueschel & Murphy, 1976; Guralnick, 1982; Wolraich, 1982). McDonald, Carson, Palmer, & Slay (1982) have reported some improvement in the support provided by physicians to parents; however, much more progress needs to be made in this area.

An important source of psychological support for families is the community network of other families with a retarded relative (Springer & Steele, 1980; Eheart & Ciccone, 1982; Suelzle & Keenan, 1981; Pizzo, 1983). Members of the local

Association for Retarded Citizens should be contacted and invited to meet with parents of a newborn retarded infant. Immediate crisis intervention at this time often makes the difference in a family's decision to care for their child at home or to consider programs for alternative care (Lavelle & Keogh, 1980; Skelton, 1972; Townsend & Flanagan, 1976).

Family counseling will be needed to assist members in the decision to institutionalize or deinstitutionalize a retarded son or daughter. Family members are often confused and fearful regarding the meaning of such terms as *deinstitutionalization* and *normalization* (Vitello & Atthowe, 1982). Genetic counseling should be available not only to at-risk parents, but also to other family members who suspect that they may be carriers of deleterious genetic material. Legal counseling will be helpful to families on matters dealing with guardianship, estate planning, and life insurance. Where parents feel that the rights of their retarded relative are being denied, access to legal counseling should also be available. Retarded persons themselves can benefit from school, vocational, marriage, and legal counseling services.

It is important to emphasize that the counseling of families with retarded members should involve the entire family, including the retarded person, whenever possible. As noted earlier, many decisions (e.g., institutionalization, sterilization) that are supposedly made in the best interests of the retarded member are in fact in the best interests of other family members. The interests of all family members need to be considered by the counselor. Despite their importance, counseling services still remain unavailable to large numbers of retarded persons and their care-providers (Bruininks, Williams, & Morreau, 1978; Gollay et al., 1978).

Parent education. It is said that parents are a child's first teachers. Parents (and siblings) of retarded children must assume this role earlier in their child's life, and with more intensity and skill. Supportive services are needed to assist the family members in the management of the retarded child's physical, emotional, social, and cognitive development. It has been clearly demonstrated that not only do early educational interventions have a positive effect on the development of the child, but also that they reduce family crises and disorganization (L. B. Vitello, 1977; M. Hansen, 1976; Heber, Garber, Harrington, Hoffman, & Falendar, 1972; Ray, 1974; Stone, 1975).

Parent education can take place in the child's home, community child development centers, or both. Family-training activities might include instruction in the use of prosthetic equipment, the management of inappropriate behavior, and the development of instructional activities to stimulate cognitive and social development. Meetings with school personnel to develop their child's IEP can provide parents additional educational opportunities to learn more about the needs of their child. Equally important, these sessions can alleviate stress, increase family coping, and improve relationships within the family (Turnbull & Turnbull, 1982).

Respite care. Respite care involves the temporary care of a retarded person outside of or inside the family home by another person, in order to provide relief for family members who care for the individual on a 24-hour basis (Katz, 1968). Respite care may be necessary when a family experiences a crisis situation, such as a serious illness, a death, or marital or financial difficulties. The availability of respite care would enable parents to give more attention to their nonretarded children and to each other. Weekend trips and summer vacations may be easier to plan (Aanes & Whitlock, 1975). Respite care services outside the home are provided by foster families, group homes, and when necessary, the local institution (Rodman & Collins, 1974). Respite care within the home is provided by sitter or homemaker services (Arnold & Goodman, 1966). In those situations where placement may be long-term (more than 30 days), provisions should be made for extended care and programming (Borchart & Brooks, 1978).

Wikler and Hanusa (1980) found that providing respite care to families with retarded children reduced family stress. Families also developed more positive attitudes toward their retarded child. Cohen (1982) reported improved mental health and social relationships among parents receiving respite services. Twenty-four percent of the families indicated they would have been unable to care for their retarded child at home without respite services. Additional studies support the assumption that respite services can prevent the institutionalization or reinstitutionalization of mentally retarded persons. In a Massachusetts study of 359 families using respite services, Upshur (1982) reported the following findings: (1) Respite care was used by 44 percent of the families for relief from physical or emotional strain of care, 20 percent for family vacations, 16 percent for family emergencies, and 13 percent for planned special circumstances. (2) Care during the day or evening in the family's own house (less than overnight) was the most frequently used type of care. (3) Problems encountered in providing respite care included client reluctance to leave family members (34.2 percent), family members not returning at agreed time (31.4 percent), and lack of transportation (25.7 percent).

Whereas Gollay and colleagues (1978) found that 60 percent of the families in their study received respite services, Bruininks, Williams, & Morreau (1978) reported that 75 percent of their respondents felt respite-care servcies were unavailable or available only on a limited basis.

Transportation. To enable mentally retarded persons to gain access to community services and activities, it is necessary to provide a variety of transport modes. Conventional public transportation services (e.g., buses, subways, cabs, trains) can be used by most retarded persons. Many mildly retarded persons can be taught to operate a motor vehicle in public school driver-education programs. For severely retarded persons with mobility problems, however, adaptations are necessary in existing transport modes, or else specialized forms of transportation are required (Hull, 1979). Several earlier studies have indicated that a large number of retarded persons placed in the community did not have access to public transportation (A. Browder et al., 1974; O'Connor, 1976; Bruininks, Williams, & Morreau, 1978). This situation presents a formidable barrier both to access to community services and to efforts to further the social integration among retarded and nonretarded persons.

Community education. Supportive services must be available to promote the public awareness and acceptance of retarded persons as neighbors, employees, and fellow citizens (Horejsi, 1975). Negative community attitudes toward the retarded are often based on lack of information and understanding. Formal campaigns of public education must be instituted to provide the community with accurate information and with increased opportunities to come into contact with retarded persons. Public education can be undertaken by parent and community groups. Private nonprofit public education centers, such as Horizon House Institute (1977) in Philadelphia, have conducted community forums throughout Pennsylvania in an effort to improve attitudes toward the mentally disabled. However, such programs are lacking in most states (Bruininks, Williams, & Morreau, 1978). Recently, the mass media (newspaper, radio, and television) have undertaken campaigns to provide the public with information about the needs and rights of the mentally retarded. Community planning for the housing and educational needs of mentally retarded persons provides an excellent forum for public education. In addition, statewide "Disability Awareness Fairs" and local "Mayors' Forums" are other strategies that can be used to promote public education.

Developmental Services

Developmental services are the direct services designed to further the physical, social, and cognitive development of retarded persons. These services include health care, special education, vocational training, employment, recreation, and religious instruction.

Health care. Health-care services assist people in dealing with their medical and psychological problems. Health-care services are critically needed by these retarded persons who have concomitant neurological problems (e.g., seizures), or orthopedic, cardiac, or respiratory problems. Such conditions require immediate medical attention to prevent further disability and to facilitate the family's management of the child.

Infants born severely retarded or at high risk (e.g., premature infants) require that their condition be monitored over an extended period of time. This monitoring can be performed by a pediatrician and visiting nurse who are trained to deliver health care to retarded infants and their families. A desirable arrangement would be for a pediatrician to periodically examine a retarded child at an outpatient community hospital, with follow-up home visits by a pediatric nurse. The visiting nurse could further assist the family by: (1) providing instruction in the correct handling of a physically handicapped child; (2) supervising the administration of medication; (3) assisting in the preparation of special diets; (4) checking that immunizations are received; and (5) recommending dentists and ophthalmologists who serve retarded children. Similar health-care services need to be made available to the increasing number of older retarded citizens who suffer ailments attributable to aging.

In addition to providing general health-care services for retarded persons, outpatient community hospitals can provide short-term medical treatment (e.g., surgery, physical therapy), thereby eliminating the dependency on institutional services. Mentally retarded persons and other family members experiencing mental health problems also need access to outpatient and inpatient community mental health clinics that provide psychological and psychiatric services (i.e., family and group therapy). The unavailability of these services is a major cause for the institutionalization and reinstitutionalization of mentally retarded persons (Jacobsen & Swartz, 1983).

Preventive health-care programs that address such topics as exercise, nutrition, sex education, dental care, and weight and stress control would be beneficial to many retarded persons. Reports show that health services are becoming increasingly available to retarded persons in the community (Bruininks, Williams, & Morreau, 1978; Gollay et al., 1978). However, insufficiencies still exist in rehabilitative therapies (e.g., physical therapy), speech, and mental health services for retarded persons (Intagliata, Kraus, & Willer, 1980; Jacobson & Schwartz, 1983). More will be said about health services in Chapter 6.

Special education.   As discussed in Chapter 3, P.L. 94-142 mandates that free, publicly supported educational services be provided children from 6 to 17 years of age. The law mandates that services should be provided in the least restrictive school setting. The "cascade" of educational settings where special education services would be delivered at the elementary and secondary levels is depicted in Figure 5-3 (Deno, 1970). Most mildly retarded children can receive their instruction in *regular classes.* A regular classroom teacher trained in special education should be able to make the necessary instructional accommodations to ensure pupil progress. In those regular classes where the teacher lacks training in special education, consultant and/or itinerant-teacher services can be provided. Some schools have *resource rooms* that service mildly retarded children enrolled in regular classes. Resource rooms are under the direction of a special educator who provides intensive supplemental instruction for one or a small number of children. Some mentally retarded children receive *part-time special class* instruction (perhaps a half a day) and are integrated into regular class activities (e.g., art, music, physical education) for the remainder of the school day. This administrative option is commonly found at the junior and senior high school levels for mildly and moderately retarded students. As discussed earlier, *full-day special classes* have been the commonly used setting to provide instruction for the mildly retarded. This is no longer the preferred placement for this group of children. Special classes in regular public schools, however, are appropriate placements for moderately, severely, and profoundly retarded children who require full-day special educational programming. When appropriate educational programs cannot be provided in the above settings, it may become necessary to serve retarded children in separate *public or private schools.* P.L. 94-142 requires that state departments of education make provisions to provide appropriate educational services for retarded children residing in these facilities. This has resulted in efforts to transport institutionalized children to

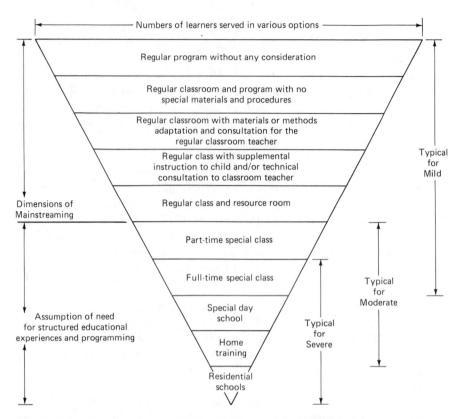

FIGURE 5-3 A Cascade System of Educational Placements. (From E. Deno, *Special Educa-tion as Developmental Capital. Exceptional Children*, 1970, *37*, p. 235. Re-printed by Permission.)

community public school programs. The settings described above represent a continuum for providing educational services for mentally retarded children. Clearly, the preference is to place as many retarded children as possible in less restrictive, integrated educational settings and to prevent their segregation from other children.

While a variety of educational services for school-age retarded children (between 6 and 17) are now available in the public schools, and the services for preschoolers and pupils between ages 18 and 21 are increasing, there is an unmet need for services at the ends of the age continuum (Thurlow, Bruininks, Williams, & Morreau, 1978). Infant stimulation programs have had demonstrable effects in enhancing the cognitive, social, and motor development of severely retarded new-borns (Bruininks, Thurlow, Thurman, & Fiorelli, 1980). In the past, this service was provided primarily by private agencies (e.g., local Association for Retarded Citizens), hospitals, and a few school districts. Five states now mandate educa-tional services for handicapped children, beginning at birth; an additional 28 states permit the establishment of such programs (U. S. Department of Education, 1982). At the other end of the age continuum, mentally retarded adults (the so-called "aging out" population) can derive increased benefits from extended learning opportunities offered by adult and continuing-education classes in the local high schools (Gollay et al., 1978). In addition, community and junior colleges, as well as four-year colleges, can provide courses geared to slower learners (Jones & Moe, 1980). Social services agencies should encourage retarded persons to use other community configurations (e.g., libraries, museums) that provide educational opportunities. The availability of lifelong educational services will not only prevent the need for institutionalization, but also will enable mentally retarded persons to obtain higher levels of independence and satisfaction in community living.

Vocational training.   The goal of vocational-training programs for mentally retarded persons should be to prepare them for gainful employment in the community. Work not only enables one to be economically independent, but it also provides a sense of worth and accomplishment, even enjoyment. Society also benefits from the employment of retarded persons, in the form of increased tax revenues and decreased welfare costs. Going to work affords a retarded person many normalizing opportunities to interact with people, make friends, and participate in recreational and social activities. Because success on the job requires appropriate work attitudes and social behavior as well as technical skills, the *career-education* concept has been proposed as a guide to curriculum development for mentally retarded students (Brolin & Alonzo, 1979; Davis & Ward, undated). Career education has been defined as the totality of experiences through which one learns about and prepares to engage in work as part of his or her way of living. In the early school years, the curriculum emphasizes the development of nonvocational skills (e.g., money management, use of transportation) that are prerequisites to employability. While skill development continues in the higher grades, career exploration and preparation are given more attention.

Several pieces of federal legislation have provided an impetus for the implementation of the career-education concept. The Vocational Rehabilitation Act of 1973, the Education for All Handicapped Children Act of 1975, and the Vocational Educational Act (1976 Amendments) encourage more cooperative efforts among vocational education, special education, and rehabilitation services (Brolin & Alonzo, 1979; Davis & Ward, undated). For example, a provision in the 1976 vocational amendments reads:

> The (vocational education) program provided each handicapped child will be planned and coordinated in conformity with and as a part of the child's individualized educational program as required by the Education for All Handicapped Children Act. (20 U.S.C. & 2301 et. seq.)

This act also requires that states match the federal funds that are set aside to be used for the vocational education of handicapped students.

In adherence to the normalization and mainstreaming principles, *regular vocational education* services should provide programs for the mentally retarded and prepare them for competitive employment in the community (Albright, 1979) (see Figure 5-4). The inclusion of retarded students in regular vocational programs

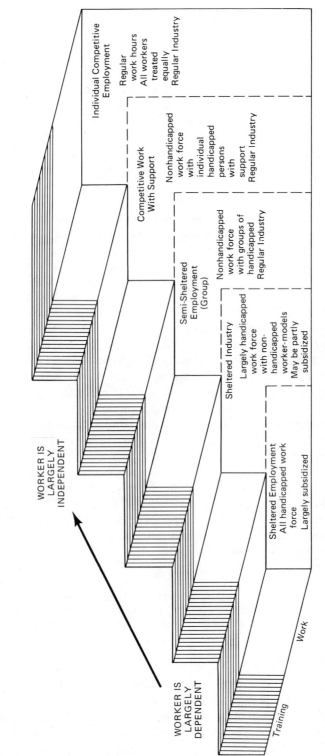

FIGURE 5–4 Continuum of Employment Options from Dependent to Independent. (Adapted from J. DuRand and A.H. Neufeldt. Comprehensive Vocational Services. In R.J. Flynn and K.E. Nitsch (Eds.), *Normalization, Social Integration and Community Services.* Baltimore: University Park Press, 1980. Reprinted by Permission.)

will necessitate the adaptation of instructional materials and strategies. In addition, supportive special services (e.g., resource rooms) may be needed. For those retarded students who cannot benefit from placement in regular vocational education programs, *special vocational programs* should be available. Both regular and special vocational education programs should provide work-study programs to assist the student in bridging the gap between school and work. Regular and special vocational educational programs for mildly and moderately retarded students are currently available in comprehensive high schools, county and vocational and technical schools, and community colleges. However, in a study of 92 public school projects providing vocational education services to special-needs students, Walsh (1975) found that (1) a nonproductive relationship existed between vocational education and special education; (2) in 70 percent of the projects, the special vocational education programs provided for the handicapped showed very little evidence of integration into regular programs; (3) only limited work-study experiences were available; and (4) 63 percent of the handicapped students were enrolled in non-skill-training courses that would not prepare them to compete in the open labor market. This study suggests that much remains to be done to improve vocational education programs for mentally retarded students in the public schools.

Sheltered workshop programs are offered in public and private schools as well as in institutions for mentally retarded persons. In addition, public and private rehabilitation agencies (e.g., Goodwill, Inc.; Association for Retarded Citizens) secure contract work that provides retarded persons sheltered employment and training in the community. In the past, because of the unavailability of public school vocational education programs, the only alternative for training many high-functioning retarded persons was placement in a sheltered workshop. Retarded persons who could have been trained to seek competitive employment were required to perform jobs involving low-level skills where the chief objective was production, not training. Consequently, many higher-functioning retarded persons remained in sheltered workshops rather than moving into the labor market (Greenleigh Associates, Inc., 1975; Department of Labor, 1977; Moss, 1977). A recent study by Berkowitz, Dean, Rubin, and Sheehy (1981) suggests that this situation still exists today.

Sheltered workshop services have been available to moderately and severely retarded persons who have been judged unable to benefit from regular and special vocational programs. It was at one time universally accepted that moderately and severely retarded persons were "unemployable" in competitive labor markets. Research has demonstrated convincingly that not only the moderately retarded but also many severely retarded persons can develop vocational skills that are marketable (Gold, 1973; Bellamy, Horner, & Inman, 1979; Wehman & Hill, 1981; Rusch & Mithaug, 1980). Sheltered employment should be viewed not as a final goal in the rehabilitation of most retarded persons, but rather as a transitional stage in preparation for competitive employment. Only those retarded persons too handicapped mentally and/or physically should be placed in adult work-activity centers where the emphasis is more therapeutic than habilitative. Lakin, Bruininks, Doth, Hill, & Hauber (1982) report that the number of sheltered workshop placements more than tripled between 1969 and 1977; placements in adult work-activity centers grew four fold to 105,000 between 1971 and 1979. In the future, greater efforts must be made in both the private and public sectors to prepare more retarded persons for gainful employment.

Employment. As is the case with many nonretarded persons, retarded persons encounter unemployment and underemployment in the job market, particularly during periods of national economic instability. Moreover, because they have been labeled mentally retarded, many qualified individuals are victims of prejudice and systematic discrimination in the job market (Gliedman & Roth, 1980). The Vocational Rehabilitation Act of 1973 attempts to reverse these practices. Section 503 requires affirmative action in the hiring and promotion of qualified handicapped persons by employers who have contracts with the federal government in excess of $2,500 per year. Section 504 prohibits discrimination against otherwise qualified individuals in any program or activity receiving financial assistance from the federal government. Despite the existence of these employment-discrimination statutes, the Department of Labor has received only a small number of complaints from mentally retarded persons concerning employment discrimination. This may reflect the lack of appropriate job training for mentally retarded persons, the lack of aggressive support and advocacy for mentally retarded clients by vocational-rehabilitation and sheltered-workshop counselors, or the defeatist attitude of mentally retarded persons who have been convinced that they cannot get or hold jobs. If the mentally retarded are to benefit from existing legislation, it is essential that enforcement mechanisms be established to take action against those employers who violate the law.

The President's Committee on Employment of the Handicapped serves an advocacy function by promoting employment opportunities for retarded persons. The Committee also educates potential employers and the public about the vocational abilities of retarded persons (Brewer & Kakalik, 1979). The Employment Services Program attempts to place retarded persons in jobs that match their abilities. Job-placement, follow-up, and counseling services are critical to the long-term employment of mentally retarded persons. Rehabilitation counselors are needed to work with potential employers. Despite the federal laws that encourage increased vocational education services and employment opportunities for retarded persons, unemployment remains a major factor in the unsuccessful community adjustment of many retarded persons (Bruininks, Williams, & Morreau, 1978; Willer, 1978).

Recreation. The recreational needs of retarded persons are as great as those of nonretarded persons (Day & Day, 1977; Luckey & Shapiro, 1974). Recreational activities provide retarded persons with opportunities to engage in pursuits that further their physical and social development. For many retarded children who may find schoolwork difficult, recreation can provide both enjoyable activities and easy-to-learn skills. Activities can be planned that involve the participation of other family members (e.g., the "Let's Play to Grow" program sponsored by the

Joseph P. Kennedy, Sr. Foundation). Since many retarded adults may be unemployed or may work fewer hours, it is important that they learn to manage their leisure time in a productive way. Activities restricted solely to watching television, going to the movies, or doing nothing contribute little to a retarded person's social and cognitive development (Katz & Yekutiel, 1974; Gollay et al., 1978).

Mildly retarded persons have always had access to generic community-based recreational programs such as the YMCA/YWCA, after-school programs, and recreational park programs. However, such public programs, while increasing, remain unavailable to many severely retarded persons. Special recreational programs such as scouting, Special Olympics, summer camps, and swimming for severely retarded persons are typically sponsored by parent, civic, and church groups. Volunteer groups arrange trips to a sporting event, the bowling alley, and to other community events (e.g., library exhibits, museums, fairs, festivals). Recently, considerable interest has been given to extending the community's generic recreational programs to *all* retarded persons. The Association for Retarded Citizens has defined the public's responsibility in this area by adopting the following resolution:

> Mentally retarded citizens should have equal access to publicly supported recreational facilities . . . public recreation agencies should do everything within their power to make these facilities adaptable to the needs of the retarded and other handicapped persons. (Luckey & Shapiro, 1974, p. 34)

Needless to say, the realization of this resolution can do much to further both the integration of the mentally retarded and their acceptance in the community (Salzberg & Langford, 1981).

Unfortunately, limited progress has been made in providing adequate recreational programs for retarded persons living in the community (Reiter & Levi, 1981). Unawareness of recreational programs, inaccessibility due to transportation, architectural and attitudinal barriers, and lack of funds account for the lack of progress (Bruininks, Williams, & Morreau, 1978; Willer, 1978; Corcoran & French, 1977).

Religious instruction. For many families, the church or synagogue is a focal point of community-wide religious and social activity. Oftentimes, the presence of a retarded child in the family curtails participation in church functions, particularly when the church has a policy of excluding mentally retarded persons. This situation is paradoxical in that, historically, the church has accepted and provided a haven for retarded persons. Full participation by retarded persons in church activities is inherent in religious teachings. Sunday schools, church picnics, Christmas and Easter programs should include retarded children and their families (Brockwell, 1963; Krummel, 1975). Such activities not only serve as a source of spiritual growth for retarded persons but also provides families the needed support and acceptance by the church and community (Shapiro, 1964; Theodore, 1966).

Service Delivery Systems

The shift in the locus of service delivery for increasing numbers of mentally retarded people will require not only increased access to community services but also the coordination of these services. For example, a severely retarded child living at home or in a community residential facility (e.g., group house) may require educational, medical, and recreational services. In addition, family members or other care-providers may need counseling and respite services.

Service-delivery systems are often described as fragmented, uncoordinated, and duplicative. The result is that many people are poorly served or unserved, at high human and economic costs. The present state of service delivery can be partly attributed to the rapid expansion of categorical programs for disadvantaged groups during the 1960s and 1970s. Today, local and state governments are making greater efforts to integrate these overlapping programs.

Service integration refers to the linking together of two or more service-providers to ensure a more efficient and unified system of care. Essential components of service integration include the reorganization of social services agencies; the expansion of generic services to serve special groups; and increased client participation in the planning and delivery of services. The following measures have been suggested to achieve service integration: (1) establishment of a fixed point of entry into the service system; (2) institution of a case-management system at the local level; (3) collocation of services; and (4) development of retraining programs for service-providers (Polivka et al., 1981). Pending fiscal cutbacks, concerns about job security, and active lobbying for categorical programs are a few of the obstacles that impede service integration. Given the competition for limited resources among social service agencies, the argument has been made that advocates for various disability groups should combine their efforts to ensure themselves a larger piece of the shrinking social services pie.

Service integration within the public sector needs to be complemented by linkages between the public and private sectors in the delivery of services to disabled people. Reductions in government allocations for social services have forced local and state agencies to contract with organizations in the private sector. Where gaps exist in the provision of services, this so-called privatization of social services will also require the increased participation of families and the voluntary sector.

Self-Help Networks

Throughout the United States in recent years, there has been a ground swell of self-help or mutual-aid groups (Pizzo, 1983; Whittaker & Garbarino, 1983). It is estimated that 15 million Americans belong to some 500,000 self-help groups (National Self-Help Clearinghouse, 1980). According to Glazer (1983):

> Self-help can take many forms from the direct provision of concrete assistance and sympathy, to the insistence that government do more (a common role for advocacy groups), to the insistence (particularly in the United States) that the courts establish certain rights that will lead government, individual employers, local providers of service, or voluntary agencies to do more. Thus, the new forms of voluntarism and the new growth of the non-statutory sector do not have the weaknesses that have been criticized as "Lady Bountiful" charity. They are the self-help of those who work to

escape from an overbearing government or other large bureaucratic institutions—and who wish, too, to make their institutions more responsive. (p. 87)

Naisbeth (1982) adds:

> Self-help means community groups acting to prevent crime, to strengthen neighborhoods, to salvage food for the elderly, and to rebuild homes, without government assistance or at least with local control over government help. (p. 133)

Self-help networks are not new to parents with mentally retarded children. The Association for Retarded Citizens is perhaps the prototype for the formation of a self-help group. Small groups of parents coming together with shared problems and concerns, helping one another, sharing information and resources, are the elements that are embodied in the self-help movement. In addition to parent groups, there is a growing network of self-help groups comprised of mentally retarded persons themselves.

Glazer (1983) concludes his discussion of the "self-service society" with this analysis:

> A greater degree of voluntarism and of self-help can do a great deal to provide for needs and services that, if provided through the state, require a heavy burden of taxation, high deficits, and a variety of unpleasant and increasingly dangerous economic developments. Certainly the role of the welfare state is still crucial. But it must more and more ponder partnerships with the variety of voluntary, market, nonstatutory organizations and mechanism that we find in each society. (pp. 89–90)

ADVOCACY SERVICES

Advocacy means many things to many people. The popularity of the word and the frequency of its use make all of us, no matter what we do, believe that we are advocates. Mentally retarded persons often discover that everyone, including parents, attorney, physician, social worker, social security representative, and institutional director, proclaims to be their advocate. If perceived too broadly, the term *advocacy* can become meaningless, encompassing virtually everything good that is done on behalf of an individual (Kahn, Kamerman, & McGowan, 1972).

Stated succinctly, an advocate is someone who "pleads the cause of another" (*Webster's,* 1975). More specifically, advocacy is a set of beliefs that result in action aimed at defending, maintaining, or promoting another person's cause (Paul, Wiegerink, & Neufeld, 1974). If individuals were all-powerful and could realize their wishes and remedy their grievances by mere will, there would be no need for advocacy. But the reality of the world is such that virtually all citizens at sometime require assistance in these endeavors. Advocacy is nothing more than the provision of such assistance, in numerous forms, by one's fellow individuals.

Advocacy and Mental Retardation

For the following reasons, advocacy on behalf of mentally retarded persons requires more. Mentally retarded persons, by definition, experience deficits in intellectual functioning and adaptive behavior that put them at a disadvantage in the transactions of everyday life. By the nature of their disability, many retarded persons do not know their rights or understand the legal mechanisms that can enable them to assert those rights. Much to our nation's discredit, mentally retarded persons have been systematically discriminated against and denied these basic rights and services available to all citizens. A mentally retarded person will most likely be involved with a number of social agencies (e.g., state departments of mental retardation). The complexity in dealing with even one of these bureau-cracies overwhelms the most knowledgeable citizens. Without advocates to assist them, the care of mentally retarded persons would be at the whim of society, a not-too-pleasant thought when one observes the treatment of these individuals. According to Herr (1979), "it is difficult to imagine a segment of the eligible client population more in need of specialist advocacy services on the basis of 'relative need' than mentally retarded persons."

Advocacy services are needed by mentally retarded persons residing in both institutions and in community living arrangements. Herr (1979) lists the following specific areas in which advocacy services are needed:

1. Challenges to involuntary commitment on grounds of mental retardation
2. Creation of a network of less restrictive alternatives to institutionalization
3. Representation at due process hearings under P.L. 94-142 and guardianship proceedings
4. Compliance with individualized habilitation and education plans under Medicaid (e.g., Title XIX) and P.L. 94-142
5. Protection of the right to refuse habilitation without retaliatory discharge
6. Securing damages and injunctive relief to halt abuse and brutality against residents
7. Achieving parity of access to social services for clients, regardless of their place of residence

With the need for advocacy for mentally retarded persons very much evident, it is important to focus on the various types of advocacy and to note their useful-ness and limitations. Before this is done, distinctions among protective services, guardianship, and advocacy need to be drawn.

Advocacy and Protective Services

Protective services connotes an array of services that are provided by an agency (e.g., Division of Mental Retardation) to ensure the appropriate care and treatment of mentally retarded persons. In other words, it is a system imposed from the outside to intervene on behalf of mentally retarded individuals in order to shield them from a threatening or harmful situation. As originally envisioned, protective services were a form of *systems advocacy*. Systems advocacy is "the process of influencing social and political systems to bring about change for groups of people" (Eklund, 1976). This can be accomplished by: (1) initiating, influencing, and monitoring legislation; (2) identifying services needed and/or changes sought in the service delivery system; (3) initiating, influencing, and assisting in the development of new services and in the improvement and expansion of existing services; and (4) promoting the active involvement of a diversity of consumers in planning, policy making, and monitoring of services (Moore, 1976).

Over time, the nature of protective services has changed from its initial advocacy purpose. According to Wolfensberger (1973), protective services evolved in an era in which local comprehensive human service systems had not yet developed. Thus, protective services combined within one agency both social-casework and advocacy functions. By the 1970s service systems had been created for mentally retarded persons. Protective services now constitute a system where paid employees of a public agency provided formal, social-casework-type assistance to mentally retarded persons. As Herr (1976) describes protective services, they "tend to be social services operated by and within state agencies providing habilitation, services and treatment to disabled and other classes of persons presumed to be at risk from themselves or others." Similarly, Boggs (1968) describes protective services as "social services directed toward the welfare of individuals who are not fully able to act for themselves, by an organized social agency which has the capacity to invoke legal sanctions to reinforce its efforts on behalf of the client."

In short, the development of the services system over the past few decades has transformed the concept of protective services from that of an outside force battling to create services to that of an internal agency mechanism designed to dispense services. The problem now confronted by mentally retarded persons is access to those services in a system characterized by increased bureaucratic obstacles and limited resources. Wolfensberger (1973) and Herr (1976) have argued that it was necessary to create an independent advocacy system to represent the interests of mentally retarded persons. Client interests are often in jeopardy when they conflict with the professional's loyalty to the agency that employs him (Holburn, 1982).

In summary, when mentally retarded persons lacked basic social services, the protective services approach was, in fact, advocacy. Once established, however, welfare and social services became an integral part of the system and, in a sense, took on the attributes of the bureaucracy. In this context, advocacy must function separately from protective services. Advocacy goes a step beyond the provision of social benefits and services; it assumes that these services themselves need systematic monitoring. The result is that the protective service arrangement, while valuable in itself, now becomes the target of advocacy. Though the system is serving individuals, advocacy demands that the services be improved, that the nature of services be altered, and that budgets be increased (Kahn et al., 1972).

Advocacy and Guardianship Services

Guardianship services provide a legal mechanism through which a third person can substitute as a decision maker for the good or benefit of a mentally retarded person who does not possess the capacity to make informed decisions on his own behalf. In the provision of both protective services and guardianship services, decisions are made and actions are taken on the basis of a third party's conception of what is best for the mentally retarded person. Advocacy, on the other hand, is a mechanism to enhance a person's ability to act or to advance his or her *own* interests and wishes. The impetus for the decision emanates from the individual and *not* from the third party providing assistance. Thus, advocacy is not an imposition of a third party's beliefs upon a mentally retarded person regardless of the retarded person's wishes. Advocacy is not a substituted judgment for the individual based on a third party's notion of that individual's "best interests." Furthermore, advocacy is not the provision of an array of services to an individual by a system that has *a priori* determined what that individual needs. Advocacy requires communication between a third person and the mentally retarded person, and it requires actions consistent with the interests and wishes of the mentally retarded person. This is not to say that an advocate cannot be a counselor, advising and discussing alternative choices with the mentally retarded person. But it does mean that the mentally retarded person will have freedom to act through the assistance of the advocate, even if such action is not considered the "ideal" or "preferable" course of action. Advocacy services free individuals to live as they choose, even if the results include failures or setbacks.

A parent, as a natural legal guardian for a minor, often serves in the same capacity as the child's advocate, but it must be remembered that the parent (or any other legal guardian) is not always equivalent to an advocate. The roles, though overlapping, are different; one must be careful to make this distinction, lest the parent or guardian act on vested interests that are in conflict with those of the retarded person. The advocate must insist on protecting the client's rights and not succumb to third-party desires that conflict with those rights.

Congress and the former United States Department of Health, Education and Welfare have made the distinctions between advocacy, protective services, and guardianship services in the establishment of the State Protection and Advocacy Systems under Section 113 of the Developmentally Disabled Assistance and Bill of Rights Act of 1975. Each state, pursuant to its federal developmental-disabilities funding, must establish an independent protection and advocacy system for its developmentally disabled residents. By *independent*, it is meant that the system be free from state control as well as free from the control of service-providers. From the Senate amendment, Congress deleted sections on protective services and guardianship, thereby casting Section 113 in a clear advocacy light (Herr, 1976). When some states, such as Illinois, attempted to create an agency that would also provide guardianship-type services within its protection and advocacy system, the Developmental Disabilities Office within HEW resisted. After some dispute, the federal government forcefully backed its position in its proposed regulations to implement the DD Act:

> Some States have proposed to place the protection and advocacy office in an agency which provides guardianship. The Department considers guardianship a service. Since Sec. 113[a][2] requires that the protection and advocacy system be independent of any agency which provides services to persons with developmental disabilities, we believe guardianship and protection and advocacy may not be combined. There is a potential conflict in guardianship cases because guardianship arrangements, especially involving adults, impose limitations on the ward's rights.

Guardianship has evolved into a specific role, distinct from advocacy. Frequently, states have defined it in limited forms, imposing it on mentally retarded persons in specific areas in which they cannot competently function (Dussault, 1978). Most important, it is now commonly recognized that the appointment or existence of a guardian does not preclude the need for an advocate.

ADVOCACY RESOURCES

Three major types of advocacy will be discussed below: citizen, legal, and self-advocacy.

Citizen Advocacy

In 1970 the Capitol Association for Retarded Citizens established the first citizen-advocacy service for mentally retarded persons (Novak, 1973). The following year the Greater Omaha, Nebraska, ARC established a similar program. Nationwide throughout the 1970s, the program models were being instituted by local ARCs. The efforts were stimulated by the availability of funds under the Developmentally Disabled Assistance and Bill of Rights Act.

A citizen advocate has been defined as "a mature, competent citizen volunteer representing, as if they were his own, the interests of another citizen who is impaired in his instrumental competency, or who has major expressive needs which are unmet and which are likely to remain unmet with special intervention" (Wolfensberger, 1973). Citizen advocates assume defender roles (e.g., securing access to educational services), instrumental roles (e.g., helping with money management), and expressive roles (e.g., providing emotional support) (Addison, 1976; National Association for Retarded Citizens, 1974).

Kurtz (1975) questions the reality of the "desirable" citizen advocate model:

> ... mature, competent, unpaid, committed, motivated, inspired, stable, must have continuity in the community, be willing to undergo orientation, understand his specific advocacy mission, have good moral character, have

desirable characteristics, share common interests with the retardate, have time free to carry on the relationship and have sincere humanitarian reasons for wanting to enter into the relationship. (p. 386)

Kurtz believes that it is naive to expect such people to step forward. If Wolfensberger's warnings against paid advocates are adhered to, the sheer number of volunteers needed to make these sacrifices and to volunteer their services does constitute a significant obstacle to the quality and success of citizen-advocacy programs. It has been noted recently that there are fewer than 5,000 advocate-protégé matches between volunteers and retarded persons throughout the country (Herr, 1979). Danker-Brown, Sigelman and Bensberg (1979), in a study of 25 advocacy-protégé matches, found advocates engaged in expressive roles regardless of the retarded person's age and level of retardation; little activity occurred in the areas of skill training and defense of rights. Kurtz (1975) goes on to suggest that citizen advocacy would not have had much effect without the concurrent development of legal advocacy services for mentally retarded persons.

Legal Advocacy

About the time when citizen-advocacy systems began to appear, ARCs also began to turn to legal advocacy. Typically, legal advocacy is practiced by attorneys who use the judicial process to define and enforce the rights of mentally retarded persons. As discussed in Chapters 2 and 3, early legal victories resulting from this joint effort were lawsuits to establish the right to education for mentally retarded children (*Pennsylvania Association for Retarded Children (P.A.R.C.)* v. *Commonwealth of Pennsylvania,* 1972) and the right to habilitation (*New York State Association for Retarded Citizens* v. *Rockefeller (Carey),* 1975). Herr (1979) urges lawyers to continue their efforts to support and assist consumer groups (e.g., ARCs) in securing the rights of mentally retarded persons. Unfortunately, the availability of legal-advocacy services is not keeping pace with the demand that mentally retarded persons and their families have for these services.

The opportunities that a law student has to learn about the legal issues involving mentally retarded and other disabled persons, though increasing, are still limited. Thus, law schools are not training a sufficient number of knowledgeable lawyers to provide advocacy services for mentally retarded persons and other disadvantaged groups. Furthermore, after becoming a part of the private bar, individual attorneys have little financial incentive to concern themselves with the advocacy needs of disabled persons. While the social activism of the 1960s and early 1970s offered the promise of dedicated legal advocates for the disabled, and law firms pledged to provide *pro bono* legal assistance, these promises have quickly faded. Moreover, the availability of job opportunities within the mental health field are rapidly shrinking as advocacy systems lose their funding and are forced to go out of business.

Legal Advocacy Systems

American Bar Association.   Unable to rely on individual or private commitments, legal advocacy efforts turned to established systems to train and employ legal advocates for mentally retarded persons. The American Bar Association responded in the 1970s by creating a Commission on the Mentally Disabled. This rapidly grew into numerous components, including the publication of the *Mental Disability Law Reporter* (now the *Mental and Physical Disability Law Reporter*), the establishment of a legislative reform section to develop and implement model state legislation, and the funding of various demonstration advocacy projects. The Commission held the promise of an active, influential bar that was supportive of the interests of mentally retarded persons.

Advocacy projects.   The federal government (e.g., Departments of Health and Human Services, Education) has funded legal advocacy services as a means of ensuring the protection of the rights of mentally retarded persons. Since 1972, it has helped fund several advocacy projects on a national and regional basis, including such projects as the National Center for Law and the Handicapped, the Mental Health Law Project, the Public Interest Law Center of Philadelphia, the Maryland Developmental Disabilities Law Center, and the Center for Law and Health Sciences. Several states have also funded legal advocacy projects (e.g., New York Mental Health Information Service, Ohio Legal Rights Service). In addition, private foundations have helped some public interest firms to operate (e.g., Mental Health Law Project, Education Law Center).

The inherent problem with all of these advocacy-project efforts has been uncertainties of funding. Many projects have come and gone, while others have shifted their focus, depending upon the source of funding. In the 1980s under President Reagan's new proposals, it appears that little, if any, federal money will be budgeted for legal services for mentally retarded persons or for any other activities that are perceived as "political advocacy." Furthermore, money from private foundations are extremely difficult to obtain, and state resources will be severely limited in the years ahead. Consequently, those advocacy projects that now provide legal services for mentally retarded persons will have a difficult time surviving.

Justice Department.   The Justice Department has played a meaningful but controversial role in advocacy over the past decade. Through its Office of Special Litigation in the Office of Civil Rights, the Justice Department has intervened in numerous institutional cases on behalf of mentally retarded persons (e.g., *Wyatt, NYSARC, Horacek, Halderman*). Given the limited financial resources that other advocacy groups possess, the intervention of the Justice Department as plaintiff or *amicus curiae,* with its abundant resources, has enabled a strong advocacy effort to be made in each of these cases. The resources have enabled the parties to conduct full and extensive investigations of institutional conditions and to secure expert witnesses to support claims for institutional reform.

The controversy arising from the Justice Department's role in intervention has resulted from the heated opposition by states to the federal government's interference with the running of their mental retardation facilities. While failing to have the Justice Department barred in cases which it intervened (*Horacek* v. *Exon,* 1973; *Halderman* v. *Pennhurst State School and Hospital,* 1977), the states have successfully blocked the filing of suits brought directly by the Justice Department (*U.S.* v. *Solomon,* 1977; *U.S.* v. *Mattson,* 1979). In 1980, Congress enacted a bill entitled the Civil Rights of Institutionalized Persons Act (P.L. 96-247). This statute permits the Attorney General to institute a civil action against a state or political subdivision of a state on behalf of persons residing in or confined to an institution to safeguard the individuals' rights, privileges or immunities secured or protected by the Constitution or laws of the United States. While this legislation may have significant impact on major institutional litigation on behalf of mentally retarded persons, it is generally believed that the circumstances under which these powers will be invoked will be limited, depending on the prevailing political climate. The climate in the early 1980s, with an apparent halt to active civil rights enforcement and a heightened deference to state autonomy, signals the curtailment in the use of these new powers. In fact, the Justice Department has interpreted the *Youngberg* v. *Romeo* decision to mean that the department will investigate institutional facilities to ensure that residents are guaranteed safety and freedom from unnecessary restraints, but that it will not intervene to determine whether institutions provide habilitative programs for mentally retarded persons.

State advocacy systems. With the passage of the Developmentally Disabled Assistance and Bill of Rights Act of 1975, the federal government provided substantial support to legal advocacy services for disabled persons. Section 113 of the Act mandates the creation of state protection and advocacy (P&A) systems with the "authority to pursue legal, administrative, and other appropriate remedies" for mentally retarded persons. In many states, however, the reality is that the legal authority of P&As, especially to file lawsuits, is significantly constrained. In addition, the development of legal advocacy services within each state system has been uneven, with some states establishing legal staffs of up to five or six attorneys while other states operate without a legal staff. Consequently, very few advocacy agencies are able to provide direct legal assistance. Again, a major obstacle to an effective advocacy service has been the uncertainties of funding. The scope of responsibilities, outlined in the legislation, far outstrips the meager resources that are provided (Herr, 1980). Repeated federal attempts to repeal the DD Act put the future existence of the P&A systems in continuous jeopardy.

Another promising attempt to reach institutionalized mentally retarded persons has been recently reversed. In order to implement the consent decree reached by the parties in a Massachusetts institutional suit, the federal district court judge ordered that the state provide a broad array of advocacy services, funded by the state. The appellate court, however, ruled that there was no basis under any law or within the general consent decree that would mandate such services (*Brewster* v. *Dukakis,* 1982). The result is the elimination of a promising device to ensure that advocacy services reach their intended clients.

Legal Services Corporation.   Among the legal advocacy services, the system that was viewed as the most stable financially was the Legal Services Corporation (LSC). Though limited to income-eligible persons, LSC appeared to be a prime source for legal advocacy on behalf of mentally retarded persons. The problem is that the LSC has historically given scant attention to the advocacy needs of mentally retarded persons or other disability groups. While its budget increased fourfold through the 1970s and its number of advocates threefold, the overall level of advocacy on behalf of mentally disabled persons declined (Herr, 1980). Although offices in scattered localities have established specialized units to meet these advocacy needs, these efforts, when viewed in perspective to the massive functioning of the Corporation, have been isolated and minimal. As Herr (1979) noted, "Without stronger incentives from national and regional offices, local programs are unlikely to tackle the problems of a client-group whose needs require greater outreach and patience." Yet by devoting more of its resources to such advocacy, the Corporation has the potential to play a significant role in vastly expanding the number of advocates for mentally retarded persons. LSC's plans to move in this direction were undercut by the Reagan administration's proposal to eliminate its categorical funding, thereby giving the option to the states to finance existing legal services programs under the Social Services Block Grant. While substantial opposition has surfaced to this proposal, the LSC for the immediate future faces significant budget cuts that will leave it in no position either to expand its client groups or to increase its outreach activities. In fact, in 1981-82 some 300 field offices closed down, and 1,773 LSC staff members were lost (American Civil Liberties Union, 1983). To some observers, these developments come as no surprise. It is asserted that it is naive to believe that governments are likely to implement publicly funded legal aid programs which promise to escalate the costs of health and social services which are being cut back in fiscal restraint (Vrooman, 1980).

In summary, despite their relative growth through the 1970s and the growing perception that legal advocates for mentally retarded persons abound, the truth of the matter is that very few advocates exist to meet the legal needs of the mentally retarded person. The political climate of the 1980s further threatens a drastic cutback to these limited legal services that are available. In his exhaustive study of legal advocacy for mentally retarded persons Herr (1979) observed that "by any absolute standard, legal services for mentally retarded citizens are in scarce supply," and that "need dramatically outstrips advocacy resources." Consequently, the new legal rights secured by mentally retarded persons "may prove illusory" without advocacy services to implement and enforce those rights (Herr, 1980).

Access to Legal Advocacy

Most clients seek out legal advocates, choosing a lawyer to handle their case. As mentioned earlier, many mentally retarded persons are either too disabled to know their rights or do not comprehend the need to assert their rights through an advocate. In addition, their confinement makes it difficult for many retarded persons to make contact with a lawyer. This is particularly true of retarded persons residing in institutions.

In the case of severely retarded persons, lawyers must either reach them through their own outreach efforts or rely on contacts by friends, parents, and guardians. While professional codes of ethics have deterred lawyers from seeking out clients, recently there has been a loosening in the interpretation of those restrictions (*In re Primus*, 1978). Lawyers can approach groups, give speeches, and conduct workshops, and they now can advertise in attempts to apprise disabled persons of their legal rights.

There exist several institutional projects around the country in which advocates have offices within institutions and bring their advocacy efforts directly to the residents (e.g., Washington Institutional Legal Services, New York Mental Health Information Service). Some of these are legal-services offices, while others are state projects. But given the sheer weight of the numbers of institutionalized mentally retarded persons (including nursing-home residents), the existing offices can barely attempt to provide advocacy to the persons they serve.

The creation of the state protection and advocacy systems for the developmentally disabled constitutes one major national attempt to make advocates accessible to mentally retarded persons. Recognizing the inherent difficulties in providing advocacy to institutionalized individuals, proposed regulations to the DD Act attempted to provide that:

> (c) (2) The P&A System must have the authority to institute administrative and legal proceedings to redress the rights of institutionalized persons with developmental disabilities without the necessity of representing a named client.

In addition, the proposed regulations would provide that

> (c) (3) The P&A System must have appropriate access to the personal, medical, and other records pertaining to the care of institutionalized developmentally disabled persons who have been judicially declared mentally incompetent after giving reasonable notice to the guardians of such persons. In the case of an institutionalized developmentally disabled person who is not mentally impaired, the P&A System must have appropriate access to that person's relevant records after obtaining the consent of that person.

(7) The P&A System must have the authority on its own initiative to obtain access to institutions and programs servicing persons with developmental disabilities.

Thus, some efforts have been or are presently being made to make advocates more accessible, even if the number of such advocates still remains woefully inadequate to meet the needs of mentally retarded persons.

A more serious problem is the ability to communicate with a mentally retarded person to ensure that as an advocate you are presenting your client's desires and not merely imposing your own wishes. Attorneys are governed, both by their Code of Professional Responsibility and by the normalization principle, to seek as much guidance as possible from their mentally retarded client. With mildly and moderately retarded clients, the attorney should always be able to elicit the client's opinions and desires. When those choices are expressed, the attorney is responsible—as with any other client— for representing the client's viewpoints.

Severely and profoundly retarded clients, however, raise more difficult problems of communication and representation. First, the attorney's reaction to this type of client may affect the level of representation; that is, the lawyer's reaction may be one which causes his performance to be less than diligent, owing either to shock, fear, disdain, or paternalism (Luckasson & Ellis, 1983). Secondly, the client's inability to communicate places the attorney in a bind. Since the attorney is to carry out the client's desires, the attorney must have someone with whom to discuss the problem, in order to prevent the total imposition of the attorney's own beliefs on the client. This problem can be solved by the appointment of a guardian—either a parent, lay, or professional advocate who provides full or limited guardianship or a *guardian ad litem* for the specific legal matter (Mickenberg, 1979). The guardian, representing the client's best interest, combined with the attorney, representing the client's desires (expressed through the aid of the guardian), can then effectively work to minimize the difficulties arising from the client's inability to communicate.

Self-Advocacy

Seeking guidance from a mentally retarded person is extremely crucial for all advocates. Traditionally, mentally retarded persons have been taught to be nonassertive, and they have learned to respond to pressure and coercion with submissive and acquiescent behavior. Thus, advocates could easily fall into the position of imposing their influence upon the mentally retarded person in subtle or nonsubtle ways.

Recently, however, mentally retarded persons are beginning to help one another to speak more plainly and to express their ideas more clearly through the process of self-advocacy (Canadian Association for the Mentally Retarded, 1979). The Accreditation Council for Facilities for the Mentally Retarded defines self-advocacy as the

> . . . presentation of the rights and interests of one's self to bring about change, in order that barriers in meeting identified needs be overcome . . . all developmentally disabled persons should be provided an opportunity to reach the most desirable level of advocacy which is self-preservation, an inherent right. (Zonca, 1980, pp. 120–121)

In recent years, throughout the United States and Canada, numerous self-help groups have been formed in which mentally retarded persons are helping one another to advocate for themselves and to express their wishes to both lay (citizen) advocates and legal advocates. These self-advocacy groups can be described as "mentally retarded persons who are tired of being over-protected . . . (and who) have begun to object when professionals and non-professionals make decisions for them and speak for them, when, with a little time and patience, they could have decided and spoken for themselves" (President's Committee on Mental Retardation, 1978).

The appearance of the self-advocacy movement requires a different approach to advocacy for mentally retarded persons. Advocates must make themselves accessible to mentally retarded persons when they are needed, but at the same time they must assist mentally retarded persons in becoming their own advocates. One promising project is the program conducted in California by the Sonoma County Advocacy System, which provides self-advocacy training and makes information on rights easily available and comprehensible to mentally retarded persons (Zonca, 1980). As these self-advocacy efforts expand, mentally retarded persons themselves will be able to shoulder some of the demands being placed upon the short supply of legal advocacy services. More important, mentally retarded persons will be able to dictate the direction of those advocacy efforts. One of the first such groups to organize is People First in Salem, Oregon. In 1974, the group arranged a state assembly that attracted 560 mentally retarded persons. This was followed by increasingly larger statewide conventions, and organizations were formed in California, Kansas, Washington, Nebraska, Ontario, and Alberta. Representing a new consumer movement, these organizations have exerted increasing political power by (1) encouraging handicapped persons to speak for themselves on issues affecting their lives; (2) demanding representation on boards of local, state, and national handicapped-advocacy and handicapped-service organizations; and (3) challenging the attitudes and actions of professionals when these do not further the interests of handicapped people (President's Committee on Mental Retardation, 1978).

SUMMARY

The successful deinstitutionalization and mainstreaming of mentally retarded persons into our social institution is contingent upon the development of a comprehensive network of specialized and generic services. The public, private and voluntary sectors must coordinate their efforts to provide mentally retarded persons decent housing, habilitative services and available advocacy resources.

CHAPTER SIX
PREVENTION

Mental retardation is one of the nation's most serious health, social, and economic problems. Therefore, prevention through greater understanding of its causes and management is both socially desirable and economically justified.

In 1972, the President's Committee on Mental Retardation (PCMR) set as a national goal a 50 percent reduction in mental retardation by the year 2000. It was believed this could be accomplished by using extant knowledge and techniques from the biomedical and behavioral sciences. While it is debatable whether the incidence of mental retardation has, in fact, declined in recent years, it is acknowledged that PCMR's goal was overoptimistic (Clarke & Clarke, 1977; Zigler, 1978; Moser, 1982). This state of affairs can be attributed to our failure to apply available preventive interventions, and the nation's failure to make increased investments in medical and behavioral research (General Accounting Office, 1977). Consequently, the estimated 11.7 billion dollars spent annually to care for retarded persons is the price paid for our society's failure to invest in prevention.

The prevention of mental retardation depends upon three basic prerequisites: (1) recognition of causes, (2) development of a preventive strategy, and (3) implementation of the strategy. In the past, reports have suggested that 60 to 70 percent of all mental retardation results from unknown causes. However, with advances in the fields of medical genetics, infectious diseases, and neonatal intensive care more recent reports indicate that perhaps as low as 25 percent of the cases of mental retardation have an unknown etiology (Moser, 1977).

With the increased understanding of causes of mental retardation have come the development of preventive strategies. A useful way to categorize these strategies is in terms of primary, secondary, and tertiary levels of prevention. *Primary prevention* removes the causative factors resulting in the occurrence of a disorder (e.g., diagnosing the carrier of a defective gene, eliminating the ingestion of lead). *Secondary prevention* attempts to treat or prevent the expression of the disorder after it has been recognized (e.g., instituting a special diet for a child with a metabolic disorder). *Tertiary prevention* deals with continuous interventions to mitigate the consequences of the disorder which has occurred (e.g., surgery, providing habilitative services).

In the following sections, an emphasis will be given to these three levels of prevention within the context of selected biogenic and psychosocial determinants of mental retardation, with the recognition that these etiological factors interact with each other.

BIOGENIC DETERMINANTS: MEDICAL INTERVENTIONS

Three major categories of genetic factors are responsible for the production of mental retardation. These categories include: (1) chromosomal anomalies (e.g., Down syndrome), (2) single-gene disorders (e.g., tuberous sclerosis) and disorders with biochemical markers (e.g., Tay-Sachs disease), and (3) multifactorial genetic inheritance. Subcategories of genetic disorders have been identified within each of these major categories.

Chromosomal Anomalies

The prevention of chromosomal disorders must begin with the identification and characterization of the genetic aberration. The normal chromosomal complement for males is 46 XY and for females, 46 XX. Aberrations from these normal complements will result in two basic types of chromosomal defects: (1) numerical anomalies, such as trisomy (where there is an additional chromosome) and monosomy (where there is one less chromosome); and (2) structural anomalies, in which a certain section of a given chromosome may be duplicated, deleted, rearranged, or damaged.

Down syndrome. The most common autosomal (non-X-linked) chromosomal cause of moderate to severe mental retardation is Down syndrome (DS). It is estimated that 5,000 cases of DS occur each year. While the incidence of DS is decreasing, its prevalence is increasing, owing to the increased life expectancy among DS persons (Moser, 1977). Three basic chromosomal aberrations are associated with DS: (1) trisomy 21, with an extra chromosome 21 in all the cells; (2) a translocation of chromosome 21 onto another chromosome, usually chromosome 14; and (3) a mixture of chromosomally normal cells and trisomy 21 cells, which is referred to as the mosaic type of Down's syndrome. The chromosomal defect not only impairs brain development, but it also is manifested in a number of recognizable phenotypic characteristics, as shown in Figure 6-1. The causative relationship between chromosomal aberrations and DS is still not understood.

Maternal age, and more recently parental age, have been correlated with the occurrence of DS. Women over 35 and younger than 17 have a significantly higher risk of having a DS child (Hook & Chambers, 1977); the risks of mutation may also increase where the biological father is over 40 years old (Stene, Stene, Stengel-Rutkowski, & Murken, 1981). Also at higher risk of giving birth to a DS child are women who have given birth to a DS child, DS females, and nonaffected carriers (i.e., males and females) of the inherited translocation-type chromosome.

Prevention. Genetic counseling is a form of primary prevention for at-risk individuals. Genetic counseling usually includes an analysis of the family history and pedigree, a physical examination, and a laboratory work-up, including chromosomal and biochemical studies. When a diagnosis is obtained, information is provided for family members for their decision making and planning. In some cases,

FIGURE 6-1   Facial Appearance of a Child with Down Syndrome. (From D.W. Smith, Journal of Pediatrics, 70:474, 1967. Reprinted by Permission of the C.V. Mosby Company.)

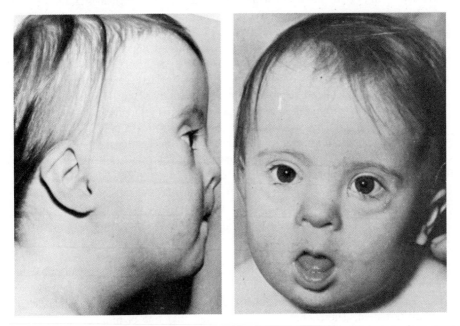

voluntary sterilization may be elected by a high-risk family member who wants to avoid any possibility of having a DS child.

Chromosomal defects, with the possible exception of some mosaics, can be detected prenatally by amniocentesis. Presently, amniocentesis is restricted to high-risk pregnancies. Amniocentesis is a procedure performed during the 16th week of pregnancy whereby fluid from the amniotic cavity surrounding the fetus is drawn out by a small needle and syringe. By studying the cells in the fluid, it is possible to determine the presence of a chromosomal defect in the fetus. The combined fetal-maternal risk for amniocentesis is calculated to be less than 1 percent. The major complications include infection, bleeding, and potential damage to the fetus. A more recently developed technique, chorionic villis biopsy, samples fetal tissue directly and can be performed between the 8th and 12th week of pregnancy. Secondary prevention of DS would entail the decision by the mother to terminate the pregnancy where there are positive signs of a chromosomal defect. Tertiary prevention, in the form of cosmetic surgery and infant stimulation, has enhanced the social and cognitive development of DS children.

Turner's and Klinefelter's syndromes. Several well-known chromosomal anomalies of the sex chromosomes produce mild to severe mental retardation. Turner's syndrome occurs in approximately 1 out of 3,000 female births. These individuals are phenotypically females and have only one X chromosome (XO). Clinically, they are generally of short stature (less than 60 inches tall), have incomplete development of gonads, fail to develop secondary sexual characteristics, and have a webbing of the neck and wide-spaced nipples. Although mental retardation is not a frequent characteristic of Turner's syndrome, some cases with mild retardation have been reported (Haddad & Wilken, 1959).

Klinefelter's syndrome occurs in about 1 out of 450 live male births. This condition is produced by having two or more X chromosomes in the presence of a Y chromosome (XXY). Clinically, the affected male is characterized by small sex organs, with increased development of mammary glands. Mild to moderate mental retardation is found in most cases; severe mental retardation is rare.

Prevention. Tertiary prevention is the only form of intervention with sex chromosome defects. In cases of Turner's syndrome, estrogen therapy usually results in enhanced development of secondary sex characteristics, menstrual spotting, and sexual responsiveness (Vogel & Moltulsky, 1979). Similarly, tertiary prevention for Klinefelter's, in the form of testosterone-replacement therapy, is recommended for improvement of the secondary sex characteristics, generally increased body development, penis enlargement, and a deepening of the voice (Smith, 1976).

Fragile-X syndrome. In an early study, Penrose (1938) reported an excess of males among institutionalized mentally retarded persons. Turner and Turner (1974) found that more brothers than sisters of mentally retarded siblings were similarly affected. These observations suggested that one or more X-linked genes for mental retardation might be responsible for the disproportionate number of affected males. Lubs (1969) described a family in which four mentally retarded males possessed a constriction at the end of the q (long) arm of the X chromosome. This resulted in a small "knob" that was separated from the main portion of the chromosome by a thin, stalklike structure. Hainey, Judge, and Wiener (1977) later confirmed this observation. Sutherland (1977) suggested that the constriction could be identified readily by growing the tissue in media depleted of folate and thymidine. The incidence of fragile-X syndrome is now estimated to be 1 in 346 live male births. Common phenotypic features of this syndrome include mental retardation, a prominent jaw, enlarged testes, ears, and head. Interestingly, an estimated 20 percent of males with this genetic defect may not express mental retardation or other features of the syndrome.

Prevention. Primary prevention of families at risk for Fragile-X syndrome would require locating the female relatives of affected males. Recently, Jenkins, Brown, Duncan, Brooks, Ben-Yishay, Giordano, and Nitowsky (1981) reported successful prenatal diagnosis of fragile-X syndrome by amniocentesis and cell-culture cytogenetic studies.

Single-Gene Disorders

Over 3,000 traits and diseases are known to be caused by single genes (Mc-Kusick, 1978). These single-gene disorders can be classified under four subcategories: autosomal dominant, autosomal recessive, X-linked dominant, and X-linked recessive.

Autosomal dominant-gene disorders. Autosomal dominant refers to those genetic diseases that can affect a person of either sex who possesses a single dominant copy of a mutated or altered gene that exerts a deleterious effect on the phenotype. The three most frequently observed autosomal dominant-gene disorders are neurofibromatosis, tuberous sclerosis, and Sturge-Weber syndrome.

The incidence of neurofibromatosis (NF) is estimated at 1 in 3,000 in live births. Recently, this condition has received increased attention owing to the popular play and film *The Elephant Man.* In one-half of all NF cases, there is evidence that the defective gene was inherited from the mother or father; the other half are the result of gene mutations (Bornberg, 1951). The diagnosis of NF is usually based on the appearance of light brown patches on the skin (i.e., café-au-lait spots) and the presence of cutaneous and subcutaneous brain tumors. In approximately 10 percent of NB cases, there is mental retardation accompanied by seizures, owing to the presence of a brain tumor.

Tuberous Sclerosis (TS) is a disorder with wide clinical variability in both physical and mental involvement. The condition occurs in 1 per 100,000 live births. In one-third of the cases, TS is due to the inheritance of an autosomal dominant gene; two-thirds of the cases are the result of sporadic gene mutations. The physical features consist of a "butterfly rash" (i.e., ademona sebaceum) in the region surrounding the nose, which may not appear until the child is 5 years old. There are also intracranial calcifications, which can be detected by a skull X-ray. Evidence of severe mental retardation and seizures may not appear until the child is 3 years of age.

Sturge-Weber syndrome (SW) occurs less frequently than NF and TS; however, it manifests characteristics similar to those two conditions. A prominent dark red skin rash called "port wine stain" appears on the face, and calcifications occur in the brain. The child's level of retardation may range from severe to mild, and the condition is typically accompanied by seizures (Gorlin, Pindborg, & Cohen, 1976).

Prevention. Most of the autosomal dominant-gene defects cannot be diagnosed prenatally (i.e., by amniocentesis). If the parent is affected, even minimally, there is 50 percent risk to the offspring for each pregnancy. The risk of occurrence could be avoided by having affected males produce children only by means of artificial insemination, using semen from donor males who presumably have no family history of genetic diseases (McCormack, Lieblum, & Lazzarini, 1983). Once one of these conditions is diagnosed at birth, tertiary prevention, in the form of medical and surgical intervention, can be instituted. These interventions include craniofacial surgery, surgical removal of neurofibroma, and medication to control seizures.

Autosomal recessive-gene disorders. Parents who are both carriers of the same autosomal recessive-gene defect have a 25 percent chance of having an affected child with each pregnancy. These disorders are attributed to a specific biochemical defect, the absence of a critical enzyme, which disrupts metabolic processes resulting in central nervous system impairment. Some of the more frequently recognized inborn errors of metabolism are phenylketonuria (PKU), congenital hypothyroidism, maple syrup urine disease, and Tay-Sachs disease (McKusick, 1978).

Phenylketonuria occurs in 1 in 11,500 live births. PKU is an inherited defect in amino-acid metabolism that is due to the absence of the phenylalanine hydroxylase enzyme, which converts phenylalanine into tyrosine. Consequently, the buildup of phenylalanine in the blood stream reaches a toxic level, resulting in brain damage. In addition, decreased protein synthesis may result in hypomyelination, which is detrimental to brain growth. If allowed to go untreated, a PKU child will be severely retarded. Common phenotypic characteristics include blond hair, blue eyes, microcephaly (i.e., a small head), and broadly spaced teeth. A peculiar smell in the urine can also be detected.

Congenital hypothyroidism (CH), or cretinism, occurs in approximately 1 in 5,000 live births; it is twice as common as PKU. CH can be detected in the newborn by the measurement of the thyroxine level and/or thyroid-stimulating hormone in the bloodstream. An endocrine deficiency affects central nervous system development; it is still unclear as to what mechanism accounts for this damage. Clinical features associated with CH include constipation, prolonged jaundice, lethargy, poor eating, and the failure to gain weight and height.

Maple syrup urine disease (MSUD) occurs in 1 in 200,000 live births. Infants with MSUD experience vomiting, muscular hyperactivity and a peculiar maple syrup odor to their urine during the first few weeks of life. These children manifest ataxia, seizures, and severe mental retardation; survival without treatment is rare beyond 2 years of age. The disease appears to be due to a decreased activity of a decarboxylase enzyme involved in the metabolism of the branched amino acids (i.e., leucine, isoleucine and valine).

Tay-Sachs disease is due to an enzyme deficiency of hexosaminidase A that is found primarily in the ancestry of the Ashkenazi Jewish population. The incidence of a carrier of the recessive gene, in the Eastern European Jewish population is approximately 1 in 30 persons, whereas the incidence of a carrier in the general population is 1 in 300. Children with Tay-Sachs disease have deposits of a fatlike substance in various tissues, including the central nervous system. After a period of normalcy, a progressive neurodegenerative disease culminate in death by the age of 5 years. Typically, these infants become blind, deaf, and severely mentally retarded (McKhann, 1979).

Prevention. Primary prevention requires genetic counseling of parents who are carriers of the deleterious recessive genes. Adult females who carry both recessive genes for PKU, but who are unaffected because a special diet was instituted at birth, may have high levels of phenylalanine. In these known cases, the resumption of diet therapy may be advisable when the woman becomes pregnant. Prenatal diagnosis of PKU is now possible by DNA studies of the amniotic fluid cells (Woo, Liasky, Güttler, Chandra, & Robson, 1983). However, the predominant mode of secondary prevention is the screening of all newborns for PKU by urine and/or blood testing (e.g., by the Guthrie test) and immediate dietary intervention in the cases where the newborn is affected. The diet should restrict phenylalanine intake and include a supplement of high-tyrosine food substances. There is presently a debate as to how long children with PKU should be maintained on the diet. It appears that children can be weaned from the diet at age 6, but periodic neurological, biochemical, and psychometric examinations are recommended to detect any changes in status that may require the reinstitution of the diet. Early dietary management can prevent retardation; however, any intrauterine damage that precedes the initiation of the diet cannot be reversed.

Screening at birth for congenital hypothyroidism has become routine in most states. Treatment can avert mental retardation if instituted during the first 3 months of life (La Franchi, Murphy, Foley, Larson, & Buist, 1979). If the disorder is suspected but is unconfirmed by laboratory testing, replacement therapy to supply the suspected missing hormone should be initiated and continued until 1 to 2 years of age. Medication can then be discontinued, and diagnostic testing reinitiated. Secondary preventive strategies include the replacement therapy with thyroid preparations such as dessicated thyroid (Committee on Drugs, 1978).

Although dietary therapy has been proposed for maple syrup urine disease, therapy is complicated by the need to regulate three amino acids and the requirement to continue the diet permanently. Dietary therapy can control the intake of the branched-chain amino acids found in certain fruits, vegetables, and cereal products (Snyderman & Davies, 1979). MSUD is prenatally diagnosible by amniocentesis; testing for MSUD, however, has been incorporated in only a few newborn-screening programs because of the condition's low incidence and its rather poor prognosis.

Primary intervention of Tay-Sachs disease requires the identification of possible carriers of the deleterious gene and genetic counseling. Amniocentesis can detect a Tay-Sachs fetus and provide the mother with the option to abort the pregnancy.

X-linked disorders. X-linked disorders are due to mutant genes located on the X chromosomes. The gene may be dominant or recessive; most are known to be recessive. Since females have two X chromosomes, a single copy of a mutant X-linked gene on one chromosome would normally be overshadowed by the non-mutant X chromosome. However, males have only one X chromosome, and if they possess an X-linked mutant gene, they generally manifest a genetic disorder. The most widely known X-linked recessive disorder is Lesch-Nyhan syndrome, which is transmitted to sons whose mothers carry the defective gene. It occurs in 1/50,000 male births. It is characterized by severe mental retardation, spasticity, and self-mutilation. Biochemically, the disease is due to a deficiency of an enzyme, hypoxanthineguanine phosphoribosyl transferase which results in brain malfunctioning.

Prevention. For women who carry the X-linked recessive gene, secondary prevention of an X-linked recessive disorder in their sons is possible by sex determination through amniocentesis, and the decision can be made to abort all male fetuses. Except in cases like Lesch-Nyhan snydrome, where a biochemical defect is known, the presence or absence of an X-linked disorder generally cannot be detected in male fetuses, since no biochemical marker has yet been identified.

Multifactorial Genetic Inheritance

Multifactorial inheritance represents the cumulative effect of numerous genes (sometimes referred to as *genetic predisposition*) and one or more environmental factor(s), which interact to produce a specific phenotype. Several major studies on mental retardation have shown that the incidence of mental retardation is significantly higher among close relatives of mildly mentally retarded persons than among the general population. The degree of risk has been identified by the extensive studies of Elizabeth and Sheldon Reed (1965) from the University of Minnesota. The typical risk figures, derived from their study for the different types of marriages and matings, are listed in Table 6-1. These data have been extremely useful in providing genetic counseling to families in which mild mental retardation frequently occurs. At this time, no precise biochemical or chromosomal explana-

TABLE 6-1   Occurrence of Familial Mental Retardation Empiric Risk
Figures for Normal and Retarded Persons

TYPE OF UNION	RISK OF FIRST CHILD'S BEING RETARDED	RISK OF SUBSEQUENT CHILDREN'S BEING RETARDED
Normal (with all normal siblings) X Normal	0.53%	5.7%
Normal (with retarded sibling) X Normal	2.5%	12.9%
Normal X Retarded	–	19.9%
Normal (with retarded sibling) X Retarded	23.8%	–
Retarded X Retarded	–	42.1%

Adapted from E.W. Reed and S.C. Reed. *Mental Retardation: A Family Study.* Philadelphia: W.B. Saunders Company, 1965, p. 56. Reprinted by permission.

tion is available for this type of mental retardation, but the genetic factor is both real and measurable. The contribution of detrimental social and environmental factors, which will be discussed later, cannot be excluded from consideration in the etiology of mild multifactorial mental retardation.

Neural-tube defects. Neural-tube defects (NTDs) are a group of multifactorial congenital gene defects primarily affecting the closure of the neural tube (a structure that ultimately develops into the head and spinal cord). Approximately 90 percent of the cases occur in families without a previous family history of this defect, and the incidence is approximately 1 in 1,000 live births. However, some evidence suggests that NTDs may occur more frequently among lower socioeconomic classes due to a vitamin deficiency. After a couple have a child affected with a NTD, the risk of having a second child with NTD is 3 percent, and for a third child it is 15 percent. If the parent is afflicted with a NTD, the risk is approximately 4 percent. There are three major types of NTD: (1) anencephaly, with failure to complete development of the cranium and brain; (2) encephalocele, with an occipital protrusion of the brain; and (3) spina bifida, characterized by cystic lesions of the spinal cord (see Figure 6-2). The first two types of NTD are incompatable with life; however, some spina bifida infants who have surgical intervention to close the cystic lesion may survive. For those who do survive, severe mental retardation may result due to hydrocephaly.

Prevention. Two secondary preventive measures have been developed for NTDs: (1) prenatal diagnosis of NTD by measurement of maternal serum alpha-fetoprotein (AFP) in all pregnant women, and (2) measurement of AFP in amniotic fluid of women at high risk for NTD. Elevated levels of AFP indicate that the fetus may have a neural tube defect, but a positive result should be confirmed by

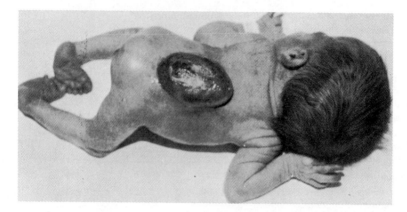

FIGURE 6-2 A Typical Neural Tube Defect Observed in a Child with Spina Bifida. (From D.W. Smith, *Recognizable Patterns of Human Malformation,* Third Edition, W.B. Saunders, Philadelphia: 1982, p. 463. Reprinted by Permission.)

other procedures including ultrasonography and amniocentesis. (The mass marketing of ATP kits has been quite controversial.) At this time, the only option to prevent the NTD is the termination of the pregnancy. Prenatal screening of all pregnant women would detect 90 percent of all NTD; the other 10 percent of NTDs are covered by skin, and no AFP leaks into the amniotic fluid. Tertiary prevention of hydrocephalus consists of placement of an intracranial shunt to dissipate any accumulating pressure from cerebrospinal fluid that otherwise cannot drain because of blocked channels. This surgical procedure can be performed in utero or shortly after birth.

NEW ADVANCES IN MEDICAL DIAGNOSIS AND TREATMENT

The so-called new medicine or new biology is resulting in rapid advances in the medical diagnosis and treatment that promise to reduce the incidence of mental retardation. In the following section a brief discussion of these advances will be presented.

Ultrasonography

Ultrasound or ultrasonography refers to a process whereby sound waves that are above the frequencies audible to the human ear are used to generate echos wherever there is interference with the passage of ultrasonic energy (Hobbin, Grannum, Berkowitz, Silverman, & Mahoney, 1979). The amount of time that it takes for an echo to return to the monitor is directly proportional to the distance traveled, that is, to the depth of the human structure under study. A sonogram provides a pictoral representation of the fetal and placental structures. Recently, the resolution of the image produced by ultrasound equipment has improved dramatically. It is not possible to delineate various features of the fetal anatomy and detect maldevelopment.

Ultrasonography has been used in the diagnosis of such congenital abnormalities as hydrocephaly, anecephaly, and other multiple congential anomalies. In addition, ultrasonography has been used to assess features of the skeletal system in utero. The use of ultrasonography in the prevention of mental retardation will undoubtedly include the earlier diagnosis of gross anatomical defects in fetuses suspected of having a genetic disorder. However, ultrasonography should not be used routinely because of the potential risks of fetal damage.

Fetoscopy

Fetoscopy is a procedure used to evaluate fetuses that are at risk for certain genetic diseases. A fetoscope, a surgical instrument equipped with a fiber-optic lens for viewing the fetus is inserted into the amniotic sac. This feature can be useful in determining whether a fetus has a congenital malformation that may be associated with mental retardation. The fetoscope can also be fitted with a 26-gauge needle attached to a syringe for drawing fetal blood and tissue samples. This intervention has the potential of identifying metabolic disorders that can only be diagnosed in fetal blood. At the present time the risk of fetal loss resulting from fetoscopy is about 5 percent and is largely due to amnionitis, fetal trauma, exsanguination (total loss of blood), or placenta abruption (detachment of the placenta).

Fetal Surgery

The early identification of congenital defects has often prompted physicians to wonder whether potential therapeutic strategies may be useful to treat the fetus affected with congenital malformation or genetic disease while in utero. Progress in this area has been delayed primarily because of the lack of appropriate techniques that would both correct the fetal abnormality and leave the fetus and placenta in adequate condition for the completion of gestational development. Recently, successful treatments have been reported in cases of certain congenital malformations, including obstruction of the bladder, hydrocephaly, and cleft palate. These have required special microsurgical techniques to release the increased pressure, in the intercranial area in the case of hydrocephaly, or within the bladder in the case of bladder obstruction (Clewell, Johnson, Meier, Newkirk, Zide, Hendee, Bowers, Hecht, O'Keefe, Henry, & Shikes, 1982). Of such cases reported to date, the number with successful outcomes has been substantial. It will be some time, however, before these procedures are routinely available. Experimentation with monkeys is currently in progress to treat neural tube defects by removing the fetus from the womb, performing the needed surgery, and then returning the fetus to the womb for the completion of the gestational period. Another area of research that may have implications for the treatment of mental retardation is the work involving fetal brain transplants among rats.

Enzyme Replacement Therapy

The inborn errors of metabolism represent one of the most intriguing known causes for mental retardation. As discussed in this chapter, they included such familiar disorders as Tay-Sachs disease and phenylketonuria. For the past 30 years, the primary focus in the area of biochemical genetics research has been the elucidation of the heterogeneity within the inborn errors of metabolism. Attempts have been made (primarily in experimental animal models) to correct the inborn error of metabolism. The procedure requires the replacement of the missing enzymes in the organ, so that important metabolic functions can occur.

This modality of therapy provides an excellent potential for the treatment of metabolic disorders associated with mental retardation. However, several technical hurdles need to be overcome, including the identification and purification of specific enzymes, the suppression of immunological response to enzymes, the stabilizing of the enzyme, and the addressing of the enzyme to allow it to proceed to the site where its activity normally occurs.

Genetic Engineering

The field of molecular genetics, recombinant DNA, and gene cloning offers promises for the reversal of potential genetic disorders. The concept of genetic-molecular diseases stems from the identification of specific genetic lesions that produce either abnormal proteins or totally nonfunctional proteins, which, in turn, produce either grossly malformed anatomical features, or abnormal central nervous system functioning, or both. With the recent advances in the cloning of genes, the isolation of a specific gene, and gene substitution, there comes the possibility of correcting these gene lesions. Present data suggest that the implementation of such a strategy may not have to wait for the all-too-distant future, a forecast based on recent reports of successful gene transplantation to effectively treat a hemoglobin disorder (Beta Thalassemia Major). More research will be needed, however, before this technique can be applied to the treatment of genetic disorders that cause mental retardation (e.g., Lesch-Nyhan).

ECONOMIC AND LEGAL ISSUES

Economic Issues

Mental retardation is a major social problem, and its prevention is a public concern. We desire to diminish human suffering and improve the quality of human life. The social costs for the care and education of mentally retarded persons draw heavily on the public purse. The use of preventive strategies is often determined by the outcome of a cost-benefit analysis. Cost-benefit analysis is a methodology that attempts to quantify and weigh all the costs and benefits derived from a particular program (e.g., prevention, education). Generally, if benefits outweigh costs and if the program is politically acceptable, it will be adopted.

Cost-benefit analyses have been conducted for preventative procedures for several frequent causes of mental retardation. To be cost-efficient, prenatal screening for fetuses at risk must have benefits that exceed the costs of this preventive procedure. A cost-benefit calculation for Down syndrome must consider the following factors: (1) the risk of Down syndrome at various maternal ages; (2) the financial cost of amniocentesis itself; (3) the risk of complications from the amniocentesis procedure; (4) the costs for caring for a Down syndrome person throughout his life; and (5) the opportunity costs (e.g., employment) foreclosed to family members who care for the Down syndrome person. These economic considerations are exclusive of any human-suffering component. One cost-benefit study sets a break-even point for amniocentesis screening for Down syndrome at a maternal age of 28 years (Hook & Chambers, 1977). Thus, we find that a cost-benefit analysis would encourage us to lower the cutoff age for amniocentesis, now set at 35 years. However, various factors, such as the limited availability of laboratory services, prohibit performing an amniocentesis on all women at this lower maternal age limit. Similar types of cost-benefit analysis have found benefits to outweigh costs for the preventive screening of PKU, lead poisoning, congenital hypothyroidism, spina bifida, and maternal rubella. Recognition of the savings in the cost of caring for mentally retarded persons has resulted in recent state plans to prevent mental retardation.

Legal Issues

Related to the prevention of mental retardation is the legal liability of physicians and genetic counselors in wrongful birth and wrongful life cases. *Wrongful birth* is an action by the parents who claim that they would have avoided conception or terminated the pregnancy had they been properly advised of the risk of birth defects to the potential child. On the other hand, *wrongful life* is an action by the deformed child who argues that but for the inadequate advice, he would not have been born to experience the pain and suffering attributable to the deformity (Foutz, 1980).

Wrongful birth suits are typical medical malpractice cases brought by parents who claim that a physician's negligence caused the birth of their physically or mentally handicapped child. Most courts now accept a cause of action for wrongful birth, permitting parents to establish a right to damages for economic and medical expenses in caring for the handicapped child, for emotional expenses for the parents' pain and suffering, or for both. The major issue in wrongful birth suits is the question of the type of damages to be collected. In *Becker* v. *Schwartz* (1978), the New York Court of Appeals upheld a suit by the parents against an obstetrician who negligently failed to advise a pregnant woman older than 35 years of age of the increased risk of having a Down syndrome child; the physician also failed to advise the parents of the availability of amniocentesis. However, while the court permitted the parents to recover damages for the costs of caring for their Down syndrome child, it did not permit them to collect damages for their own emotional suffering. Six months later, the New Jersey Supreme Court in *Berman* v. *Allan* (1979) allowed parents in a similar situation to collect damages for their emotional suffering but did not permit them to collect for the cost of their child's care. Yet in *Schroeder* v. *Perkel* (1981) the New Jersey Supreme Court, in upholding a wrongful birth action, permitted the parents to collect damages both for emotional distress and for their extraordinary medical expenses resulting from their child's handicaps. The supreme courts of Pennsylvania (*Speck* v. *Finegold, 1981)* and Virginia (*Naccash* v. *Burger, 1982*) have also permitted parents to recover the expenses of caring for their child, as well as damages for mental distress and physical inconvenience caused by the birth of a genetically defective infant.

Courts that have recognized wrongful birth suits have typically rejected wrongful life suits. In *Phillips* v. *U.S.* (1980, 1981), a federal district court in South Carolina issued two opinions less than a month apart. While permitting the parents to sue for wrongful birth, it cited an overwhelming majority of cases in support of prohibiting the defective child from suing for wrongful life. The court refused to base its decision either on the difficulty of ascertaining damages to the child or on the legal questions of the physician's duty to the infant. Rather, the court focused specifically on public policy in recognizing the preciousness and sanctity of human life. The court reasoned that with life being more precious than nonlife, no cause of action could exist for negligence that resulted in life over nonlife, no matter how flawed that life was. Until very recently, the leading decision to the contrary was that of a California appellate court, *Curlender* v. *Bio-Science Laboratories* (1980). In this case, the court permitted a wrongful life suit resulting from negligence in genetic testing for Tay-Sachs disease. The parents accepted a $1.5 million settlement from the laboratory before the case went to trial. However, a federal court (*Robak* v. *U.S.,* 1981), and also another California appellate court (*Turpin* v. *Sortini,* 1982), have rejected *Curlender*; the court in *Turpin* concluded that whether impaired but living children can sue for injury of birth is an issue that is better left to legislative determination. Even when a New York appellate court tried to recognize the wrongful life cause of action (*Park* v. *Chessin,* 1977), it was quickly reversed on the basis that the child did not suffer an injury cognizable at law (*Becker* v. *Schwartz,* 1978). There are, however, indications that this judicial resistance may be weakening. The California Supreme Court has reversed the decision in *Turpin* v. *Sortini* (1982) and has ruled that a wrongful life suit may proceed, though limiting the damages to the related expense of the handicap (deafness) and rejecting as too speculative the assessment of general damages for the deprivation of the right not to be born disabled. In addition, the Pennsylvania Supreme Court, in *Speck* v. *Finegold* (1981), failed to establish the validity of a wrongful life suit by a mere single vote, splitting 3-3 and thus upholding the lower court's decision that had denied such an action. Finally, Washington became the second state to permit a wrongful life suit, when its Supreme Court permitted a handicapped child to sue (*Harbeson* v. *Parke-Davis, Inc.,* 1983).

SOCIOCULTURAL DETERMINANTS:
SOCIAL INTERVENTIONS

A causal link between poverty and mental retardation has been established (Hurley, 1963; Wortis, 1970; Ramey & Finkelstein, 1981). Approximately 75 percent of the cases of mental retardation are of the mild type; mild mental retardation is associated with psychosocial disadvantage.

A child born into urban or rural poverty is 15 times more likely to be labeled mentally retarded. However, while the risk of being affected with mental retardation is higher among the poor, it is estimated that only 10 percent of the population is so labeled (Begab, 1981). According to Fuchs (1974):

> Poverty at birth by no means irrevocably dooms a child to social judgment of infirmity, stupidity, or demoralization—there are millions of witnesses to the contrary—but it makes all three of these outcomes more likely. (p. xi)

Thus, it is not poverty *per se* that causes mental retardation; rather, the causes are the host of proximate environmental conditions that combine with, and are affected by, more remote socialization factors, with the result of reducing the educability of some children (Chan & Rueda, 1979). Because the cumulative effects of these interactive sociocultural determinants are not so well understood as the effects of single biogenic determinants, and because their impact is more indirect than direct, the prevention of psychosocial retardation is a more intractable problem.

The Culture of Poverty

Many of the estimated 13 million children of poverty endure physical, sociological, and psychological conditions that interfere with their chances for normal growth and development. According to studies conducted by the Carnegie Council on Children, poor children have the deck stacked against them for a decent life; poverty shrinks their future life chances (Keniston, 1977; de Leone, 1979). The hazardous physical environment in which these children live is one of substandard housing, crowded living conditions, high-density automobile traffic, epidemic diseases, contaminated water, and nearby toxic-waste sites. Sociologically, poor children (many of whom are from minority groups with different cultural values and languages) feel alienated from the mainstream of community life. Segregated low-income housing units and placement in special classes contribute further to their feelings of isolation and inferiority. Many poor children are the victims of broken homes, inadequate educational and health services, chronic parental unemployment, family violence, and the drug market. Most harmful is the stigma associated with being poor and living under destitute conditions relative to the rest of society. According to Harrington (1963) "the warping of the will and spirit" is a consequence of living in poverty. Over time, children develop negative self-concepts and have little motivation and hope of improving their lives (Ogbu, 1978; de Leone, 1979). Oscar Lewis (1968) writes:

> Once the culture of poverty has come into existence it tends to perpetuate itself. By the time children are six or seven they have usually absorbed the basic attitudes and values of their subculture, therefore they are psychologically unready to take full advantage of changing conditions to improve opportunities that may develop in their lifetime. (p. 409)

In the following sections we will examine the nexus between poverty and mental retardation. The focus will be on some of the known sociocultural determinants of mild mental retardation. Again, it should be noted that these causative factors interact with biogenic factors in producing retardation (Knoblock & Pasamanick, 1969). Preventive strategies designed to eliminate and lessen mental retardation will be emphasized.

Poor Health Care: Premature Births

Health care in the United States can be characterized as a two-tier system —one for the poor and the other for the nonpoor. The poor have limited access to good-quality health services, and this is the major contributor of high mortality and morbidity rates among newborns to low-income families (Erickson & Bjerkaldal, 1982). The following facts were reported in a study conducted by the Children's Defense Fund (Edelman, 1980):

1. A black baby is three times as likely as a white baby to have a mother who dies in childbirth, and twice as likely to be born to a mother who has had no prenatal care.
2. Some 600,000 babies are born annually to teenage mothers; the mothers are disproportionately black. These mothers often lack adequate counseling, nutrition, education, and parenting skills.
3. Thousands of black children are not fully immunized against measles, polio, and other childhood diseases.
4. Black children suffer from low hemoglobin levels and other indicators of malnutrition at twice the rate of white children.

The findings can be generalized to other groups of children (e.g., Hispanics, rural whites) who live in poverty.

Limited access and use of prenatal health services is a major factor in the high incidence of premature births among the poor (General Accounting Office, 1977b; President's Committee on Mental Retardation, 1980). The risk of having a premature baby is six times greater among mothers at the lower socio economic level. Premature babies (i.e., infants with birth weights less than 5½ lbs.) are about 10 times more likely to be mentally retarded than are babies of normal birth weight (President's Committee on Mental Retardation, 1962). Recent advances in neonatal intensive care, however, are reducing significantly the incidence of both physical and mental disabilities among premature infants. Nevertheless, as medical technology makes it possible for more babies with birth weights as low as 1½ lbs. to survive, the risk of neurological impairment may increase.

In addition to inadequate prenatal care, prematurity is associated with a number of interrelated causal factors in mental retardation, including maternal and child nutrition, maternal age, and maternal health. Several but not all of these factors have a strong association with poverty.

Maternal and child nutrition.   The evidence is convincing that a pregnant woman's poor diet is a major cause of prematurity and mental retardation. Deficiencies in vital nutrients such as protein, iron, and vitamins (e.g., B_{12}, B_6, and thiamine) can adversely affect the development of the fetus's central nervous system. The developing infant is particularly vulnerable to malnutrition between the fourth and eighteenth weeks of gestation, and postnatally during the first 18 months of life. It is during these periods that rapid myeliniation of the brain occurs. Moreover, maternal undernutrition makes the mother more susceptible to infection, hemorrhage, and inadequate weight gain during pregnancy. Poor maternal diet resulting in obesity, diabetes, or anemia can also have negative prenatal influences on the developing fetus.

Maternal age.   As reflected in the Children's Defense Fund study, an increasing number of teenagers are having babies, a trend that increases the risk of premature births. This risk can be attributed not only to the lack of knowledge regarding good prenatal care, but also to the emotional and biological immaturity of teenagers.

Maternal health.   A number of chemical agents (i.e., teratogens) can affect central nervous system development when exposure to the fetus occurs at critical periods in pregnancy (usually in the first trimester). The mother's excessive smoking, drug use, and consumption of coffee and alcohol can result in prematurity and mental retardation. Studies conducted in the United States and Canada attribute 20 to 40 percent of the cases of prematurity to maternal smoking (U.S. Department of Health and Human Services, 1981). The more cigarettes a woman smokes during pregnancy, the lower the birth weight of the baby. Damage to the fetus appears to occur as a result of *nicotine* and carbon monoxide interfering with the delivery of oxygen to the brain and to other body tissues (Witter & King, 1980). *Addictive drugs* (e.g., heroin, LSD) and other pharmaceutical substances (e.g., painkillers, vitamins, narcotics, sedatives) may also affect fetal development. Some evidence, by no means conclusive, suggests that excessive coffee drinking produces high levels of *caffeine* in the bloodstream, which can have detrimental effects on the fetus (Borlée, LeChat, Bouckaert, & Mission, 1978). Alcohol consumption can result in prematurity and the childhood diagnosis of *fetal alcohol syndrome* (FAS).

It is estimated that 4,000 to 5,000 births a year have FAS (Eisenberg & Parron, 1979). Patterns of malformation observed in FAS include distinctive facial features, central nervous system disorders, and sensory and organ defects (Figure 6-3). Although the degree of mental retardation in FAS varies, studies suggest a correlation between the degree of physical deformity and brain damage (Streissguth, Landesman-Dwyer, Martin, & Smith, 1980). Quellette, Rossett, Rosman, & Weiner (1977) found that in 74 percent of the cases of FAS, the mother consumed more than 10 alcoholic drinks a day. However, even small amounts can result in FAS. While an association between alcoholic consumption and fetal maldevelopment has been established, it is still unclear how it affects the developing fetus.

Two other teratogenic agents, ionizing radiation and bilirubin, although not associated with social class, should also be mentioned. Fetal exposure to *ionizing radiation* may result in growth retardation (i.e., microcephaly) and congential malformation. X-ray dose exposure of 10 rads or less involves minimal risk of congenital defect, whereas exposure of more than 10 rads can be considered a threshhold for induction of birth defects. Most radiographic examinations subject the fetus to less than 1 rad; it is highly unlikely that the small dosage will affect the fetus. *Rh blood incompatibility* is another condition that can result in neurological damage to the fetus. The damage occurs when a Rh-negative mother, who has been sensitized by a previous Rh-positive fetus and thus has formed antibodies in her blood, subsequently has another Rh-positive baby. The antibodies cross the placenta and destroy the fetus's red blood cells (i.e., erythroblastosis fetalis), which produces *hyperbilirubinemia* (excess of bilirubin) and a reduction of oxygen going to the brain. The result is jaundice and severe mental retardation.

Both the general physical health and the mental health of a pregnant woman are important to the well-being of the fetus. Maternal infectious diseases and hypertension can cause premature births and possible mental retardation. Most of the infections that occur during pregnancy are caused by bacterial, viral, or protozoan agents. It is estimated that 2.0 to 2.5 percent of congenital defects among infants are the result of the mother's infection during the first trimester. These infections are often considered "silent," since many of them manifest no or only minimal symptoms in the mother, while having devastating effects on the developing fetus. *Cytomegalovirus* (CMV), *rubella* (german measles), and *toxoplasmosis* are infections that are transmitted from the mother to the fetus. Depending on the onset of fetal brain infection and the extent of damage, mental retardation may range from mild to severe. Other infectious agents that appear to exert a harmful affect on the fetus include *treponema pallidum* (the agent involved in syphilis) and *herpes virus hominis* (HVH). Studies have shown that up to 60 percent of fetuses with known syphilis infections experience central nervous system involvement (Ingall & Nouns, 1976). Most cases of the herpes infection are transmitted to the fetus at delivery as a result of maternal vaginal infection with the herpes virus. It is estimated that 25 percent of the fetuses surviving this infection will suffer neurologic impairment with mental retardation.

The existence of a modest hypertension appears to affect infant mortality

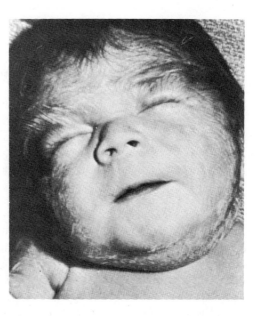

FIGURE 6-3
Facial Appearance of Child with Fetal
Alcohol Syndrome. (From K.L. Jones
and D.W. Smith, *The Lancet,* 2:999,
1973. Reprinted by Permission.)

and morbidity. Several studies have attempted to evaluate the effect of increased
dyastolic blood pressure on the incidence of complications during the perinatal
period (Naeye & Freedman, 1979). There appears to be an increase in the incidence
of placental infarction, placenta abruptio, retardation of placental growth, and
acute infection of amniotic fluid (Mendoza, Beck, & Griswold, 1981). A study by
Felding (1968) reported a perinatal mortality rate that was increased from 8 percent to 31 percent in pregnancies where the mother was hypertensive. The rate of
prematurity also increased, from 12 percent to 37 percent.

Prevention. The primary prevention of premature births associated with
mental retardation requires accessible prenatal, perinatal, and postnatal health-
care services for the poor. Nutritional counseling, family planning, and health-
education services are needed.

More specifically, the primary prevention of mental retardation due to
those toxic agents discussed above is relatively simple—avoidance of exposure.
Pregnant women should avoid ingestion of all medications during pregnancy,
except where the needs of medical treatment supersede the risk of teratogenic
effects. Consumption of drinking alcohol should be limited, since even small
amounts could be potentially harmful to the developing fetus. Pregnant women
should avoid exposure to radiation as much as possible.

Primary prevention of Rh incompatibility is possible by obtaining information about the parent blood types when applying for a marriage license. A Rh-
negative mother and a Rh-positive father increase the risk of Rh incompatibility.
The primary prevention of Rh blood incompability is possible by immunization
of the Rh-negative mother with Rhogam 72 hours after giving birth to the first

Rh-positive baby (Zarafu, 1980). In those cases where primary preventive intervention has not been instituted, amniocentesis can be used to detect the presence of hyperbilirubinemia in the affected fetus; a blood transfusion can be given in utero or immediately after delivery to prevent damage to the central nervous system.

Primary prevention of maternal infectious diseases requires avoiding the contraction of the pathogenic agent. Precautions regarding toxoplasmosis generally include reduced contact with animals (e.g., cats and dogs, particularly their excrement). It is also suggested that red meat be cooked perhaps more thoroughly than usual to avoid exposure to the toxoplasmosis protozoan. Mass innoculation of women with the rubella vaccine prior to conception would be a precautionary measure, as would reduced contact with persons having an infectious disease. The treatment for syphilis in both the pregnant and nonpregnant person is oral penicillin G. Benzathine penicillin G can be administered as a single large dose and is capable of curing a maternal infection. If administered during the first trimester, the treatment prevents fetal infection; if given to the pregnant woman beyond the first 3 months of gestation, it is usually capable of curing the infection. Alternative drugs are available for those who are allergic to penicillin.

The diagnosis of herpes virus is difficult, since the lesions typically seen in this type of infection occur in one third of those infected; at least one half of those infected are totally asymptomatic or show no symptoms (e.g., cervical inflammation or pelvic pain). Serological testing may be useful in identifying the presence of the infection. The optimum screening approach for infants with a suspected congenital infection must include an attempt to isolate the infectious agent. Treatment of herpes virus infection includes administration of drugs such as iododeoxyuridine, cytosine, and adenine arabinosides. Adenine arabinoside is preferred, since it appears to be less toxic and less immunosuppressive. Primary prevention, however, is the best means of alleviating the potential complications of this infection. Since effective therapy of recurrent maternal infection is not readily available at this time, the possibility of primary prevention lies primarily in early identification of at-risk cases and the use of caesarean delivery to avert fetal exposure by passage through the infected vaginal tract.

Appropriate medical treatment of maternal hypertention during pregnancy can prevent infant mortality and morbidity.

Harmful Environmental Influences

A number of harmful environmental influences that are associated with poverty can disrupt and impede cognitive functioning. These harmful influences include lead poisoning, pollutants, accidents, infectious diseases, and lack of cognitive stimulation.

Lead poisoning. Children of low-income families who live in old, central-city dwellings in close proximity to congested highways and air-polluting industries have a higher risk of elevated blood lead levels and lead encephalopathy. It is estimated that between 3 and 20 percent of children below age six are affected with lead poisoning. Approximately 500,000 children a year have elevated blood-lead levels that, depending on the elevation, can cause learning disabilities, severe mental retardation, and even death (President's Committee on Mental Retardation, 1980). The primary sources of lead intoxication are the ingestion of lead-based-paint chips (i.e., picca), exposure to high levels of atmospheric lead from automotive and industrial exhaust emissions, cigarette smoke, and cosmetics.

In addition to lead poisoning, today's industrialized society has introduced a wide spectrum of chemical substances (e.g., mercury, cadmium), some of which are toxic and can have potentially harmful mutagenic effects, (including mental retardation). These chemicals take numerous forms, including toxic wastes, pesticides, and aerosols. Pregnant women who drink contaminated water and breathe contaminated air can accumulate sufficient levels of toxins in their blood, and this can seriously affect the fetus.

Prevention. The best primary approach to preventing lead poisoning is the removal of children from environments where there is a high risk of lead ingestion. Since this is an impractical approach, efforts should be undertaken to reduce the amount of lead in a particular geographical area. The Lead-Based Poisoning Prevention Act of 1971 prohibits the use of lead-based paint and requires its removal in old buildings. The 1971 law also requires blood-level screening of children at least annually in high-risk residential areas. It has been recommended that these screenings occur more frequently, particularly during the summer months, when young children are likely to have increased contact with lead substances (e.g., lead in soil). Additional environmental-protection legislation has been passed that requires new cars to use lead-free gasoline; industries are also required to control for lead pollution. Stronger legislation is needed to protect the environment from becoming contaminated not only with lead but also with other harmful pollutants.

While recent reports have shown a significant decrease in atmospheric lead levels as a result of these measures, 4 percent of all preschool children and 19 percent of black children from poor families have blood-lead levels above the threshold for lead poisoning ("High Lead Levels," 1982). For these children who are affected by lead poisoning, chelation injections constitute a secondary preventive approach. These injections reduce the blood level by drawing the lead out of the circulatory system, so that it can be excreted from the body.

Accidents. Much of the trauma experienced by young children is due to accidents (e.g., falls, automobile injuries) and physical abuse. The risks of accidents among poor children is increased by their living in delapidated and often crowded households. In addition, they are more likely to be a victim of an auto accident in cities where the volume of traffic tends to be high.

Child abuse, while by no means limited to the poor, appears to occur more frequently in families in which the parents experience long-term stressful environmental and living conditions.

Prevention. Increased adult supervision of young children's activities, adherence to fire and safety regulations, and enforcement of the Child Abuse, Prevention and Treatment Act of 1974 can help reduce the risks of mental retardation attributable to physical trauma. An increasing number of states are passing laws that require all children under the age of 4 to be restrained by car seats or seat belts while traveling in motor vehicles.

Infectious diseases. Unsanitary and crowded surroundings, failure to be immunized, malnutrition, and poor hygiene are some of the factors that may predispose children to infectious diseases. Severe mental retardation can result from viral and bacterial infections that cause high fevers (i.e., brain infection) during the neonatal period. The known etiological agents causing *bacterial meningitis* include *E. coli* and beta-hemolytic streptococci; Type I herpes virus is the viral agent producing *encephalitis*. German measles, or *rubella,* is a common childhood disease that occurred at an annual rate of 4 million cases in the United States, prior to the implementation of vaccination programs. This significantly high incidence of measles resulted in 4,000 cases of encephalitis, 1,300 cases of mental retardation, and approximately 400 deaths (Papageorgiou, 1980). Nonimmunized children affected with rubella are not only at risk of sustaining neurological impairment, but they also serve as a reservoir for the virus, which may infect pregnant women.

Prevention. Immunization programs designed to reduce the incidence of measles have proven to be extremely successful. Antibiotics in treatment of affected children can also reduce the harmful effects of a high fever associated with an infectious disease. More importantly, improvements in living conditions and personal health habits can reduce the occurrence of infectious diseases.

Inadequate cognitive stimulation. The cognitive development of children of lower socioeconomic status is affected by both the inadequate quantity and the inadequate quality of sensory stimulation that is provided to them. The cumulative result of ineffective parenting and inferior schooling is a major cause of developmental attrition among poor children. If parents are limited both intellectually and economically, they are unable to provide the type of learning experiences that would equip their children with the cognitive and social skills that are needed to succeed in the public schools.

Prevention. Early intrafamilial education programs have demonstrated that psychosocial mild mental retardation can be prevented. Both the Milwaukee (Garber & Heber, 1977) and Abecedarian (Ramey & Campbell, 1977) longitudinal studies continue to report significant IQ differences between poor children in experimental and control groups. Experimental children are markedly above the IQ cutoff for mild mental retardation. Infants selected for inclusion in these studies came from low-income families where the mothers had an IQ lower than 80. Experimental-group children received enriched day-care programs; their mothers received instruction in childrearing, as well as other supportive services. Project Head Start, a federally supported program that provides compensatory education for economically disadvantaged children and parent training, has also produced beneficial outcomes, although there is disagreement about the long-lasting benefits of the program (Westinghouse Learning Corporation, 1969; Consortium for Longitudinal Studies, 1978; Zigler & Valentine, 1979). What is clear is that preschool and day-care programs should not be viewed as one-shot innoculation interventions, but that they must be followed by high-quality education programs in the public schools.

LARGE SCALE
SOCIAL INTERVENTIONS

Mass Education

The success of any program to prevent mental retardation will depend on the mass education of those in their reproductive years, so that they are aware of the known causes of mental retardation and the available strategies to avert this condition. Prospective biological parents should understand the dangers associated with poor maternal and infant nutrition, substance abuse, and advanced maternal and paternal age. The importance of obtaining good obstetrical and pediatric care should become common knowledge. Parents need to become more knowledgeable about the potentially harmful effects of lead poisoning, hazardous living conditions, and inadequate cognitive stimulation. Much of the available information on prevention can be disseminated to junior and senior high school students in their sex- or family-life education courses. Others can receive instruction at family-planning clinics. Litch (1980) has developed a model education program for high school students entitled *Prevention: To Be Born Well*. The program presents the causes of mental retardation and attempts to instill in the students a sense of responsibility for decreasing their chances of reproducing a mentally retarded child. It is particularly important that health professionals (e.g., physicians, nurses, public health specialists) who serve families be knowledgeable about recent developments in the etiology and treatment of mental retardation.

Social Programs

For the general population to be knowledgeable about how to prevent mental retardation will prove inconsequential, if our society lacks the will to commit the necessary resources to correct or eliminate the social conditions that produce this disability. The Great Society social programs initiated during the 1960s were designed to declare "a war on poverty" and its consequences (e.g., mental retardation). Table 6-2 lists some of the major social welfare programs aimed at assisting those families whose income is below the poverty line. These programs provide income (e.g., cash assistance) as well as in-kind services (e.g., health) to ensure a minimally adequate standard of living. Depending upon the level of income and severity of disability, an individual or family may be eligible for more than one of these social programs. As can be seen from a description of the program bene-

TABLE 6-2   Major Social Welfare Programs

PROGRAMS	BENEFITS
Aid to Families with Dependent Children (AFDC)	Cash assistance to poor families with needy children
Medicaid	Health services for the poor and their children (e.g., hospital costs, doctor's visits, prenatal and perinatal care)
Early Periodic Screening, Diagnosis, and Treatment Program (EPSDT)	Early detection and treatment of childhood physical and health problems; screening for lead poisoning, malnutrition, and immunization
Maternal and Child Health (MCH), Crippled Services (Title V)	Comprehensive pre- and postnatal care for mother and children (e.g., family planning, nutritional counseling, immunization, medical care for high-risk infants)
Community Health Centers Program	Health services for poor mothers and children, family planning, health education, prenatal care
Food Stamps	Scrip provided to low-income families to enable them to purchase sufficient food for an adequate diet
Special Supplemental Food Program for Women, Infants and Children (WIC)	Provides supplemental food to low-income pregnant women and children up to the age of 5 years who are nutritional risks; nutritional counseling to pregnant and nursing women, infants, young children
National School Breakfast and Lunch Program	Nutritional programs for needy children
Head Start	Comprehensive educational, social, health, and nutrition services for children (3 to 5 years old) from low-income families
Housing Subsidies	Financial assistance to provide decent housing for low-income families

fits, they attack the causes of psychosocial mental retardation discussed earlier in this chapter. During the 1960s and '70s, access to health and educational services increased significantly for thousands of low-income families, and this access contributed to the prevention of mental retardation (Davis & Schoen, 1978; Children's Defense Fund, 1983).

The gains made toward reducing poverty and psychosocial mental retardation over the past 20 years have been reversed by recent shifts in federal welfare policy. The implementation of this policy has resulted in the elimination or substantial reduction of social programs for the poor. The Reagan administration's new federalism and "safety net" policies give the states the major responsibility for the type of social programs they choose to provide. The administration proposed that the states assume the entire cost of the food stamp and AFDC programs. Reduced federal assistance to the states is provided through block grants rather than through categorical program grants. While these block grants must be used to help finance the costs for health services, preventive health, social services, and elementary and secondary education, there is no guarantee that state and local governments will use the limited funds to continue those programs that contribute to the prevention of mental retardation.

The Children's Defense Fund conducted a national survey of the impact that federal health budget reductions had on state maternal and child health services (Rosenbaum & Weitz, 1983). Listed below are some of their major findings:

1. About 725,000 people, 64 percent of whom are children and women of childbearing age, lost services at community health centers.
2. Cutbacks in vital public health services are contributing to a significant rise in infant mortality among the poor.
3. About 1.5 million children lost some or all AFDC benefits; 700,000 children have lost Medicaid coverage.
4. Forty-four states reduced prenatal and delivery services for pregnant women and reduced primary and preventive services for women of childbearing age, infants, and children.

The number of children living in poverty is increasing (it is now approximately 20 percent), and the negative consequences are surfacing in health statistics (e.g., more hunger) and personal tragedies throughout the country. Unquestionably, the new federalism policies are having a detrimental effect on the poor and are increasing the risks of mental retardation.

Concern about these developments has resulted in the drafting of the Children's Survival Bill, which has been introduced into both the House (H.R. 1603) and the Senate (S. 572). This bill is designed to restore and strengthen those social programs that have been cut by the President and the Congress. Title I of the bill enumerates those "essential preventive programs for children." Specific programs include: Child Abuse Preventive and Adoption Opportunities, Head Start, Family Planning, Immunization, Supplemental Food (Women, Infants, and Children), Food Stamps, and AFDC. At this writing, the Congress has yet to deliberate on the substance of the proposed legislation.

A SYNERGISTIC APPROACH
TO PREVENTION

As noted earlier, progress in the prevention of psychosocial mental retardation has proven considerably more elusive and difficult than has the reduction of severe mental retardation attributable to biogenetic causes. Whereas the identification of a single-factor cause of severe mental retardation can lead to prevention, the cumulative, polycausal factors associated with mild retardation make prevention more difficult to achieve. This distinction may lead some to advocate more support for the prevention of severe retardation (and its catastrophic effects) than for mild retardation. Moreover, the prevention of severe retardation requires medical engineering involving a single client, whereas the prevention of mild retardation requires large-scale social engineering affecting the entire populace. Advocates who are inclined to support prevention through medical engineering may be reluctant to encourage social engineering.

It is unlikely that psychosocial mental retardation will be significantly reduced without a comprehensive synergistic program to eradicate poverty (Zigler, 1978), that is, a comprehensive program in which all components are coordinated with one another. Such a program would include preschool education, health care, public assistance to needy families, job training, urban renewal, and the enforcement of the civil rights of all citizens. Grubb and Lazerson (1982) argue that to eliminate poverty, more progressive transformations in American society are required. The improvement in the quality of life of poor children and their families "requires looking beyond children's institutions and families to necessary transformations in the economic and political system—in macroeconomic policy, in the relationship between public and private ownership and employment, and political democracy. Ultimately, reforms to improve children's institutions or to strengthen families will lack much content without these larger transformations" (p. 302).

CHAPTER SEVEN
FUTURES

The year 1984 has arrived and the world is not quite the one George Orwell predicted. It is obvious how wrong a futurist can be in his prediction about the long term. The best that we can do is to look to "megatrends" and social indicators to forecast what things might be like in the short term. We do this in a world of increasing uncertainty where a single event (e.g., a war, an energy crisis, an assassination) may alter our expectations and aspirations. Yet, we do have a choice of futures.

What can be predicted with some degree of certainty is that nothing will remain the same for very long—human relationships will change, jobs will be taken and left, Republicans will be succeeded by Democrats, even golf balls will take on different colors. While similar changes have occurred in the past, what will be different in the future is the rapidity of their occurrence. Each of us will have to deal with rapid change within many spheres of our private and public lives. Now in the "third wave," we may soon be entering a fourth wave. In the following sections we will note some social trends, their likely impact on the lives of mentally retarded persons and future choices.

TECHNOLOGY

Technological advances have had, and will continue to have, a profound impact on the lives of physically and mentally disabled persons. Electric wheelchairs, functional artificial limbs, and robots are a few examples of technological breakthroughs that can reduce or eliminate handicapping conditions caused by physical disability. Similar technological advances have the potential to improve the lives of mentally retarded persons.

According to Linstone (1980):

> It is very apparent that the technology of a communicative-information society can serve to integrate the mentally retarded person into society, serving as an extension—more correctly an enhancement—of his or her mind. This role is perhaps comparable to prosthetic equipment for the physically handicapped. (p. 132)

The educability of mentally retarded persons can be enhanced by rapid developments in the computer technology and telecommunications fields. Computer assisted instruction (CAI) and instructional television can provide software programs designed for slow learners. This technology will make available to mentally retarded persons individualized learning packages that will accelerate their learning rate (Vitello & Bruce, 1979). Moreover, these devices can become available to mentally retarded persons not only in schools and at the workplace, but in their own homes. Consequently, the freedom to learn can take place anywhere, at any time. The technology can also serve as a source of entertainment, as it presently does for many nonretarded persons.

In addition to benefiting mentally retarded persons directly, computer technology can also benefit their service-providers. Teachers and parents can gain rapid access to diagnostic and curricular information that will enable them to plan a child's educational program. Computers are being increasingly used in the schools to monitor pupil progress. It is now possible to identify what community services are available for mentally retarded persons, track a person's use of the system, and maintain an account of the costs and benefits of service delivery. Such a computer-based system will not only provide mentally retarded persons more rapid access to needed services, but it will also enable the service agency to reduce operational costs while increasing program accountability.

Technological advances in the fields of genetic engineering, nuclear magnetic resonance, and laser surgery have the potential to reduce the incidence of mental retardation.

Technological development will also have its negative effects. Robotics will result in many manual jobs no longer being available to mentally retarded persons. The lack of access to computers and appropriate software programs could cause wider gaps between retarded and nonretarded learners.

In the years ahead, humanity will be confronted with the choice to use technology to improve the quality of life on earth or to continue the madness of developing costly weaponry that can end life. In a world in which nations are capable of developing technology to enable people to live in space, it certainly is within the realm of the possible to develop the technology to significantly reduce the effects of severe physical and mental disability.

INTEGRATION/SEGREGATION

The deinstitutionalization and mainstreaming movements represent moral imperatives to integrate increasing numbers of mentally disabled persons into our social
institutions. Disabled persons are one in a series of minority groups who in the last
two decades have sought equal opportunity. As history has shown, their progress
has been slow, and it has encountered (and continues to encounter) a number of
barriers. We are a society where ethnic, racial, class, and sex discrimination is still
pervasive. Despite our declarations and our Constitution that espouses social justice,
we are a society in which contrasts in the quality of life among people can be wit-
nessed in our schools, neighborhoods, and health care facilities. Therefore, it should
not have been unanticipated that efforts to integrate disabled, formerly segregated
persons into our social structure would meet with resistance.

While the implementation of the normalization principle has been successful
in the Scandanavian countries, some predict its failure in the United States. Zipperlin (1975) contends:

> It is hard to integrate anyone, normal or not, into a disintegrating society
> based on egotism. Deinstitutionalization does not constitute normalization
> unless it goes together with the use of some appropriate, integrated structure.
> (p. 271)

Kurtz (1977) also strikes a doubtful note on the social integration of mentally
retarded persons:

> At this point one can only speculate about whether the American public is
> ready to accept the drastic changes in social patterns which implementation
> of the normalization principle would necessitate. There is little doubt that the
> public would be willing to accept the principle on a theoretical and idealistic
> level since it is consistent with the general American value system, but it may
> not be willing to make the practical every day adjustments which would be
> necessary if it was to be implemented in social and economic activities.
> (p. 141)

These pessimistic sentiments are confirmed by continued neighborhood resistance
to housing for mentally retarded persons.

If we are unable to create a psychological sense of community, disabled
persons may choose the course of other minority groups who have grown impa-
tient with efforts at integration and now seek separate, but high-quality living
conditions. In the future, we may see an expansion in planned community living
for disabled persons very similar to some European models (e.g., the L' Arche
and Camphill programs).

PROFESSIONAL AND
COMMUNITY EDUCATION

A major reexamination is required in the scope and sequence of the professional
education of individuals interested in working with disabled persons. Our training

of teachers and other allied professional groups has been much too narrow. For example, we continue to prepare "teachers of the mentally retarded" and "teachers of the learning-disabled," even though we acknowledge the noncategorical attributes of these disabled children. More mindless are college and university programs that require an overdose of "special" courses for teachers of handicapped children. Consequently, the student has little opportunity to study important theoretical principles found in child development, human learning, and social psychology that can be applied to the learning situation. We have yet to articulate the nature of clinical experiences that will further the competence of teachers, and to make these experiences an integral part of the professional training program. Teacher educators may find some direction from the clinical-experience models used in the training of other professionals in other fields (e.g., physicians, social workers, lawyers).

One way to attract brighter students into the teaching profession is to make the program more intellectually challenging and stimulating. Of course, as most agree, a substantial increase in the salaries paid teachers would be the strongest incentive. While wider political participation is required to achieve the latter objective, there is much that professional educators can do to change and improve present training programs. The requirements of a liberal arts base in the professional education of all students entering the teaching field is a step in the right direction. Teachers should not only be able to teach well, but they should also be well-educated in the broadest sense. Teachers should not be among those scoring the lowest in a recent survey of persons knowledge about public and international affairs. The status of teachers will be enhanced not only by larger salaries but also by the more rigorous selection and preparation of those choosing to work in our schools and other social agencies.

Leadership training in the field of education and human services is critical to the future welfare of disabled persons. Personnel must be prepared to work with a number of constituencies—consumers, researchers, and policy makers. A familiarity with a number of knowledge bases (e.g., economics, organizational behavior, politics, law) must be included in leadership-training programs. In addition, internship programs need to be designed in collaboration with local, state, and federal agencies to enable the student to acquire effective interpersonal skills and an understanding of how "the system" operates.

Many myths and misconceptions about disabled persons still exist in the public mind. For example, there is the still prevalent belief that mentally retarded persons are "crazy" and a danger to the community. This misconception poses a major barrier in obtaining public support for investment in community residential alternatives for mentally retarded persons. Programs of public education will be needed to reduce the ignorance about disabled persons. Informal gatherings (e.g., at church and civic meeting places), special courses (e.g., in high schools and community colleges) and the use of the media (e.g., newspaper, TV) are a few of the mechanisms that can be used to educate the public. These approaches need to focus on the nature of particular disabilities and what can be done in the areas of prevention and habilitation. The public needs to understand that investments in human capital have payoffs, not only for disabled persons but also for the taxpaying society at large. Moreover, the nondisabled need to realize that they are only "temporarily able bodied" (Bowe, 1978). Disease, accidents, old age, may result in any one of us becoming a disabled person. We can expect no better care than that which we now provide disabled persons.

INTERNATIONAL DEVELOPMENTS

It is estimated that there are 40 million mentally retarded disabled people in the world. Each society chooses to deal with its disabled population in a somewhat different way. Wherever retarded persons are neglected, and their human rights violated, the international community must voice their concerns. In 1971 the United Nations adopted the Declaration on the Rights of the Mentally Retarded, which states:

> The mentally retarded person has a right to proper medical care and physical therapy and to such education, training, rehabilitation and guidance as will enable him to develop his ability and maximum potential. (p. 93)

In the future, offices within the United Nations must provide countries the necessary support to develop services for disabled persons.

There is much to be learned from those countries that provide exemplary services for mentally retarded persons. The United States has benefited from Scandanavian influences in the care of mentally retarded persons. In the future, communication must improve among countries in the areas of research, education, and service delivery. International forums such as the meetings of the Congress of the International Association for the Scientific Study of Mental Retardation and the International League of Societies for Persons with Mental Handicaps can provide excellent opportunities for these exchanges to occur. Foreign exchange study programs and collaborative research programs should also be undertaken. In short, we must begin to think internationally.

RESEARCH

Throughout this text, relevant research has been cited that has furthered our understanding of the sociological, psychological, and medical aspects of mental retardation. Medical and behavioral research has improved the quality of lives of mentally retarded persons. Interventions such as amniocentesis and special diets can now prevent mental retardation. The application of behavioral principles has enhanced the cognitive and vocational development of mentally retarded persons. In decision making, the courts and policy makers have increasingly relied on social science data. For example, evidence on the educability of severely retarded children was pivotal in the *PARC* decision; the *Larry P.* decision relied heavily on research findings showing the discriminatory effects of IQ testing. School policies have been influenced by the research on special class placement and mainstreaming; deinstitutionalization policy has been influenced by studies of the successful placement of retarded persons in community programs.

More sophisticated research is needed to improve the lives of mentally retarded persons and to increase our knowledge base for the generation of sound social policy. The following broad areas have been identified as requiring further inquiry:

1. The causes of mild mental retardation and the development of interventions to mitigate its effects (Zigler, 1978).
2. Program-evaluation studies to determine what type of programs and services improve the lives of mentally retarded persons and their families. More specifically, research is needed on the efficacy of person-setting interactions (Zigler, 1978; Baumeister, 1981). Cost-benefit analyses should be included in the evaluation design (Haywood, 1976).
3. Basic research on human learning and cognitive development and its relationship to teaching strategies in enhancing the adaptive behavior of mentally retarded persons (Haywood, 1976).

Edward Zigler has addressed the problem of the present "crisis in mental retardation research." By this he means the reluctance of the federal government to make the investments in research, particularly in the behavioral and social sciences, which have the potential to improve the lives of mentally retarded persons. In the future, reseachers as well as practitioners will have to continue their lobbying to secure a balance between the funds expended for services and research. Furthermore, the argument will have to be made that these two areas are interdependent, not mutually exclusive.

Procedures need to be developed to reduce the time gap between the accumulation of academic knowledge and its dissemination in our schools, residential settings, and other social agencies serving mentally retarded persons. Despite our past efforts in this area, we have been disappointingly unsuccessful. We must become more creative in finding ways to put knowledge into the heads and hands of those who provide direct services to mentally retarded persons.

SOCIAL VULNERABILITY

In his 1981 address to the American Association on Mental Deficiency, H. Carl Haywood discussed at length the "special social vulnerability of mentally retarded persons" in the United States. According to Professor Haywood, "retarded persons are vulnerable to a wide variety of negative social forces, most of which act either to limit their personal and psychological development or to limit their access to and participation in social institutions" (1981, p. 192). The following are among the negative social forces that increase the vulnerability of mentally retarded persons.

1. The labeling of a person as mentally retarded "makes one even more retarded as time goes on" (Haywood, 1981, p. 191). As less is expected of mentally retarded persons, less is provided for them. Consequently, environments function not to enhance their development but to retard it. The special vulnerability of mentally retarded persons is further compounded by cuts in educational and social services that delimit their educability.

    What arises as a dangerous future concern is the growing debate over the habilitation and educability of severely and profoundly mentally retarded persons. By subdividing the class of mentally retarded persons, factions within our society have begun to argue that limited resources should not be invested in individuals whose limited abilities will not yield a social benefit. In other words, based on a cost-benefit analysis, funds should support those programs for individuals who can benefit the most, with *benefit* defined as increased productivity. This future trend may well be a threat to the recent advances in education and community living for severely and profoundly mentally retarded persons and may signal an attempt to relegate those persons back to the safety and isolation of institutional settings.

2. Mentally retarded persons continue to be specially vulnerable to residential segregation. While the number of retarded persons released from public institutions has increased significantly in the past 15 years, recidivism rates for some placements are high. Recidivism may increase as funds decrease for the development of appropriate community programs. Mentally retarded persons are vulnerable to expedient depopulation plans and to placement into inferior nursing and boarding homes.

    Mentally retarded persons living in the community are also specially vulnerable. They may be subject to negative community attitudes, discrimination in access to services, victimization (e.g., personal, financial, sexual) and mistreatment in the criminal justice system.

3. Mentally retarded persons are specially vulnerable because of their increased dependency on others. Their dependency may be too heavy a burden for their families and lead to their placement outside the home. In some cases they may become the victim of neglect or child abuse. The shrinking of advocacy services also increases their vulnerability.

    Mentally retarded persons are included among the poor who are dependent on the welfare system for their economic well-being. While increasing numbers of mentally retarded persons can perform in competitive jobs, many are unable to find employment in our capitalistic society. Consequently, they cannot earn the amount of income needed to reduce their dependency on the state. Other retarded persons, due to the severity of their disability, will be unable to engage in meaningful employment and, therefore, will permanently depend on society for economic assistance. Thus while in the abstract, mentally retarded persons may gain equality and equal access to society, what this means, in reality, is that mentally retarded persons are being provided equality and equal access to the lowest socioeconomic segment of society, where they will remain. In short, they will become part of what is referred to as the "underclass" in American society (Auletta, 1982).

    Mentally retarded persons are specially vulnerable to the influences of living in poverty and to the policies the government fails to adopt to reduce poverty. In the future, any significant change in the social position of mentally retarded persons will require policies that restructure our society to eliminate poverty and to ensure each citizen a decent quality of life. According to B. Farber (1968):

Just how serious we are in wanting to solve social problems relating to surplus populations (in particular the mentally retarded) will determine exactly how much effort and sacrifice we are willing to undergo in order to revise modern society. (p. 270)

4. Severely mentally retarded persons are specially vulnerable to decisions that may result in their early death. The defective-newborn and Phillip Becker cases discussed in this text are examples of this vulnerability. Wolfensberger (1980) voices his concern about "a new wave of euthanasia of severely impaired people." The tightening of the economic screws must be watched carefully, because a real danger exists that fiscal policy may dictate moral and ethical judgments. Thus, as resources become scarcer and groups battle for those reduced funds, quality of life may become a factor dictating the allocation of resources.

   Haywood (1981) concluded his presidential address by noting that our most significant challenge for the 1980s will be our efforts to increase the social participation and decrease the social vulnerability of mentally retarded persons.

NATIONAL LEADERSHIP

In 1963 President John F. Kennedy summoned the nation to develop a plan to combat mental retardation. In the last 20 years tremendous progress has been made in the education and habilitation of retarded persons and in the prevention of this disability; yet more remains to be done. Another call is needed, at the national level, to combat mental retardation. The Congress has shown some leadership by establishing the Select Committee on Children, Youth and Families in the House and the Children's Caucus in the Senate. In the years ahead, a different kind of presidential leadership will be required to bring greater attention to the needs of disabled persons and their families. It is simply not enough to draw national attention to the needs of one disabled person. It is equally foolish to speak about "new ideas" when so many old-valued ideas—liberty, justice, and a measure of happiness —have not been released by too many Americans.

SUMMARY

This text has traced two decades of unprecedented progress toward improving the quality of life of mentally retarded persons and their families. More retarded people are sharing the benefits of American citizenry—public education, decent housing and better health care. More families have access to community services, support networks and knowledgeable professionals. These advances have come not from acts of benevolence, but from the struggle to secure human and legal rights for all mentally retarded persons. Today, the struggle to further define and enforce these rights continues in a sociopolitical climate that reminds us of the vulnerability of mentally retarded people. Just as the history of mentally retarded people cannot be understood without a study of America's social history, their future cannot be predicted without a plan for America's future. While the future is hopeful for many of us, advocates must remain vigilant lest our society become careless in its treatment of mentally retarded persons.

GLOSSARY

Adenoma Sebaceum: multiple yellow nodules on the face

Affirm: to uphold a lower court's decision

Alpha-Fetoprotein: a biochemical substance useful in detecting the presence of severe malformations in the fetus like spina bifida

Amicus Curiae: friend of the court; process by which an interested organization can assist a court by filing, in the form of a brief (with the parties' or court's permission), information and arguments that it believes are important in helping the court to decide difficult issues

Amnionitis: inflamation of the membrane enclosing the embryo or fetus

Anencephaly: a neural tube defect with absence of cranial vault and a rudimentary brain

Autosome: any chromosome other than the X and Y chromosomes. Humans have 22 pairs of autosomes. Compare **X-linked**.

Block-Grant Funding: funding process by which federal funds for numerous programs are lumped together, leaving to the state or locality the decision as to which programs to support and how much to fund each one

Café-au-lait Spots: lightly pigmented spots on the skin seen in neurofibromatosis.

Certiorari (cert.): the process by which the U.S. Supreme Court agrees to review a case (cert. granted) or declines to review a case (cert. denied).

Class Action: a method by which a lawsuit can be brought on behalf of large numbers of persons, too numerous to name, in order that all of their rights may be remedied through a favorable court decision. Plaintiff class includes all persons who would benefit from a favorable decision (such as all mentally retarded persons at a state institution).

Concurring Opinion: opinion of a judge who agrees with the court's decision, but who desires to emphasize certain points considered especially important or to expand upon certain points

Consent Decree: the process by which a lawsuit is settled between the parties in the form of an agreement enforced by the judge. This is in lieu of a trial, where all final decisions would be imposed upon the parties by the court.

Contempt of Court: disciplinary action by a judge against a party who has violated the orders of the court. It may result in fines, imprisonment, or both.

Dissenting Opinion: the views of a judge who disagrees with the court's decision

Dominant: In genetics, a trait is dominant if it is expressed in the heterozygote. When only 1 copy of the gene is present.

Encephalocele: a neural tube defect with a protrusion of the brain through a congenital opening of the skull

Entitlements: the rights to receive specific moneys and benefits under a law

Exsanguination: complete withdrawal of the body's blood

Genetic Heterogeneity: multiple distinct genetic causes for a similar phenotype

Guardian/Guardian *ad litem*: a person appointed to represent the interests and, often, care for one who is incompetent to do this himself. When appointed by a court for a specific legal process, the guardian is *ad litem*.

Heterozygote: for a given trait, an individual who has two different alleles at a given locus on a pair of homologous chromosomes; that is, a perons whose two genes for that trait are different from each other, one being dominant, the other recessive

Hydrocephaly: an abnormal accumulation of fluid in the cranial vault, accompanied by enlargement of the head, brain deterioration, and convulsions

Incompetent: legal term indicating a person's inability to make decisions or take actions on his own behalf

Injunction: judicial order, either ordering a party to take certain actions or prohibiting a party from doing certain acts. This may be temporary (in an emergency situation), preliminary (covering a relatively short period of time), or permanent.

Intervening Party: a party that becomes involved in a lawsuit after it has begun (often the Justice Department) in order to assist or to better present a specific side of the suit or to protect the interests of a larger group of persons not directly involved in the suit (such as all mentally retarded persons)

Master/Review Panel: mechanisms by which a judge can enforce compliance with the court's decision in a lawsuit. A master is a single person who acts under the judge's authority to work out the details of compliance. A review panel is usually formed from the parties' nominees and works to carry forth the court decision or order. These compliance mechanisms are usually utilitized after orders in complex lawsuits that will need to be monitored over a period of time.

Monosomy: a condition in which one chromosome of a single pair is missing, as in Turner's syndrome (XO)

Mosaic: the presence of at least two distinctive cell lines, derived from a single zygote

Mutation: an alteration in the structure of a gene or chromosome

Neurofibroma: a tumor of the peripheral nerve cells

***Parens Patriae*:** process by which the state, as parent, acts on behalf of its residents (children) for their own good and welfare; often used to support civil commitment laws

Phenotypic: the physical appearance of an individual, as determined by genetic and environmental factors

Placenta Abruptio: premature detachment of the placenta

Pro Bono: without charge; applies to attorneys willing to take cases and represent persons in court without fee

Q: long arm of a chromosome

Recessive: a gene that is expressed only when homozygous

Restrictive Covenant: a clause in a deed or contract that prohibits the property from being used in a specific way (such as to be utilized as a group home for mentally retarded persons)

Restrictive Zoning: process by which a state or locality limits a neighborhood or region to certain kinds of facilities. Single-family residential zones are usually utilized to attempt to prevent mentally retarded persons in group homes from residing there.

Remand: the returning of a case to a lower court for further consideration or action in light of the decision by the higher court

Reverse: to overturn a lower court's decision

Rh: a blood-group type

Translocation: the transfer of a segment of one chromosome to a nonhomologous chromosome

Treponema Pallidum: the causative agent of human syphilis

Trisomy: the state of having three of a given chromosome instead of the usual pair, as in trisomy 21 (Down's syndrome)

X-Linked: genes on the X chromosome (the sex chromosome); also, traits determined by such genes. Compare **autosome.**

REFERENCES

AANES, D., and MOEN, M. Adaptive behavior changes of group home residents. *Mental Retardation,* 1976, *14,* 36–40.

AANES, D., and HAAGENSEN, L. Normalization: Attention to a conceptual disaster. *Mental Retardation,* 1978, *16,* 55–56.

AANES, D., and WHITLOCK, A. A parental relief program for the MR. *Mental Retardation,* 1975, *13,* 36–38.

ADAMS, G. L. Referral advice by physicians. *Mental Retardation,* 1982, *20,* 16–20.

ADAMS, M. Foster care for mentally retarded children: How does child welfare meet the challenge? *Child Welfare,* 1970, *49,* 260–269.

ADDISON, M. Citizen Advocacy. *Amicus,* 1976, *1,* 9–10.

ALBRIGHT, L. *Administering vocational programs for handicapped students.* Arlington, Va.: The American Vocational Association, Inc., 1979.

"A Legal Knot in Baby Case" *New York Times,* November 7, 1983, pp. B1, B38.

ALLEN, D. F., and ALLEN, V. S. *Ethical issues in mental retardation: Tragic choices/living hope.* Nashville: Abingdon, 1979.

ALLEN, R. *Legal rights of the disabled and disadvantaged.* Washington, D.C.: Department of Health, Education, and Welfare, 1969.

American Academy of Pediatrics v. *Margaret M. Heckler,* 561 F. Supp. 395 (D.D.C. April 14, 1983)

AMERICAN CIVIL LIBERTIES UNION. *No justice for the poor.* Washington, D.C., 1983.

ANDRON, L., and STURM, M. L. Is "I do" in the repertoire of the retarded? A study of the functioning of married retarded couples. *Mental Retardation,* 1973, *11,* 31–34.

ANINGER, M., and BOLINSKY, K.   Levels of independent functioning of retarded adults in apartments. *Mental Retardation,* 1977, *15*, 12-13.

ANTHONY, P.   A Critique of Rowley by a special educator. *Education Law Reporter,* 1982, *6*, 867.

APPOLONI, A. H., and TRIEST, G.   Respite Services in California: Status and recommendations for improvement. *Mental Retardation,* 1983, *21*, 240-243.

Armstrong v. *Kline,* 476 F. Supp. 583 (E. D. Pa. 1979). aff'd sub nom. *Scanlon* v. *Battle, 629* F. 2d. 269 (3rd Cir. 1980) cert. den., 422 U.S. 968, 1981.

ARNOLD, I. L., and GOODMAN, L.   Homemaker services to families with young retarded children. *Children,* 1966, *13*, 149-152.

ASSOCIATION FOR RETARDED CITIZENS. *The right to choose: Achieving residential alternatives in the community,* Arlington, Va.: 1973.

Association of Retarded Citizens in Colorado v. *Frazier,* 517 F. Supp. 105 (D. Colo. 1981).

AULETTA, K.   *The underclass.* New York: Random House, 1982.

BAKEN, J. W., ZIRING, P. R., STEINDORF, D. R., TILLOW, J., and HOWE, E. M.   *The Willowbrook consent decree: Its impact on and implications for noninstitutionalized persons with developmental disabilities.* Unpublished manuscript, 1979. Available from Staten Island Borough Developmental Services Office, New York.

BAKER, B. L., SELTZER, G. B., and SELTZER, M. M.   *As close as possible: Community residences for retarded adults.* Boston: Little, Brown, 1977.

BALLA, D., BUTTERFIELD, E. C., and ZIGLER, E.   Effects of institutionalization on retarded children: A longitudinal cross-institutional investigation. *American Journal of Mental Deficiency,* 1974, *78,* 530-549.

BALLA, D., and KLEIN, M. S.   Labels for taxonomies of environments for retarded persons. In H. Carl Haywood and J. R. Newbrough (Eds.), *Living environments for developmentally retarded persons.* Baltimore: University Park Press, 1981.

BAROFF, G.   *Mental Retardation: Nature, cause, and management.* Washington, D.C.: John Wiley, 1974.

BAROFF, G. S.   Predicting the prevalence of mental retardation in individual catchment areas. *Mental Retardation,* 1982, *20*, 133-135.

BASS, M. S.   Marriage and parenthood. In M. S. Bass (Ed.), *Sexual rights and responsibilities of the mentally retarded.* Santa Barbara: Channel Lithographs, 1973.

Bartley v. *Kremens,* 402 F. Supp. 1039 (E. D. Pa. 1975), vacated and remanded, 431 U.S. 119 (1977), redecided, *Institutionalized Juveniles* v. *Secretary of Public Welfare,* 459 F. Supp. 30 (E. D. Pa. 1977) reversed, 99 S. Ct. 2523 (1979).

BAUMEISTER, A. A.   Mental retardation policy and research: The unfulfilled promise. *American Journal of Mental Deficiency,* 1981, *85*, 449-456.

BAUMEISTER, A. A., and MUMA, J. R.   On defining mental retardation. *The Journal of Special Education,* 1975, *9*, 293-306.

BAUMEISTER, A. A., and MacLEAN, W. E.   Brain damage and mental retardation. In N. R. Ellis (Ed.), *Handbook of mental deficiency: Psychological theory and research.* Hillsdale, N.J.: Erlbaum, 1979.

BECKER, H.   *Outsiders: Studies in the sociology of deviance.* New York: The Free Press, 1963.

Becker v. *Schwartz,* 386 N. E. 2d 807 (N.Y. 1978).

BECKMAN, P. L.   Influence of selected child characteristics on stress in families of handicapped children. *American Journal of Mental Deficiency,* 1983, *88,* 150-156.

BEGAB, M. J. *The mentally retarded child: A guide to services of social agencies.* Washington, D.C.: U.S. Government Printing Office, 1963.

BEGAB, M. J. The mentally retarded and society: Trends and issues. In M. J. Begab and S. A. Richardson (Eds.), *The mentally retarded and society: A social science perspective.* Baltimore: University Park Press, 1975.

BEGAB, M. J. The major dilemma of mental retardation: Shall we prevent it? (Some social implications of research in mental retardation). *American Journal of Mental Deficiency,* 1979, *78,* 519–529.

BEGAB, M. J. Issues in the prevention of psychosocial retardation. In M. Begab, C. Haywood, and C. H. Garber (Eds.), *Psychosocial influences in retarded performance: Issues and theories in development.* Baltimore: University Park Press, 1981.

BELLAMY, G. T., HORNER, R., and INMAN, D. *Vocational training of severely retarded adults.* Baltimore: University Park Press, 1979.

BENOIT, E. P. Towards a new definition of mental retardation. *American Journal of Mental Deficiency.* 1959, *63,* 559–565.

BENOIT, E. P. Rationale of a social center for employed limited adults. In R. K. Eyrran, C. E. Meyers, and G. Tarjan (Eds.), *Sociobehavioral studies in mental retardation.* Washington, D.C.: American Association on Mental Deficiency, 1973.

BERCOVICI, S. M. *Barriers to normalization: The restrictive management of retarded persons.* Baltimore: University Park Press, 1983.

BERGER, B., and BERGER, P. L. *The war over the family: Capturing the middle ground.* New York: Anchor Press, 1983.

BERKIANSKY, H. H., and PARKER, R. Establishing a group home for the adult mentally retarded in North Carolina. *Mental Retardation,* 1977, *15,* 8–11.

BERKOWITZ, E. D. The policies of mental retardation during the Kennedy Administration. *Social Science Quarterly,* 1980, *61,* 128–143.

BERKOWITZ, M., DEAN, D., RUBIN, J., and SHEEHY, S. Wages in sheltered workshops. In *Report of the minimum wage study commission.* 1981, *5,* 465–515.

Berman v. Allan, 404 A. 2d 8 (N.J. 1979).

BIKLEN, D. The case for deinstitutionalization. *Social Policy,* 1979, *10,* 48–54.

BIRENBAUM, A. *Non-institutionalized rules and role formation: A study of mothers of mentally retarded children.* Unpublished doctoral dissertation, Columbia University, 1968.

BIRENBAUM, A. On managing a courtesy stigma. *Journal of Health and Social Behavior,* 1970, *11,* 196–206.

BIRENBAUM, A. The mentally retarded in the home and the family cycle. *Journal of Health and Social Behavior,* 1971, *12,* 55–65.

BIRENBAUM, A., and RE, M. A. Resettling mentally retarded adults in the community—Almost 9 years later. *Mental Retardation,* 1979, *83,* 323–329.

BJAANES, A. T., and BUTLER, E. W. Environmental variation in community care facilities for mentally retarded persons. *American Journal of Mental Deficiency,* 1974, *78,* 429–439.

BJAANES, A. T., BUTLER, E. W., and KELLY, B. R. Placement type and client functional level as factors in provision of services aimed at increasing adjustment. In R. H. Bruininks, C. E. Meyers, B. B. Sigford, and K. C. Lakin (Eds.), *Deinstitutionalization and community adjustment of mentally retarded people.* Washington, D.C.: American Association on Mental Deficiency, 1981, No. 4 Monograph.

BLANTON, R. L.   Historical perspectives on classifications of mental retardation. In N. Habbs (Ed.), *Issues in the classification of children* (Vol. 1). San Francisco: Jossey-Bass, 1976.

BLATT, B.   Introduction: The legal rights of the mentally retarded. *Syracuse Law Review,* 1972, *23,* 991–994.

BLATT, B.   *The family papers: A return to purgatory.* New York: Longman, 1979.

BLATT, B., BOGDAN, R., BIKLEN, D., TAYLOR, S.   From institution to community. In E. Sontag (Ed.), *Educational programming for the severely and profoundly handicapped.* Reston, Va.: Council for Exceptional Children, 1977.

BLATT, B., and KAPLAN, F.   *Christmas in purgatory: A photographic essay on mental retardation.* Boston: Allyn & Bacon, 1966.

Board of Education of the Hendrick Hudson Central School District v. *Rowley,* 102 S. Ct. 3034 (1982).

BOGDAN, R.   What does it mean when a person says, "I am not retarded"? *Education and Training of the Mentally Retarded,* 1980, *15,* 74–79.

BOGGS, E.   The need for protective services for the mentally retarded and others with serious long-term disabilities. In United Cerebral Palsy Association, *Conference Proceedings on Protective Supervision and Services for the Handicapped, 1968.*

BOGGS, E.   Economic factors in family care. In R. H. Bruininks and G. C. Krantz (Eds.), *Family care of developmentally disabled members: Conference proceedings.* Minneapolis: University of Minnesota, August 1979.

BORCHART, K. R., and BROOKS, S.   *Operating respite care homes for children and adults who are developmentally disabled.* Paper presented at the meeting of the American Association on Mental Deficiency, Denver, Colorado: May 1978.

BORLÉE, I., LeCHAT, M. F., BOUCKAERT, A. C., and MISSION, C.   Le Café, facteur de risque pendant la grossesse. *Louvain Medicine,* 1978, *97,* 279–284.

BORNBERG, A.   Clinical and genetic investigation in Tuberous Sclerosis and Recklinghausen's Neurofibromatosis. *Acta Psyschiatrica et Neurologica Supp.,* 1951, *71,* 11–239.

BOWE, F.   *Handicapping America: Barrier to disabled people.* New York: Harper & Row, 1978.

BRADDOCK, D.   *Opening closed doors: The deinstitutionalization of disabled individuals.* Reston, Va.: The Council for Exceptional Children, 1977.

BRADDOCK, D.   Deinstitutionalization of the retarded: Trends in Public Policy. *Hospital and Community Psychiatry,* 1981, *32,* 607–615.

BRADLEY, V. S.   *Deinstitutionalization of developmentally disabled persons: A conceptual analysis and guide.* Baltimore: University Park Press, 1978.

BRADLEY, V.   Deinstitutionalization: Social justice or political expedient? *Amicus,* 1980, *5,* 82–87.

BRANDON, M. W. G.   The intellectual and social status of children of mental defectives. *The Journal of Mental Science,* 1957, *103,* 710–738.

Brandon Township v. *North Oakland Residential Services,*   312 N. W. 2d 238 (Mich. Ct. App. 1981).

BRESLIN, E. R.   Backlash against the disabled. *Mental Disability Law Reporter,* 1980, *4,* 345–355.

BREWER, G. D., and KAKALIK, J.   *Handicapped children: Strategies for improving services.* New York: McGraw-Hill, 1979.

Brewster v. *Dukakis,*   687 F.2d 495 (lst Cir. 1982).

"Bringing up superbaby." *Newsweek,* March 28, 1983, p. 62.

BROCKMEIR, W. E. Attitudes and opinions of relatives of institutionalized mentally retarded individuals toward institutional and noninstitutional care and training. *Dissertation Abstracts International,* 1975, *35,* 516 3A.

BROCKWELL, C. *Challenge and opportunity for the churches.* Columbia S.C.: Governor's Interagency Council on Mental Retardation, 1963.

BROLIN, D. E., and ALONZO, B. Critical issues in career education for handicapped students. *Exceptional Children,* 1979, *45,* 246–253.

BROWDER, A., ELLIS. L., and NEAL, J. Foster homes: Alternatives to institutions? *Mental Retardation,* 1974, *12,* 33–36.

BROWDER, J. A. Adoption and foster care of handicapped children in the United States. *Developmental Medicine and Child Neurology,* 1975, *17,* 614–620.

BROWN, J. S., and GUARD, K. A. The treatment environment for retarded persons in nursing homes. *Mental Retardation,* 1979, *17,* 77–81.

Brown v. Board of Education, 347 U.S. 483 (1954).

BRUININKS, R., HAUBER, I. A., and KUDLA, M. J. *A national survey of community residential facilities: A profile of facilities and residents in 1977* (Report by the Developmental Disabilities Project on Residential Services and Community Adjustment). Minneapolis: University of Minnesota, 1979.

BRUININKS, R. H., HILL, B. K., and THORSHEIM, M. J. *A profile of specially licensed foster homes for mentally retarded people in 1977.* Minneapolis: University of Minnesota, 1980.

BRUININKS, R., and KRANTZ, G. G. (Eds.). *Family care of developmentally disabled members: Conference proceedings.* Minneapolis: University of Minnesota, August 1979.

BRUININKS, R. H., C. E. MEYERS, B. B. SIGFORD, and K. C. LAKIN (Eds.), *Deinstitutionalization and community adjustment of mentally retarded people.* Washington, D.C.: American Association on Mental Deficiency, 1981, No. 4, Monograph.

BRUININKS, R. H., and RYNDERS, J. E. Alternatives to special class placement for educable mentally retarded children. *Focus on Exceptional Children,* 1971, *3,* 1–12.

BRUININKS, R. H., THURLOW, M. I., THURMAN, S. K., and FIORELLI, J. S. Deinstitutionalization and community services. In Wortis, J. (Ed.), *Mental retardation and developmental disabilities* (Vol. 12). New York: Brunner/ Mazel, 1980.

BRUININKS, R. H., WILLIAMS, S. M., and MORREAU, L. E. *Issues and problems in deinstitutionalization in H. E. W. Region V.* University of Minnesota: Information and Technical Asssistance Project on Deinstitutionalization, 1978.

Buck v. Bell, 274 U.S. 200 (1927).

BUDOFF, M. Engendering change in special education practices. *Harvard Educational Review,* 1975, *45,* 507–526.

BUDOFF, M., and ORENSTEIN, A. Special education appeals hearings: Are they fair and helping? *Exceptional Education Quarterly,* 1981, *2,* 37–48.

BURDA, M. Residential services: The Pennsylvania paradox. *AMICUS,* 1977, *2,* 34–40.

BURT, R. A. Beyond the right to habilitation. In M. Kindred (Ed.), *The mentally retarded citizen and the law.* New York: The Free Press, 1976.

BUTLER, E. W., and BJAANES, A. T. A typology of community care facilities and differential normalization outcomes. In P. Mittler (Ed.), *Research to practice in mental retardation (Vol. 1): Care and intervention.* Baltimore: University Park Press, 1977.

BUTTERFIELD, E. C. The role of environmental factors in the treatment of institutionalized mental retardates. In A. A. Baumeister (Ed.), *Mental retardation: Appraisal, education and rehabilitation.* Chicago: Aldine Publishing Co., 1967.

BUTTERFIELD, E. C. Institutionalization and its alternatives for mentally retarded people in the United States. *International Journal of Mental Health.* 1977, *6*, 21–34.

Cain v. Delaware Securities Investments and *Piendak* v. *Delaware Securities Investments, Inc.* No 5. 7236, 7239 (Del-Chancery Ct., August 11, 1983).

CALDWELL, B. M., and GUZE, B. A study of the adjustment of parents and siblings of institutionalized and noninstitutionalized retarded children. *American Journal of Mental Deficiency,* 1960, *64*, 845–861.

CANADIAN ASSOCIATION FOR THE MENTALLY RETARDED. We are people first, listen please. *Mental Retardation,* (special issue), 1979, *29*, 8.

CAVALIER, A. R., and McCARVER, R. B. Wyatt v. Stickney and mentally retarded individuals. *Mental Retardation,* 1981, *19*, 209–214.

CENTER FOR RESIDENTIAL AND COMMUNITY SERVICES–1982. *National survey of residential facilities for mentally retarded people.* University of Minnesota. Unpublished paper, 1983.

CENTERWALL, S. A., and CENTERWALL, W. R. A study of children with mongolism reared in the home compared to those reared away from the home. *Pediatrics,* 1960, *25*, 678–685.

CHAN, K. S., and RUEDA, R. Poverty and culture in education: Separate but equal. *Exceptional Children,* 1979, *3*, 422–428.

CHILDREN'S DEFENSE FUND. *A children's defense budget: An analysis of the President's FY 1984 budget and children.* Washington, D.C.: Children's Defense Fund, 1983.

City of White Plains v. *Ferraioli,* 34 N.Y. 2d 300 (1974).

CLARKE, A. D., and CLARKE, A. M. Prospects for prevention and amelioration of mental retardation: A guest editorial. *American Journal of Mental Deficiency,* 1977, *81*, 523–533.

CLAUSEN, J. Mental deficiency: Development of a concept. *American Journal of Mental Deficiency,* 1967, *71*, 727–745.

CLAUSEN, J. The continuing problem of defining mental deficiency. *Journal of Special Education,* 1972, *6*, 97–106.

CLEVELAND, D. W., and MILLER, N. Attitudes and life commitments of older siblings of mentally retarded adults: An exploratory study. *Mental Retardation,* 1977, *15*, 38–41.

CLEWELL, W. H., et al. A surgical approach to the treatment of fetal hydrocephalus. *New England Journal of Medicine,* 1982, *306*, 1320–1325.

CLOSE, O. W. Community living for severely and profoundly retarded adults: A group home study. *Education and Training of the Mentally Retarded,* 1977, *12*, 256–262.

Coffey v. *Baltimore Dept. of Social Services,* No. 471 (Md. ct. Special Appeals 1979).

COHEN, S. Supporting families through respite care. *Rehabilitation Literature,* 1983, *43*, 7–11.

COLE, R. W., and DUNN, R. A new lease on life for education of the handicapped: Ohio copes with 94-142. *Phi Delta Kappan,* 1977, *59*, 3–6.

COLOMBATTO, J. J., ISETT, R. O., ROSZKOWSKI, M., SPREAT, S., PIGNO-FRIO, A., and ALDERFOR, R. *Survey of the National Association of Superintendents of Public Residential Facilities for the Mentally Retarded on Deinstitutionalization.* Philadelphia: Temple University, Developmental

Disabilities Program, Woodhaven Center for Education and Research Technical Report, 1980, 80-5-(2).

COMMITTEE ON DRUGS. Treatment of congenital hypothyroidism. *Pediatrics,* 1978, *62*, 413–417.

CONLEY, R. *The economics of mental retardation.* Baltimore: Johns Hopkins University Press, 1973.

Connecticut Association for Retarded Citizens, Inc. v. *Mansfield Training School,* CA. No. 78-653 (D. Conn. 1978).

CONROY, J. W. Trends in deinstitutionalization of the mentally retarded. *Mental Retardation,* 1977, *15*, 44–46.

CONROY, J. W. and LATIB, A. Family Impacts: Pre-post attitudes of 65 families of clients deinstitutionalized. Unpublished paper. Temple University Developmental Disabilities Center, August 31, 1982.

CONSORTIUM FOR LONGITUDINAL STUDIES. *Lasting effects after preschool* (Final Report for HEW Grant 90C-1311). Ithaca, N.Y.: Cornell University, Community Services Laboratory, October 1978.

CORCORAN, E. L., and FRENCH, R. W. Leisure activity for the retarded adult in the community. *Mental Retardation,* 1977, *15*, 21–23.

COVAL, T. E., GILHOOL, T., and LASKI, F. Rules and tactics in institutionalization proceedings for mentally retarded persons: The role of the courts in assuring access to services in the community. *Education and Training of the Mentally Retarded,* 1977, *12*, 177–185.

CRAIG, P. A. Provision of related services: A good idea gone awry. *Exceptional Education Quarterly,* 1981, *2*, 11–15.

Crane Neck Association, Inc., et al. v. *NYC/Long Island County Services Group, et al.,* 466 N.Y.S. 2d 69 (N.Y. Sup. Ct. App. Div. 2d Sept. 1983).

Crawford v. *Pittman,* 708 F. 2d 1028 (5th Cir. 1983).

CRAWFORD, J. L., AIELLO, J. R., and THOMPSON, D. E. Deinstitutionalization and community placement: Clinical and environmental factors. *Mental Retardation,* 1979, *17*, 59–62.

CRNIC, K. A., FRIEDRICH, W. N., and GREENBERG, M. T. Adaptation of families with mentally retarded children: A model of stress, coping, and family ecology. *American Journal of Mental Deficiency,* 1983, *88*, 125–138.

CRONBACH, L. J., ET AL. *Toward reform of program evaluation: Aims, methods, and institutional arrangements.* San Francisco: Jossey-Bass Publishers, 1981.

CULLINANE, M. M. Sequential program needs of an individual with mental retardation and other developmental disabilities. Boston: Developmental Evaluation Clinic, Children's Hospital Medical Center, Undated.

CULVER, M. Intergenerational social mobility among families with a severely mentally retarded child. Unpublished doctoral dissertation, University of Illinois, 1967.

Curlender v. *Bio-Science Laboratories,* 165 Cal. Rptr. 477 (Cal. App. 1980).

Cuyahoga County Association for Retarded Children and Adults v. *Essex,* 411 F. Supp. 46 (N. D. Ohio 1976).

DANKER-BROWN, P., SIGELMAN, C., and BENSBERG, G. T. Advocate-protege pairings and activities in three citizen advocacy programs. *Mental Retardation,* 1979, *17*, 137–140.

DARLING, R. B. *Families against society: Reactions to children with birth defects.* Beverly Hills, Calif.: Sage Publications, 1979.

DAVIES, S. P. *The mentally retarded in society.* New York: Columbia University Press, 1959.

DAVIS, K., and SCHOEN, C. *Health and the war on poverty: A ten-year appraisal.* Washington: Brookings Institute, 1978.

DAVIS, S., and WARD, M. *Vocational education of handicapped students: A guide for policy development.* Reston, Va.: The Council for Exceptional Children, undated.

DAY, R. M., and DAY, H. M. Leisure skills instruction for the moderately and severely retarded: A demonstration program. *Education and Training of the Mentally Retarded,* 1977, *12,* 128–131.

de LEONE, R. H. *Small futures.* New York: Harcourt Brace Jovanovich, 1979.

DEMPSEY, J. J. *The family and public policy: The issues of the 1980's.* Baltimore: Paul Brookes Co., 1981.

DENNY, M. R. Research in learning and performance. In H. A. Stevens and R. Heber (Eds.), *Mental retardation: A review of research.* Chicago: University of Chicago Press, 1964.

DENO, E. Special education as developmental capital. *Exceptional Children,* 1970, *37,* 229–237.

DEPARTMENT OF LABOR, *Sheltered workshop study* (Vol. I). Washington, D.C.: 1977.

Der KALOUSTIAN, V. M., and KURBAN, A. K. *Genetic diseases of the skin.* New York: Springer-Verlag, 1975.

de SILVA, R., and FAFLAK, P. From institution to community—A new process. *Mental retardation,* 1976, *14,* 25–28.

DEUTSCH, A. *The mentally ill in America: A history of their care and treatment from colonial times* (2nd ed). New York: Columbia University Press, 1949.

DEVELOPMENTALLY DISABLED ASSISTANCE AND BILL OF RIGHTS ACT, 42 U.S.C. 6001 et seq (1975).

DeVIZIA, J. Success in a foster home program for mentally retarded children. *Child Welfare,* 1974, *53,* 120–125.

DEXTER, L. A. On the politics and sociology of stupidity in our society. In H. S. Becker (Ed.), *The other side in perspectives on deviance.* New York: The Free Press, 1964.

Diana v. *State Board of Education,* Civil Action No. C70 37 RFP (N. D. Cal. January 7, 1970, and June 18, 1973).

DINGMAN, H. F., and TARJAN, G. Mental retardation and the normal distribution curve. *American Journal of Mental Deficiency,* 1960, *64,* 991–994.

DOLL, E. A. The essentials of an inclusive concept of mental deficiency. *American Journal of Mental Deficiency,* 1941, *46,* 214–219.

DOLL, E. A. *The Vineland scale of social maturity.* Minneapolis: American Guidance Service, 1964.

Driscoll v. *Goldberg.* No. 72. Cl 1259 (Mohooning Cty. Ct. of Comm. Pleas 1970).

DUFF, R., and CAMPBELL, S. Moral and ethical dilemmas in the special care nursery. *New England Journal of Medicine,* 1973, *289,* 890–894.

DUGDALE, R. *The Jukes: A study in crime, pauperism, disease, and heredity.* New York: G. P. Putnam, 1910.

DUNLAP, W. R., and HOLLINGSWORTH, J. S. How does a handicapped child affect the family? Implications for practitioners. *The Family Coordinator,* 1977, *26,* 286–293.

DUNN, L. M. Special education for the mildly retarded—Is much of it justifiable? *Exceptional Children,* 1968, *35,* 5–22.

DUNN, L. (Ed.), *Exceptional children in the schools: Special education in transition* (2d ed.). New York: Holt, Rinehart & Winston, 1973.

178   *References*

DURAND, J., and NEUFELDT, A. H. Comprehensive vocational services. In R. J. Flynn and K. E. Nitsch (Eds.), *Normalization, social integration and community services.* Baltimore: University Park Press, 1980.

DUSSAULT, W. L. E. Guardianship and limited guardianship in Washington state: Application for mentally retarded citizens. *Gonzaga Law Review,* 1978, *13,* 585–624.

DYBWAD, G. Action implications, U.S.A. today. In R. D. Kugel and W. Wolfensberger (Eds.), *Changing patterns in residential services for the mentally retarded.* Washington, D.C.: President's Committee on Mental Retardation, 1969.

East Brunswick Board of Education v. *New Jersey State Board of Education,* C. A. 81-3600 (D. N. J. July 7, 1982).

EDELMAN, M. W. *Portrait of inequality: Black and white children in America.* Washington, D.C.: Children's Defense Fund, 1980.

EDGERTON, R. B. *The cloak of competence: Stigma in the lives of the mentally retarded.* Berkeley: University of California Press, 1967.

EDGERTON, R. B. Issues relating to the quality of life among mentally retarded persons. In M. J. Begab and S. A. Richardson, *The mentally retarded and society: A social science perspective.* Baltimore: University Park Press, 1975.

EDGERTON, R. B. *Mental retardation.* Cambridge, Mass.: Harvard University Press, 1979.

EDGERTON, R. B. Deinstitutionalizing the mentally retarded: Values and conflict. In A. W. Johnson, O. Grusky, and R. H. Roven, (Eds.), *Contemporary Health Services: Social Science Perspectives.* Boston: Auburn House, 1982.

EDGERTON, R., and BERCOVICI, S. The cloak of competence: 12 years later. *American Journal of Mental Deficiency,* 1976, *80,* 482–497.

EDGERTON, R. B., EYMAN, R. K., and SILVERSTEIN, A. B. Mental retardation system. In N. Hobbs (Ed.), *Issues in the classification of children.* San Francisco: Jossey-Bass, 1975.

EDUCATION ADVOCATES COALITION. *Report on federal compliance activities to implement the Education for All Handicapped Children Act (Public Law 94-142),* April 16, 1980.

EDUCATION FOR ALL HANDICAPPED CHILDREN ACT OF 1975 (P.L. 94-142) 20 U.S.C. S1401 et seq

EDUCATIONAL AND HUMAN SERVICES RESEARCH CENTER. *Local implementations of P.L. 94-142: Third year report of a longitudinal study.* SRI International, Menlo Park, Ca.: 1982.

EDUCATION TURNKEY SYSTEMS. *Case study of the implementation of Public Law 94-142: Preliminary findings and summary.* Washington, D.C.: Author, June 30, 1978.

EHEART, B. K., and CICCONE, J. Special needs of low-income mothers of developmentally delayed children. *American Journal of Mental Deficiency,* 1982, *87,* 26–33.

EISENBERG, L., and PARRON, D. Strategies for the prevention of mental disorders. In *Healthy people: The Surgeon General's Report on health promotion and disease prevention. Background papers.* Washington, D.C.: U.S. Department of Health, Education and Welfare, 1979.

EKLUND, E. *Systems advocacy.* University of Kansas, Lawrence, Kansas University Affiliated Facility, 1976.

ELKIND, D. *The hurried child: Growing up too fast too soon.* Reading, Mass.: Addison-Wesley, 1981.

ELLIS, N. R. Memory processes in retardates and normals. In N. R. Ellis (Ed.), *Interventional review of research in mental retardation* (Vol. 4). New York: Academic Press, 1970.

ELLIS, N. R. (Ed.), *Handbook of mental deficiency, psychological theory and research* (2nd ed). Hillsdale: Erlbaum, 1979. (a)

ELLIS, N. R. The Partlow case: A reply to Dr. Roos. *Law & Psychology Review*, 1979, *5*, 15–30. (b)

ELLIS, N., MOORE, S., TAYLOR, J., and BOSTICK, G. A follow-up of severely and profoundly retarded children after short-term institutionalization. *Mental Retardation*, 1981, *19*, 31–35.

ERICKSON, J. D., and BJERKALDAL, T. Fetal and infant mortality in Norway and the United States. *Journal of the American Medical Association*, 1982, *247*, 987–991.

ERIKSON, K. T. *Wayward puritans*. New York: John Wiley, 1966.

EYMAN, R. K., and BORTHWICK, S. Patterns of care for mentally retarded persons. *Mental Retardation*, 1980, *18*, 63–66.

EYMAN, R. K., DEMAINE, J. C., and LEI, T. J. Relationship between community environments and resident changes in adaptive behavior: A path model. *American Journal of Mental Deficiency*, 1979, *83*, 330–338.

EYMAN, R. K., SILVERSTEIN, A. B., McLAIN, R., and MILLER, C. Effects of residential settings on development. In P. Mittler (Ed.), *Research to practice in mental retardation* (Vol. 1). Baltimore: University Park Press, 1977.

FANNING, F. Coordinating community services. *Mental Retardation*, 1973, *11*, 46–47.

FARBER, B. *Prevalence of exceptional children in Illinois in 1958*. Springfield, Ill: Superintendent of Public Instruction, 1959.

FARBER, B. Effects of a severely mentally retarded child on family integration. *Monograph of the Society for Research in Child Development*, 1959, 24.

FARBER, B. Perceptions of crisis and related variables in the impact of a retarded child on the mother. *Journal of Health and Human Behavior*, 1960, *1*, 108–118.

FARBER, B. *Mental retardation: Its social context and social consequences*. Boston: Houghton Mifflin, 1968.

FARBER, B. Family adaptations to severely mentally retarded children. In M. J. Begab and S. A. Richardson (Eds.), *The mentally retarded and society: A social science perspective*. Baltimore: University Park Press, 1975.

FARBER, B. Sociological ambivalence and family care. In R. H. Bruininks and G. C. Krantz, *Family care of developmentally disabled members: Conference proceedings*. Minneapolis: University of Minnesota, August 1979.

FARBER, B., and RYCKMAN, D. B. Effects of severely mentally retarded children on family relationships. *Mental Retardation Abstracts*, 1965, *2*, 1–17.

FEATHERSTONE, H. *A difference in the family: Living with a disabled child*. New York: Basic Books, 1980.

FELDING, C. F. The obstetric prognosis in chronic renal disease. *Acta Obstetrica Gyneologica Scandaniva*, 1968, *47*, 166–172.

FERLEGER, D., and BOYD, P. A. Anti-institutionalization: The promise of the Pennhurst case. *Stanford Law Review*, 1979, *31*, 717–752.

FERNALD, W. E. The history of the treatment of the feeble-minded. *Proceedings of the National Conference for Charities and Correction*, 1883, 203–221.

FERNALD, W. The burden of feeble-mindedness. *Journal of Psycho-Asthenics*, 1912, *17*, 87–111.

FERNALD, W. E. After-care study of the patients discharged from Waverly for a period of twenty-five years. *Ungraded*, 1919, *5*, 25–31.

FERRARA, D. Attitudes of parents of mentally retarded children toward normalization activities. *American Journal of Mental Deficiency*, 1979, *84*, 145–151.

Fetzer v. *Mandau Public School District*, No. A1-80-40 (D.N.Dak. Oct. 17, 1980).

FIORELLI, J. S., and THURMAN, S. K. Client behavior in more and less normalized residential settings. *Education and Training of the Mentally Retarded*, 1979, *14*, 85–88.

FISHER, M. M., and ZEAMAN, D. Growth and decline of retardate intelligence. In N. R. Ellis (Ed.), *International review of research in mental retardation* (Vol. 4). New York: Academic Press, 1970.

FLETCHER, J. Abortions, euthanasia, and care of defective newborns. *New England Journal of Medicine*, 1975, *292*, 75–78.

FLOOR, L., BAXTER, D., ROSEN, M., and ZISFEIN, L. A survey of marriages among previously institutionalized retardates. *Mental Retardation*, 1975, *13*, 33–37.

FLYNN, J. R., GACKA, R. C., and SUNDEA. Are classroom teachers prepared for mainstreaming? *Phi Delta Kappan*, 1978, *59*, 562.

Forrest v. *Ambach* (Special Term of the Supreme Court of New York, May 10, 1982).

FORSSMAN, H., and AKESSON, H. O. Mortality of the mentally deficient: A study of 12,903 institutionalized subjects. *Journal of Mental Deficiency Research*, 1970, *14*, 276–296.

FOTHERINGHAM, J. B., and CREAL, D. Handicapped children and handicapped families. *International Review of Education*, 1974, *20*, 355–371.

FOTHERINGHAM, J. B., SKELTON, M., and HODDINOTT, B. A. *The retarded child and his family.* Toronto: The Ontario Institute for Studies in Education, Monograph Series 11, 1971.

FOTHERINGHAM, J. B., SKELTON, M., and HODDINOTT, B. A. The concept of social competence as applied to marriage and child care in those classified as mentally retarded. *Canadian Medical Association Journal*, 1971, *104*, 813–816.

FOUTZ, T. K., "Wrongful life": The right not to be born. *Tulane Law Review*, 1980, *54*, 480–499.

FOWLE, C. M. The effect of the severely mentally retarded child on the family. *American Journal of Mental Deficiency*, 1968, *73*, 468–473.

FRANCIS, S. H. Behavior of low-grade institutionalized mongoloids: Changes with age. *American Journal of Mental Deficiency*, 1970, *75*, 92–101.

FRANKLIN, D. S., and MASSARIL, F. The adoption of children with medical conditions: Part II—The families today. *Child Welfare*, 1969, *48*, 459, 533–539.

FREEMAN, H. Foster home care for mentally retarded children: Can it work? *Child Welfare*, 1978, *57*, 113–121.

FRIEDMAN, P. R. *The rights of mentally retarded persons.* New York: Avon Books, 1976.

FRIEDRICH, W. N., and FRIEDRICH, W. L. Psychosocial assets of parents of handicapped children. *American Journal of Mental Deficiency*, 1981, *85*, 551–553.

FRITH, G. H. "Advocate" vs. "professional employee." A question of priorities for special educators. *Exceptional Children*, 1981, *47*, 486–493.

FRITZ, M., WOLFENSBERGER, W., and KNOWLTON, M. *An apartment living plan to promote integration and normalization of mentally retarded adults.* Toronto: Canadian Association for the Mentally Retarded, 1971.

FROHBOESE, R., and SALES, B. D. Parental opposition to deinstitutionalization: A challenge in need of attention and resolution. *Law and Human Behavior*, 1980, *4*, 1–83.

FUCHS, V. R. *Who shall live: Health, economics and social choice.* New York: Basic Books, Inc., 1974.

GALLAGHER, J. J. The special education contract for mildly handicapped children. *Exceptional Children,* 1972, *38*, 527–535.

GALLAGHER, J. J., BECKMAN, P., and CROSS, A. H., Families of handicapped children: Sources of stress and its amelioration. *Exceptional Children,* 1983, *50*, 10–17.

GARBER, H., and HEBER, R. The Milwaukee Project: Indications of effectiveness of early intervention in preventing mental retardation. In P. Mittler (Ed.), *Research to practice in mental retardation (Vol. 1): Care and intervention.* Baltimore: University Park Press, 1977.

Garcia v. *Siffrin Residential Association,*   407 N. E. 2d 1369 (Ohio 1980).

GARDNER, J. M. Community residential alternatives for developmentally disabled. *Mental Retardation,* 1977, *15*, 3–8.

GARDNER, P. *Community acceptance of alternative living arrangements for the developmentally disabled mentally retarded citizen of Ohio.* (Research report). Columbus, Ohio: Association for Developmentally Disabled, 1981.

Gary B. v. *Cronin,*   542 F. Supp. 102 (N.D. Ill. 1980).

GATH, A. The impact of an abnormal child upon the parents. *British Journal of Psychiatry,* 1977, *130*, 405–410.

GELMAN, S. A system of services. In C. Cherington and G. Dybwad (Eds.), *The retarded citizen in quest of a home.* Washington, D.C.: President's Committee on Mental Retardation, 1974.

GENERAL ACCOUNTING OFFICE. *Returning the mentally disabled to the community: Government needs to do more.* Washington, D.C.: Department of Health, Education and Welfare, January 7, 1977. (a)

GENERAL ACCOUNTING OFFICE. *Preventing mental retardation: More can be done.* (Comptroller General's Report to the Congress). Washington, D.C.: U.S. Government Printing Office, 1977. (b)

GENERAL ACCOUNTING OFFICE. *Disparities still exist in who gets special education.* Washington, D.C.: U.S. Government Printing Office, 1981. (a)

GENERAL ACCOUNTING OFFICE. *Unanswered questions of educating handicapped children in local public schools.* Washington, D.C.: U.S. Government Printing Office, 1981. (b)

Georgia Association for Retarded Citizens v. *McDaniel,*   511 F. Supp. 1263 (N.D. Ga. 1980).

GETTINGS, R. M., and MITCHELL, D. *Trends in capital expenditures for mental retardation facilities: A state by state survey.* Arlington, Va.: National Association of State Mental Retardation Program Directors, Inc., 1980.

GILHOOL, T. The right to community services. In M. Kindred (Ed.), *The mentally retarded citizen and the law.* New York: Free Press, 1976.

GLAZER, N. Towards a self-service society. *Public Interest,* 1983, *70*, 66–90.

GLENN, L. The least restrictive alternative in residential care and the principle of normalization. In M. Kindred (Ed.), *The mentally retarded citizen and the law.* New York: Free Press, 1976.

GLIEDMAN, J., and ROTH, W. *The unexpected minority: Handicapped children in America.* New York: Harcourt Brace Jovanovich, 1980.

GODDARD, H. H. *The Kallikak family.* New York: Macmillan, 1912.

GOFFMAN, I. *Asylums.* Garden City, N.Y.: Anchor Books, 1961.

GOLD, M. W. Research on the vocational habilitation of the retarded: The present, the future. In N. R. Ellis (Ed.), *International review of research in mental retardation* (Vol. 6). New York: Academic Press, 1973.

GOLDBERG, I., and CRUICKSHANK, W. The trainable but noneducable: Whose responsibility? *National Education Association Journal,* 1958, *47*, 622–623.

GOLDBERG, I. I., and LIPPMAN, L. Plato had a word for it. *Exceptional Children*, 1974, *40*, 325–334.
GOLDSTEIN, J., FREUD, A., and SOLNIT, A. *Beyond the best interests of the child*. New York: Free Press, 1973.
GOLDSTEIN, S. STRICKLAND, B., TURNBULL, A. P., and CURRY, L. An observational analysis of the IEP conference. *Exceptional Children*, 1980, *46*, 278–286.
GOLLAY, E. Deinstitutionalized mentally retarded people: A closer look. *Education and Training of the Mentally Retarded*, 1977, *12*, 137–144.
GOLLAY, E., FREEDMAN, R., WYNGAARDEN, M., and KURTZ, N. *Coming back: The community experiences of deinstitutionalized mentally retarded people*. Cambridge, Mass.: Aut Books, 1978.
GOODLAD, J. I. A study of schooling: Some findings and hypotheses. *Phi Delta Kappan*, 1983, *64*, 465–470.
GORHAM, K. A. A lost generation of parents. *Exceptional Children*, 1975, *3*, 521–525.
GORLIN, R. G., PINDBORG, J. J., and COHEN, M. M. *Syndromes of the head and neck*. New York: McGraw-Hill, 1976.
GOTTLIEB, J. Mainstreaming: Fulfilling the promise. *American Journal of Mental Deficiency*, 1981, *86*, 115–126.
GOTTLIEB, J., GAMBEL, D. H., and BUDOFF, M. Classroom behavior of retarded children before and after integration into regular classes. *The Journal of Special Education*, 1975, *9*, 307–315.
GOTTLIEB, J., GOTTLIEB, B. W., SCHMELKIN, L., and CURCI, R. Low- and high-IQ learning disabled children in the mainstream. *Analysis and Intervention in Developmental Disabilities*, in press.
GOULD, S. J. *The mismeasure of man*. New York: Norton, Co., 1981.
GREENLEIGH ASSOCIATES, INC. *The role of the sheltered workshop in the rehabilitation of the severely handicapped* (Vol. 1). New York: Executive Summary, 1975.
GROSSMAN, F. K. *Brothers and sisters of retarded children: An exploratory study*. Syracuse, N.Y.: Syracuse University Press, 1972.
GROSSMAN, H. J. (Ed.) *Manual on terminology and classification in mental retardation*. Washington, D.C.: American Association on Mental Deficiency, 1973.
GROSSMAN, H. J. (Ed.), *Classification in mental retardation*. Washington, D.C.: American Association on Mental Deficiency, 1983.
GRUBB, W. N., and LAZERSON, M. *Broken promise: How Americans fail their children*. New York: Basic Books, 1982.
Guardianship of Becker, 188 Cal. Rptr. 781, 785 (App. 1983).
Guempel v. State, 418 A. 2d 229 (N.J. 1980).
GUNZBURG, H. C., and GUNZBURG, A. L. Social education and the institution: The shaping of a theragenetic "non-institutional" environment. In *Proceedings of the Second International Congress on the Scientific Study of Mental Retardation*, 1971.
GURALNICK, M. Pediatrics, special education, and handicapped children: New relationships. *Exceptional Children*, 1982, *48*, 294–295.
GUSTAFSON, J. M. Mongolism, parental desires, and the right to life. *Perspectives in Biology and Medicine*, 1973, *16*, 529–557.
HAAVIK, S. F., and MENNINGER, K. A. *Sexuality, law, and the developmentally disabled person: Legal and clinical aspects of marriage, parenthood, and sterilization*. Baltimore: Paul Brookes, 1981.
HADDAD, H. M., and WILKEN, L. Congenital anomalies associated with gonadal aplasia: Review of 58 cases. *Pediatrics*, 1959, *23*, 885–902.

HAINEY, J., JUDGE, C., and WIENER, S. Familial X-linked mental retardation with an X chromosome abnormality. *Journal of Medical Genetics,* 1977, *14*, 46–50.

Halderman v. *Pennhurst State School and Hospital,* 446 F. Supp. 1295 (E.D.PA. 1977), *aff'd* 612 F. 2d 84 (3rd Cir. 1979), *rev'd* 451 U.S. 1, 101 S. Ct. 1531 (1981), *redecided* 673 F. 2d 647 (3rd Cir. 1982a), rev'd and rem. 52 U.S. L.W., 4155 (1-24-84).

Halderman v. *Pennhurst State School and Hospital,* 553 F. Supp. 661 (E.D. Pa. 1982b).

HALLAHAN, D. P., and KAUFFMAN, J. M. Labels, categories, behaviors: ED, LD, EMR reconsidered. *The Journal of Special Education,* 1977, *11*, 139–149.

HALPERN, C. The right to habilitation. In M. Kindred (Ed.). *The mentally retarded citizen and the law.* New York: Free Press, 1976.

HANSEN, A. Willowbrook. In J. Wortis (Ed.), *Mental retardation and developmental disabilities* (Vol. 9). New York: Brunner/Mazel, 1977.

HANSEN, H., BELMONT, L., and STEIN, Z. Epidemiology. In J. Wortis, (Ed.), *Mental retardation and developmental disabilities* (Vol. 11). New York: Brunner/Mazel, Inc., 1980.

HANSEN, M. Evaluations of training procedures used in a parent implemented intervention program for Down's syndrome infants. *American Association for the Education of Severely/Profoundly Handicapped,* 1976, *1*, 36–52.

Harbeson v. *Parke-Davis, Inc.,* 656 P. 2d 483 (Wash. 1983).

Harrell v. *Wilson County Schools,* 293S.E. 2d 687 (N.C. Ct. App. 1982).

HARRINGTON, M. *The other America.* New York: Penguin Books, 1963.

HAYWOOD, H. C. The ethics of doing research . . . and of not doing it. *American Journal of Mental Deficiency,* 1976, *81*, 311–317.

HAYWOOD, H. C. *Reducing social vulnerability is the challenge of the eighties. Mental Retardation,* 1981, *19*, 190–195.

HEAL, L. W., and DANIELS, B. S. *A cost-effectiveness analysis of residential alternatives for selected developmentally disabled citizens of three northern Wisconsin counties.* Paper presented at the annual meeting of the American Association on Mental Deficiency, Denver, May 1978.

HEAL, L., SIGELMAN, C., and SWITZKY, H. Community residential alternatives for the mentally retarded. In N. R. Ellis (Ed.), *International review of research in mental retardation.* New York: Academic Press, 1978.

HEBER, R. F. A manual on terminology and classification in mental retardation. *American Journal of Mental Deficiency,* 1959, *64* (Monograph Supplement).

HEBER, R. F. A manual on terminology classification in mental retardation (Rev. ed.). *American Journal of Mental Deficiency Monograph,* 1961 (Supp 64).

HEBER, R., and GARBER, H. The Milwaukee Project: A study of the use of family intervention to prevent cultural-familial mental retardation. In B. Friedlender, G. Sterritt, and G. Kirk (Eds.), *Exceptional Infant: Assessment and Intervention.* New York: Brunner/Mazel, 1975.

HEBER, R. F., GARDNER, H., HARRINGTON, S., HOFFMAN, C., and FALENDAR, C. *Rehabilitation of families at risk for mental retardation* (Progress report). Madison: University of Wisconsin, Rehabilitation Research and Training Center in Mental Retardation, 1972.

HELSEL, E. D. Residential service. In J. Wortis (Ed.), *Mental retardation and developmental disabilities* (Vol. 3). New York: Brunner/Mazel, 1971.

HENDRIX, E. The fallacies of the concept of normalization. *Mental Retardation,* 1981, *19*, 195-296.

Herbert and Patsy H. v. *Warren B.,* 188 Cal. Rptr. 781 (Cal. Ct. App. 1983).

HERNSTEIN, R. S. *IQ in the meritocracy.* Boston: Little, Brown, 1973.

HERR, S. *Advocacy under the Developmental Disabilities Bill of Rights Act.* Region III Developmental Disabilities Office discussion paper, Philadelphia, Pennsylvania, 1976.

HERR, S. The new clients: Legal services for mentally retarded persons. *Stanford Law Review,* 1979, *31,* 553-611.

HERR, S. Legal advocacy for the mentally handicapped, *International Journal of Law and Psychiatry,* 1980, *3,* 61-79.

HERR, S. *Rights and advocacy for retarded people.* Lexington: Lexington Books, 1983.

"High lead level found in 4% of preschoolers," *New York Times,* May 20, 1982, p. A15.

HILL, B. K., and BRUININKS, R. H. Maladaptive behavior of mentally retarded individuals in residential facilities. *American Journal of Mental Deficiency,* 1984, *88,* 380-387.

HINKLE, H., and VITELLO, S. J. Sterilization of mentally retarded people: A search for authority and standards. Unpublished manuscript, 1983. Available from Rutgers University, Graduate School of Education, New Brunswick, N.J. 08903.

HOBBIN, J. C., GRANNUM, P., BERKOWITZ, R., SILVERMAN, R., and MAHONEY, M. Ultrasound in the diagnosis of congenital anomalies. *American Journal of Obstetrics and Gynecology,* 1979, *134,* 311-345.

HOLBURN, C. S. Impact of a legal advocacy program on services in a state residential facility. *Mental Retardation,* 1982, *20,* 254-259.

HOLT, K. S. The home care of severely retarded children. *Pediatrics,* 1958, *22,* 744-755.

HOLT, K. S. Home care of severely retarded children. In J. Dempsey (Ed.), *Community services for retarded children: The consumer-provider relationship.* Baltimore: University Park Press, 1975.

HOOK, E. B., and CHAMBERS, G. M. Estimated rates of Down's syndrome in live births by one year maternal age intervals for mothers aged 20–49 in a N.Y. state study—implications of the risk figures for genetic counseling and cost-benefit analysis of prenatal diagnosis programs. *Birth Defects, Original Article Series,* 1977, *13,* 123-141.

Hopkins v. *Zoning Board,*   423 A. 2d 1082 (Pa. Commonwealth Ct. 1980).

Horacek v. *Exon,*   354 F. Supp. 71 (D. Neb. 1973), No. 72-6-299 (D. Neb. 1975).

HOREJSI, C. R. *Deinstitutionalization and the development of community based services for the mentally retarded: An overview of concepts and issues.* Missoula, Mont.: University of Montana, Project on Community Resources and Deinstitutionalization (Grant No. 90-C-341, Office of Child Development, U.S. Dept. of Health, Education, and Welfare), August 1975.

HOREJSI, C. R. Social and psychological factors in family care. In R. H. Bruininks and G. C. Krantz (Eds.), *Family care of developmentally disabled members: Conference proceedings.* Minneapolis: University of Minnesota, August 1979.

HORIZON HOUSE INSTITUTE. *These people: A citizen education project focusing on public response to community care for the mentally disabled,* Philadelphia: 1977, Final Report (2nd Draft).

HUBERTY, T. J., KOLLER, J. R., and TEN BRINK, T. D. Adaptive behavior in the definition of the mentally retarded. *Exceptional Children,* 1980, *46,* 256-261.

HULL, K. *The rights of physically handicapped people.* New York: Avon Books, 1979.

HUNT, J. M. *Intelligence and experience.* New York: Ronald Press, 1961.

HURLEY, R. *Poverty and mental retardation: A causal relationship.* New York: Vintage Books, 1963.

INGALL, D., and NOUNS, L. Syphilis. In J. S. Remington and J. O. Klein (Eds.), *Infectious diseases of the fetus and newborn infant.* Philadelphia: W. B. Saunders, 1976.

INGALLS, R. P. *Mental retardation: The changing outlook.* New York: John Wiley, 1978.

INHELDER, B. [*The diagnosis of reasoning in the mentally retarded*] (2d ed) (W. B. Stephens and others, trans.). New York: Chandler Publishing, 1968.

In re "A" Family, 602 P. 2d 157 (Mont. 1979).

In re Anderson, (Idaho Educ. Agency Admin. Rev. Bd., Sept. 10, 1980).

In re Baby Girl Obernauer, (Morris County N.J. Juv. Dom. Rel Ct., Dec. 22, 1970).

In re Cicero, 421 N.Y. 2d 965 (1979).

In re Green, 2174 (N.Y. Fam. Ct. 1978).

In re Lee Ann Grady, 426 A 2d 467 (N.J. 1981).

In re Orlando F., 40 N.Y. 2d 103 (1976).

In re Phillip Becker, 92 Cal App 3d 796, 156 Cal Rep 48 (1979).

In re Primus, 98 S. Ct. 1893 (1978).

In re Schmidt, 429 A. 2d. 631 (Pa. 1981).

IRELAND, W. W. *The mental affections of children: Idiocy, imbecility, and insanity.* Philadelphia: Blakiston, 1900.

INTAGLIATA, J., KRAUS, S., and WILLER, B. The impact of deinstitutionalization on a community based service system. *Mental Retardation,* 1980, *18,* 305-307.

INTAGLIATA, J., WILLER, B. S., and COOLEY, F. B. Cost comparison of institutional and community-based alternatives for mentally retarded persons. *Mental Retardation,* 1979, *17,* 134-136.

In the Matter of Treatment and Care of Infant Doe, (Appeal from the circuit court for Monroe Cty., Indiana Cause No. GU-8204-0041, 1982).

JACOBSON, J. W., and JANICKI, M. P. Observed prevalence of multiple developmental disabilities. *Mental Retardation,* 1983, *21,* 87-94.

JACOBSON, J. W. and SCHWARTZ, A. A. Personal and service characteristics affecting group home placement success: A prospective analysis. *Mental Retardation,* 1983, *21,* 1-7.

JAFFE, F. S., LINDHEIM, B. L., and LEE, P. R. *Abortion politics: Private morality and public policy.* New York: McGraw-Hill, 1981.

JANICKI, M. P., MAYEDA, T., and EPPLE, W. A. Availability of group homes for persons with mental retardation in the United States. *Mental Retardation,* 1983, *21,* 45-51.

JASTAK, J. F., MacPHEE, H. M., and WHITEMAN, M. *Mental retardation: Its nature and incidence.* Newark: University of Delaware Press, 1963.

JENCKS, C. *Who gets ahead? The determinant of economic success in America.* New York: Basic Books, 1979.

JENKINS, E. C., BROWN, W. T., et al. Feasibility of Fragile X chromosome prenatal diagnosis demonstrated. *Lancet,* 1981, *2,* 1292.

JENSEN, A. R. How much can we boost IQ and scholastic achievement? *Harvard Educational Review,* 1969, *39,* 1-123.

JERVIS, G. A. Medical aspects of mental deficiency. *American Journal of Mental Deficiency,* 1952, *57,* 175-188.

J. R. v. Parham, 412 F. Supp. 112, (M.D. Ga. 1976), rev'd 442 U.S. 584, 99 S. Ct. 2493 (1979).

JONES, J. R., and MOE, R. College education for mentally retarded adults. *Mental Retardation,* 1980, *18,* 59–62.

JONES, P. A., CONROY, J. W., FEINSTEIN, C. S., and LEMANOWICZ, J. A. A matched comparison study of cost-effectiveness: Institutionalized and de-institutionalized clients. Unpublished paper. Temple University, Developmental Disabilities Center, 1983.

Jose P. v. *Ambach,* 79 C 270 (E.D. N.Y. 1979).

J. T. Hobby and Son, Inc. v. *Family Homes of Wake County, Inc.,* 274 S.E. 2d. 174 (N.C. 1981).

JUSTICE, R. S., BRADLEY, J., and O'CONNOR, G. Foster family care for the retarded: Management concerns of the caretaker. *Mental Retardation,* 1971, *9,* 12–15.

KAHN, A., KAMERMAN, S., and McGOWAN, B. *Child advocacy.* Columbia University, School of Social Work, Child Advocacy Research Project, 1972.

KAKALIK, J. S., FURRY, W. S., THOMAS, M. A., and CARNEY, M. F. *The cost of special education: Summary of study findings.* The Rand Corporation, Santa Monica, Ca.: 1982.

KAMERMAN, S. B. *Parenting in an unresponsive society: Managing work and family life.* New York: Free Press, 1980.

KAMIN, L., and EYSENCK, H. J. *The intelligence controversy.* New York: John Wiley, 1981.

KANNER, L. Miniature textbook of feeblemindedness. *Child Care Monographs,* 1949, No. 1.

KANNER, L. *A history of the care and study of the mentally retarded.* Springfield, Ill.: Charles C. Thomas, 1964.

KARRER, R., NELSON, M. N., and GALBRAITH, G. C. Psychophysiological research with the mentally retarded. In N. R. Ellis (Ed.), *Handbook of mental deficiency, psychological theory and research.* Hillsdale: Erlbaum, 1979.

KATZ, E. *The retarded adult in the community.* Springfield, Ill.: Charles C. Thomas, 1968.

KATZ, S., and YEKUTIEL, E. Leisure time program of mentally retarded graduates of training programs. *Mental Retardation,* 1974, *12,* 54–57.

KATZMAN, S. Parental rights of mentally retarded: The advisability and constitutionability of the treatment of retarded parents in New York state. *Columbia Journal of Law and Social Problems,* 1981, *16,* 521–559.

KAUFFMAN, J. M. and KRAUSE, J. The cult of educability: Searching for the substance of things hoped for; the evidence of things not seen. *Analysis and Intervention in Developmental Disabilities,* 1981, *1,* 53–60.

KAUFFMAN, M. E. The affects of institutionalization on development of stereotyped and social behavior in mental defectives. *American Journal of Mental Deficiency,* 1966, *71,* 581–585.

KAUFFMAN, M. E., and ALBERTO, P. A. Research on efficacy of special education for the mentally retarded. In N. Ellis, *International review of research on mental retardation* (Vol. 8). New York: Academic Press, 1976.

KAUFFMAN, M. E., GOTTLIEB, J., AGARD, J. A., and KUKIC, M. B. Mainstreaming: Toward an explication of the construct. *Focus on Exceptional Children,* 1975, *7,* 1–12.

KEATING, D. J., CONROY, J. W., and WALKER, S. *Longitudinal study of the court-ordered deinstitutionalization of Pennhurst.* Philadelphia: Temple University Developmental Disabilities Evaluation and Research Group, 1980.

KENISTON, K. *All our children: The American family under pressure.* New York: Harcourt Brace Jovanovich, 1977.

Kentucky Association for Retarded Citizens v. *Conn,*   674 F. 2d 582 (6th Cir. 1982), *affirming* 510 F. Supp. 1233 (W.D. Ky. 1980).

KERENYI, T., and CHITKARA, U. Selective birth in twin pregnancy with discordency for Down's syndrome. *New England Journal of Medicine,* 1981, *304,* 1525-1527.

KEYS, V., BOROSKIN, A., and ROSS, R. T. The revolving door in MR hospital: A study of returns from leave. *Mental Retardation,* 1973, *11,* 55-56.

KIRP, D. Schools as sorters: The constitutional and policy implications of student classifications. *University of Pennsylvania Law Review,* 1973, *121,* 705-717.

KIRP, D. and JENSEN, D. N. What does due process do? *Public Interest,* 1983, *73,* 75-90.

KLABER, M. M. The retarded and institutions for the retarded: A preliminary research project. In S. B. Sarason and J. Doris, *Psychological problems in mental deficiency.* New York: Harper & Row, 1969.

KLEINBERG, J., and GALLIGAN, B. Effects of deinstitutionalization on adaptive behavior of mentally retarded adults. *American Journal of Mental Deficiency,* 1983, *88,* 21-27.

KNOBLOCH, H., and PASAMANICK, B. Environmental factors affecting human development before and after birth. *Pediatrics,* 1960, *26,* 210-218.

KOEGEL, P. and EDGERTON, R. B. Labeling and the perception of handicap among black mildly mentally retarded adults. *American Journal of Mental Deficiency,* 1982, *87,* 266-276.

KREECH, F. Adoptive outreach. *Child Welfare,* 1973, *52,* 669-675.

KRISHEFF, C. H. Adoption agency services for the retarded. *Mental Retardation,* 1977, *15,* 38-39.

Kruelle v. *New Castle County School District,*   642 F. 2d 687 (3rd Cir. 1981).

KRUMMEL, C. The mentally retarded: God's exceptional children. *The Lutheran,* 1975, *13,* 4-6.

KURILOFF, P., KIRP, D., and BUSS, W. *When handicapped children go to court: Assessing the impact of the legal reform of special education in Pennsylvania.* Philadelphia, University of Pennsylvania, Final Report, 1979.

KURTZ, R. Advocacy for the mentally retarded: The development of a new social role. In M. Begab and S. Richarson (Eds.), *The mentally retarded and society: A social science perspective.* Baltimore: University Park Press, 1975.

KURTZ, R. A. *Social aspects of mental retardation.* Lexington, Mass.: D. C. Heath and Co., 1977.

KUSHLICK, A., and BLUNDEN, R. The epidemiology of mental subnormality. In A. M. Clarke and A. D. B. Clarke (Eds.), *Mental deficiency: The changing outlook.* New York: Free Press, 1974.

LaFRANCHI, S., MURPHY, W., FOLEY, T., LARSON, P., and BUIST, N. Neonatal hypothyroidism detected by the Northwest regional screening program. *Pediatrics,* 1979, *63,* 180-191.

LAKIN, K. C. *Demographic studies of residential facilities for the mentally retarded: An historical review of methodologies and findings.* Minneapolis: University of Minnesota, Department of Psychoeducational Studies, 1979.

LAKIN, K. C., BRUININKS, R. H., and SIGFORD, B. B. Early perspectives on the community adjustment of mentally retarded people. In R. H. Bruininks, C. E. Meyers, B. B. Sigford, and K. C. Lakin (Eds.), *Deinstitutionalization and community adjustment of mentally retarded people.* Washington, D.C.: American Association on Mental Deficiency, 1981.

LAKIN, K. C., HILL, B. K., HAUBER, F. A., and BRUININKS, R. H. Changes in age at first admission to residential care for mentally retarded people. *Mental Retardation,* 1982, *20,* 216–219.

LAKIN, K. C., BRUININKS, R. H., DOTH, D., HILL, B. K., and HAUBER, F. *Sourcebook on long-term care for developmentally disabled people.* Minneapolis: Center for Residential and Community Services, 1982.

LANDESMAN-DWYER, S. Living in the community. *American Journal of Mental Deficiency,* 1981, *86,* 223–234.

LANDESMAN-DWYER, and SACKETT, G. Behavioral changes in nonabulatory, profoundly mentally retarded individuals. In E. Meyer (Ed.), *Quality of Life in Severely and Profoundly Retarded People. Research Foundation for Improvement* (Monograph No. 3). Washington, D.C.: American Association on Mental Deficiency, 1978.

LANDESMAN-DWYER, S., and SULZBACHER, F. M. Residential placement and adaption of severely and profoundly retarded individuals. In R. H. Bruininks, C. E. Meyers, B. B. Sigford, and K. C. Lakin (Eds.), *Deinstitutionalization and community adjustment of mentally retarded people.* Washington, D.C.: American Association on Mental Deficiency, 1981.

Lang v. Braintree, 545 F. Supp. 1221 (D. Mass. 1982).

Larry P. v. Riles, 343 F. Supp. 1306 (N.D. Cal. 1972) 495 F. Supp. 926 (N.D. Cal. 1979).

LARSEN, L., GOODMAN, L., and GLEAN, R. Issues in the implementation of extended school year programs for handicapped students. *Exceptional Children,* 1981, *47,* 256–263.

LAVELLE, N., and KEOGH, B. K. Expectation and attributions of parents of handicapped children. In J. J. Gallagher (Ed.), *New directions for exceptional children: Parents and families of handicapped children* (Vol. 4). San Francisco: Jossey-Bass, 1980.

LEINHARDT, G. and PALLAY, A. Restrictive educational settings: Exile or haven? *Review of Educational Research,* 1982, *52,* 557–578.

Lelz v. Kavanagh, No. 82-2164 (5th Cir. July 13, 1983).

LEMKAU, P. V., and IMRE, P. D. Results of a field epidemiologic study. *American Journal of Mental Deficiency,* 1969, *73,* 858–863.

LERMAN, P. *Deinstitutionalization and the welfare state.* New Brunswick: Rutgers University Press, 1982.

Levine v. State Department of Institutions and Agencies, 418 A. 2d 229 (N.J. 1980).

LEVINSON, E. J. *Retarded children in Maine: A survey and analysis.* Oreno: University of Maine Press, 1962.

LEVITAN, S. A., and BELOUS, R. S. *What's happening to the American family.* Baltimore: Johns Hopkins University Press, 1981.

LEVY, F., and McLEOD, W. The effect of environmental design on adolescents in institutions. *Mental Retardation,* 1977, *15,* 28–32.

LEWIS, O. The culture of poverty. In L. A. Ferman, J. L. Kornbluh, and A. Haber (Eds.), *Poverty in America.* Ann Arbor: University of Michigan, 1968.

LILLY, M. S. *Children with exceptional needs: A survey of special education.* New York: Holt, Rinehart & Winston, 1979.

LINN, B., and BOWERS, L. The historical fallacies behind legal prohibition of marriage involving mentally retarded persons: The eternal child grows up. *Gonzaga Law Review,* 1978, *13,* 625–690.

LINSTONE, H. A. The postindustrial society and mental retardation. In S. C.

Plog and M. B. Sautamour (Eds.), *The year 2000 and mental retardation.* New York: Plenum Press, 1980.

LIPPINCOTT, M. K. "A sanctuary for people": Strategies for overcoming zoning restrictions on community homes for retarded persons. *Stanford Law Review,* 1979, *31,* 767–783.

LITCH, S. A. Development and implementation of a preventive program on mental retardation: Education aspects. *Pediatric Habilitation,* 1980, *1,* 641–660.

Little Neck Community Association v. *Working Organization for Retarded Children,* (N.Y. Sup. Ct., 2nd Dept., May 3, 1976).

LUBIN, R., JACOBSON, J. W., and KIELY, M. Projected impact of the functional definition of developmental disabilities: The categorically disabled population and service eligibility. *American Journal of Mental Deficiency,* 1982, *87,* 73–79.

LUBS, H. A. A marker X chromosome. *American Journal of Human Genetics,* 1969, *21,* 231–244.

LUCKASSON, R., and ELLIS, J. Representing institutionalized mentally retarded persons. *Mental Disability Law Reporter,* 1983, 7, 49–51.

LUCKEY, R. E., and ADDISON, M. R. The profoundly retarded: A new challenge for public education. *Education and Training of the Mentally Retarded,* 1974, *9,* 123–130.

LUCKEY, R. E., and SHAPIRO, I. G. Recreation: An essential aspect of habilitative planning, *Mental Retardation,* 1974, *12,* 33–35.

LURIA, A. R. Experimental study of the higher nervous system activity of the abnormal child. *Journal of Mental Deficiency Research,* 1959, *3,* 1–22.

LURIA, A. R. Psychological studies of mental deficiency in the Soviet Union. In N. R. Ellis (Ed.), *Handbook of mental deficiency.* New York: McGraw-Hill, 1963.

LYON, R., and BLAND, W. The transfer of adult mental retardates from a state hospital to nursing home. *Mental Retardation,* 1964, *7,* 31–36.

MacMILLAN, D. L. *Mental retardation in school and society.* Boston: Little, Brown, 1977.

MacMILLAN, D. L., JONES, R. L., and ALOIA, G. F. The mentally retarded label: A theoretical analysis and review of research. *American Journal of Mental Deficiency,* 1974, *79,* 241–261.

MacMILLAN, E. S. Birth defective infants: A standard for non-treatment decisions. *Stanford Law Review,* 1978, *30,* 599–632.

MacMILLAN, D. L., and BORTHWICK, S. The new educable mentally retarded population: Can they be mainstreamed? *Mental Retardation,* 1980, *18,* 155–158.

MADDEN, N. A., and SLAVIN, R. E. *Count me in: Academic achievement and social outcomes of mainstreaming students with mild academic handicaps.* Baltimore: The Johns Hopkins University, Center for Social Organization of the Schools, 1982.

Maine Medical Center v. *Houle,* No. 74-145 (Cumberland County Super. Ct., Maine, Feb. 14, 1974).

MALONEY, M. P., and WARD, M. P. *Mental retardation and modern society.* New York: Oxford University Press, 1979.

MARINELLI, J. Critical issues in the financing of education for the handicapped. *Journal of Education Finance,* 1975, *1,* 246–269.

MARION, R. L. Communicating with parents of culturally diverse exceptional children. *Exceptional Children,* 1980, *46,* 616–623.

MARTIN, E. W. Testimony presented before the Subcommittee on Select Education, Committee on Education and Labor, U.S. House of Representatives, October 24, 1977.

MASON, B., and MENOLASCINO, F. The right to treatment for mentally retarded citizens: An evolving legal and scientific interface. *Creighton Law Review*, 1976, *10*, 124–169.

Mattie T. v. Holladay, No. DC-75-31 S (N.D. Miss. 1-26-79).

MATTINSON, I. Marriage and mental handicap. In F. de la Cruz and C. LaVeck (Eds.), *Human sexuality and the mentally retarded*. New York: Brunner/ Mazel, 1973.

MAYEDA, T., and SUTTER, P. Deinstitutionalization: Phase II. In R. H. Bruininks, C. E. Meyers, B. B. Sigford, and K. C. Lakin, *Deinstitutionalization and community adjustment of mentally retarded people*. Washington, D.C.: American Association on Mental Deficiency, 1981.

MAYEDA, T., and WAI, F. The cost of long-term developmental disabilities services. Pomona, Calif.: UCLA Research Group at Pacific State Hospital, 1975.

McALLISTER, R. J., BUTLER, E. W., and LEI, T. J. Patterns of social interaction among families of behaviorally retarded children. *Journal of Marriage and the Family*, 1973, *35*, 93–100.

McCLUNG, M. The legal rights of handicapped school children. *Educational Horizons*, 1975, *54*, 25–32.

McCORD, W. T. From theory to reality: Obstacles to the implementation of the normalization principle in human services. *Mental Retardation*, 1983, *20*, 247–253.

McCORMACK, M., BALLA, D., and ZIGLER, E. Resident care practices in institutions for retarded persons: A cross-institutional, cross-cultural study. *American Journal of Mental Deficiency*, 1975, *80*, 1–17.

McCORMACK, M. K., LIEBLUM, S., LAZZARINI, A. Attitudes regarding artificial insemination by donor in persons at-risk for Huntington's Disease. *American Journal of Medical Genetics*, 1983, *14*, 5–13.

McDEVITT, S. C., SMITH, P. M., SCHMIDT, D. W., and ROSEN, M. The deinstitutionalized citizen: Adjustment and quality of life. *Mental Retardation*, 1978, *16*, 22–24.

McDONALD, A. C., CARSON, K. L., PALMER, D. J., and SLAY, T. Physician's diagnostic information to parents of handicapped neonates. *Mental Retardation*, 1982, *19*, 12–14.

McEvoy v. Mitchell, C.A. No. 74-2768-T (D. Mass., Feb. 2, 1979).

McKHANN, G. Gmz-Ganglirosidosis with hexosaminidase A deficiency. In *Birth defects compendium* (2nd ed.). New York: A. R. Liss, 1979.

McKUSICK, V. *Mendelian inheritance in man*. Baltimore: Johns Hopkins University, 1978.

MENDOZA, S. A., BECK, C. H., and GRISWOLD, W. R. Renal disorders. In J. D. Schulman and J. L. Simpson (Eds.), *Genetic diseases and pregnancy: Maternal affects and fetal outcome*. New York: Academic Press, 1981.

MENOLASCINO, F. J. *Challenges in mental retardation: Progressive ideology and services*. New York: Human Services, 1977.

MENOLASCINO, F. J., and McGEE, J. J. The new institutions: Last ditch agreements. *Mental Retardation*, 1981, *19*, 215–220.

MERCER, J. Patterns of family crisis related to reacceptance of the retardate. *American Journal of Mental Deficiency*, 1966, *71*, 19–32.

MERCER, J. The meaning of mental retardation. In R. Koch and J. C. Dobson (Eds.), *The mentally retarded child and his family*. New York: Brunner/ Mazel, 1971.

MERCER, J. R. *Labelling the mentally retarded.* Berkeley: University of California Press, 1973. (a)

MERCER, J. R. The myth of 3% prevalence. In R. K. Eyman, C. E. Meyers, and G. Tarjan (Eds.), *Sociobehavioral studies in mental retardation.* Monographs of the American Association on Mental Deficiency, 1973, *1*, 1-18. (b)

MERCER, J., and LEWIS, J. *SOMPA: Student assessment manual.* New York: Psychological Corporation, 1978.

MESIBOV, G. B. Alternatives to the principle of normalization. *Mental Retardation,* 1976, *14*, 30-32.

MEYER, R. J. Attitudes of parents of institutionalized mentally retarded individuals toward deinstitutionalization. *American Journal of Mental Deficiency,* 1980, *85*, 478-488.

MICKELSON, P. The feebleminded parent: A study of 90 family cases. *American Journal of Mental Deficiency,* 1947, *51*, 644-653.

MICKELSON, P. Can mentally deficient parents be helped to give their children better care? *American Journal of Mental Deficiency,* 1949, *53*, 516-534.

MICKENBERG, N. The silent clients: Legal and ethical consideration in representing severely and profoundly retarded individuals. *Stanford Law Review,* 1979, *31*, 625-35.

Mills v. *Board of Education,* 348 F. Supp. 866 (D.D.C. 1972), No. 1939-71 (D.D.C. 6-18-80).

MOEN, M., BOGEN, D., and AANES, D. Follow-up of mentally retarded adults successfully and unsuccessfully placed in community. *Hospital and Community Psychiatry,* 1975, *26*, 752-754.

MOORE, M. Systems change advocacy. *Amicus,* 1976, *1*, 13-16.

"More Genetic-Defect Victims Adopted" *New York Times,* March 8, 1979.

MORONEY, R. M. *Families, social services and social policy: The issues of shared responsibility.* Washington, D.C.: U.S. Government Printing Office, 1980.

MORONEY, R. M. Public social policy: Impact on families with handicapped children. In J. L. Paul (Ed.), *Understanding and working with parents of children with special needs.* New York: Holt, Rinehart, and Winston, 1981.

MORELL, B. Deinstitutionalization: Those left behind. *Social Caseworker: The Journal of Contemporary Social Work,* 1979, *24*, 528-532.

MOSER, H. Prevention of mental retardation from biomedical causes. In *International summit on prevention of mental retardation from biomedical causes.* Washington, D.C.: Department of Health, Education and Welfare, 1977.

MOSHER, E. K., HASTINGS, A. H., and WAGNER, J. L. *Pursuing equal educational opportunity: School politics and the new activists.* New York: Institute for Urban and Minority Education, Teachers College, 1979.

MOSER, H. W. Prevention of mental retardation: A realistic and achievable goal. Paper presented to the President's Committee on Mental Retardation, Atlanta, September 17, 1982.

MOSS, J. W. Employment training of mentally retarded individuals: A proposed plan for national action. Paper submitted to the Rehabilitation Services Administration, September, 1977.

MNOOKIN, R. H. Foster care: In whose best interest? *Harvard Educational Review,* 1973, *43*, 599-638.

MURPHY, J. G. and DATEL, W. G. A cost benefit analysis of community versus institutional living. *Hospital and Community Psychiatry,* 1976, *27*, 165-176.

Naccash v. *Burger,* 290 S. E. 2d 825 (Va. 1982).

NAEYE, R. L. and FREEDMAN, E. A. Causes of perinatal death associated with gestational hypertension and poteinuria, *American Journal of Obstetrics and Gynecology,* 1979, *113*, 8-10.

NAISBETH, J. *Megatrends: Ten new directions in transforming our lives.* New York: Warner Communication Co., 1982.

NATIONAL ASSOCIATION FOR RETARDED CITIZENS. *Citizen advocacy for mentally retarded children: An introduction.* Washington, D.C., 1974.

NATIONAL ASSOCIATION FOR RETARDED CITIZENS. Information sheet, 1976.

NATIONAL ASSOCIATION OF STATE DIRECTORS OF SPECIAL EDUCATION (NASDSE). *Report on the implementation of P.L. 94-142* Unpublished report, 1980. (Available from Author, Washington, D.C.).

NATIONAL ASSOCIATION OF SUPERINTENDENTS OF PUBLIC RESIDENTIAL FACILITIES FOR THE MENTALLY RETARDED. *Contemporary issues in residential programming.* Washington, D.C.: President's Committee on Mental Retardation, 1974.

NATIONAL COMMISSION ON EXCELLENCE IN EDUCATION. *A nation at risk: The imperative for educational reform.* Washington, D.C.: U.S. Department of Education, 1983.

NATIONAL COMMITTEE FOR CITIZENS IN EDUCATION. Parents should be more involved in handicapped children law. *NCCE News,* October 11, 1979.

NATIONAL SELF-HELP CLEARINGHOUSE. *Developing a directory of self-help groups.* New York: City University of New York, Graduate School and University Center, 1980.

NEW JERSEY DEPARTMENT OF HUMAN SERVICES. *Manual for the instruction of operation of family care homes for the mentally retarded,* Trenton, 1978.

New Mexico Association for Retarded Citizens v. State of New Mexico, 495 F. Supp. 391 (D.N. Mex. 1980), rev'd 678 F. 2d 847 (10th Cir. 1982).

NEW YORK STATE COMMISSION ON QUALITY CARE OF THE MENTALLY DISABLED. *Willowbrook: From institution to community.* New York: August, 1982.

New York State Association for Retarded Citizens v. Rockefeller (Carey), 357 F. Supp. 752 (E.D.N.Y. 1973), 393 F. Supp. 715 (E.D.N.Y. 1975), 72 Civ. 356 (E.D.N.Y., Jan. 2, 1980).

NIHIRA, K., FOSTER, R., SHELLHAAS, M., and LELAND, H. *AAMD adaptive behavior scale.* Washington: American Association on Mental Deficiency, 1969.

NIHIRA, K., FOSTER, R., SHELLHAAS, M., and LELAND, H. *AAMD adaptive behavior scale* (rev. ed.). Washington: American Association on Mental Deficiency, 1974.

NIHIRA, L., and NIHIRA, K. Normalized behavior in community placement. *Mental Retardation,* 1975, *13,* 9–13.

NIRJE, B. A Scandinavian visitor looks at U.S. institutions. In R. B. Kugel, and W. Wolfensberger (Eds.), *Changing patterns in residential services for the mentally retarded.* Washington, D.C.: President's Committee on Mental Retardation, 1969.

NIRJE, B. The normalization principle. In R. B. Kugel, and A. Shearer, *Changing patterns in residential services for the mentally retarded.* Washington: President's Committee on Mental Retardation, 1976.

North v. District of Columbia Board of Education, 471 F. Supp. 136 (D.D.C. 1979).

NOTE: Implementation problems in institutional reform litigation. *Harvard Law Review,* 1977, *91,* 428–463.

NOVAK, L. Operation of the citizen advocate program in Lincoln, Nebraska.

In W. Wolfensberger and H. Zauka, *Citizen Advocacy*. Toronto: National Institute of Mental Retardation, 1973.

O'BRIEN, J. The principle of normalization: A foundation for effective services. In J. F. Gardner et al. (Eds.), *Program issues in developmental disabilities: A resource manual for surveyors and reviewers*. Baltimore: Paul H. Brookes, 1980.

O'CONNOR, G., JUSTICE, R. S., and WARREN, N. The aged mentally retarded: Institution or community care? *American Journal of Mental Deficiency*, 1970, *75*, 354–360.

O'CONNOR, G. *Home is a good place: A national perspective of community residential facilities for developmentally disabled persons*. Washington, D.C.: American Association on Mental Deficiency, 1976.

O'CONNOR, G., and SITKEI, E. G. Study of a new frontier in community services. *Mental Retardation*, 1975, *13*, 35–38.

OGBU, J. U. *Minority education and caste: The American system in cross-cultural perspective*. New York: Academic Press, 1978.

OLSHANSKY, S. Parent responses to a mentally defective child. *Mental Retardation*, 1966, *4*, 21–23.

O'REGAN, G. Foster family care for children with mental retardation. *Children Today*, 1974, *3*, 20–24; 36.

ORELOVE, F. P. Administering education for the severely handicapped after P.L. 94-142. *Phi Delta Kappan*, 1978, *59*, 699–702.

PAGEL, S. P., and WHITLING, C. A. Readmission to a state hospital for mentally retarded persons: Reasons for community placement failure. *Mental Retardation*, 1978, *16*, 164–166.

Papacoda v. *State of Connecticut*, 528 F. Supp. 68 (D. Conn. 1981).

PAPAGEORGIOU, P. Infectious diseases in the intrauterine period of development. *Pediatric Habilitation*, 1980, *1*, 385–446.

Parents in Action on Special Education (PASE) v. *Hannon*, No. 74 C 3586 (N. D. Ill. 1980).

Park v. *Chessin*, 400 N.Y.S. 2d 110 (1977), *aff'd sub. nom. Becker* v. *Schwartz*, 386 N.E. 2d 807 (N.Y. 1978).

PATRICK, J. L., and RESCHLY, D. J. Relationship of state educational criteria and demographic variables to school-system prevalence of mental retardation. *American Journal of Mental Deficiency*, 1982, *86*, 351–360.

PAUL, J., WIEGERINK, R., and NEUFELD, R. *Advocacy: a role for DD councils*. Developmental Disabilities/Technical Assistance System, Chapel Hill: North Carolina, 1974. (Monograph)

PAYNE, J. E. The deinstitutional backlash. *Mental Retardation*, 1976, *14*, 15–19.

Pennsylvania Association for Retarded Children (P.A.R.C.) v. *Commonwealth of Pennsylvania*, 343 F. Supp. 278 (E.D. Pa. 1972).

PENROSE, L. S. *A clinical and genetic study of 1,280 cases of mental defects* (Report Series No. 299). London: Medical Research Council, 1938.

People of State of New York v. *Cornwell Co.*, 508 F. Supp. 273 (E.D. N.Y. 1981).

PERSKE, R. The dignity of risk and the mentally retarded. *Mental Retardation*, 1972, *10*, 24–27.

PERSKE, R. *New directions for parents of persons who are retarded*. Nashville: Abingdon Press, 1973.

PERSKE, R., and MARGUISS, J. Learning to live in an apartment: Retarded adults from institutions and dedicated citizens. *Mental Retardation*, 1973, *11*, 18–19.

Phillips v. *U.S.*, 508 F. Supp. 537 (D.S.C. 1980); 508 F. Supp. 544 (D.S.C. 1981).

PITTENGER, J. C., and KURILOFF, P.   Educating the handicapped: Reforming a radical law. *Public Interest*, 1982, *66*, 72–96.

PIZZO, P.   *Parent to parent: Working together for ourselves and our children.* Boston: Beacon Press, 1983.

PLAMONDON, A. and SOSKIN, R.   Handicapped parents: Can they call their children their own? *Amicus*, 1978, *3*, 24–31.

POLIVKA, C. H., MARVIN, W. E., BROWN, J. L., and POLIVKA, L. J.   Selected characteristics, services, and movement of group home residents. *Mental Retardation*, 1979, *17*, 227–230.

POLIVKA, L., IMERSHEIN, A. W., WHITE, J. W. and STIVERS, L. E.   Human service organization and its effects. *Public Administration Review*, 1981, *41*, 359–365.

POLLOWAY, E. A., and PAYNE, J. S.   Comparison of the AAMD Heber and Grossman manuals on terminology and classification in mental retardation. *Mental Retardation*, 1975, *13*, 12–14.

POLLOWAY, E. A. and SMITH, J. D.   Changes in mild mental retardation: Population, programs, and perspectives. *Exceptional Children*, 1983, *50*, 149.

PRESIDENT'S COMMISSION FOR THE STUDY OF ETHICAL PROBLEMS IN MEDICINE AND BIOMEDICAL AND BEHAVIORAL RESEARCH. *Deciding to forego life-sustaining treatment.* Washington, D.C.: U.S. Government Printing Office, 1983.

PRESIDENT'S COMMITTEE ON MENTAL RETARDATION. *People live in houses.* Washington, D.C.: U.S. Government Printing Office, undated.

PRESIDENT'S COMMITTEE ON MENTAL RETARDATION. *The six-hour retarded child.* Report on a Conference on Problems of Education of Children in the Inner City, August 10–12, 1969. Washington, D.C.

PRESIDENT'S COMMITTEE ON MENTAL RETARDATION. *Mental retardation: past and present.* Washington, D.C.: U.S. Government Printing Office, 1977.

PRESIDENT'S COMMITTEE ON MENTAL RETARDATION. *MR: The leading edge: Service programs that work.* Washington, D.C.: U.S. Government Documents, 1978.

PRESIDENT'S COMMITTEE ON MENTAL RETARDATION. *Mental retardation: Prevention strategies that work.* Washington, D.C.: U.S. Department of Health and Human Services, 1980.

PRESIDENT'S PANEL ON MENTAL RETARDATION. *A proposed program for national action to combat mental retardation.* Washington, D.C.: U.S. Government Printing Office, 1962.

PRICE, M., and GOODMAN, L.   Individualized education programs: A cost study. *Exceptional Children*, 1980, *46*, 446–454.

PUESCHEL, S. M., and MURPHY, A.   Assessment of counseling practices at the birth of a child with Down's syndrome. *American Journal of Mental Deficiency*, 1976, *18*, 325–330.

QUELLETTE, E. M., ROSETT, H. C., ROSMAN, N. T., and WEINER, L.   Adverse effects on offspring of maternal alcohol abuse during pregnancy. *New England Journal of Medicine*, 1977, *297*, 528–530.

RAMEY, C. T., and CAMPBELL, F. A.   Prevention of mental retardation in high-risk children. In P. Mittler (Eds.), *Research to practice in mental retardation (Vol. 1): Care and Intervention.* Baltimore: University Park Press, 1977.

RAMEY, C. T., FARRAN, D. C., and CAMPBELL, F. A.   Predicting IQ from mother-infant interaction. *Child Development*, 1979, *50*, 804–814.

RAMEY, C. T., and FINKELSTEIN, N. W.   Psychosocial mental retardation: A biological and social coalescence. In M. Begab, C. Haywood, and H. Garber

(Eds.), *Psychosocial influence in retarded performance: Issues and theories in development.* Baltimore: University Park Press, 1981.

RAUTH, M. What can be expected of the régular education teacher? Ideals and realities. *Exceptional Education Quarterly,* 1981, *2,* 27–36.

RAY, J. S. The family training center: An experiment in normalization. *Mental Retardation,* 1974, *12,* 12–13.

RAYNES, N. V., BURNSTEAD, D. C., and PRATT, M. W. Unitization: Its effects on residential care practices. *Mental Retardation,* 1974, *12,* 12–14.

REBELL, M. A. Implementation of court mandates concerning special education: The problem and the potential. *Journal of Law & Education,* 1981, *10,* 335–356.

REED, E. W., and REED, S. C. *Mental Retardation: A family study.* Philadelphia: W. B. Saunders, 1965.

REHABILITATION ACT OF 1973, SECTION 504 (P.L. 93-112). 29 U.S.C. 704.

REID, E. S. Helping parents of handicapped child. In R. L. Noland (Ed.), *Counseling parents of the ill and the handicapped.* Springfield, Ill.: Charles C. Thomas, 1971.

REISS, S., LEVITAN, G. W., and McNALLY, R. J. Emotionally disturbed mentally retarded people. *American Psychologist,* 1982, *37,* 361–367.

REITER, S., and LEVI, A. M. Leisure activities of mentally retarded adults. *American Journal of Mental Deficiency,* 1981, *86,* 201–203.

RESCHLY, D. J. Evaluation of the effects of SOMPA measures on classification of students as mildly mentally retarded. *American Journal of Mental Deficiency,* 1981, *86,* 16–19.

RESCHLY, D., and JIPSON, F. Ethnicity, geographic location, age, sex, and urban-rural residence as variables in the prevalence of mild retardation. *American Jounral of Mental Deficiency,* 1976, *81,* 154–161.

RESEARCH TRIANGLE INSTITUTE. *Final report: A national survey of individualized education programs (IEPs) for handicapped children* (Contract No. 300-77-0529). Research Triangle Park, N.C.: Author, October 1980.

RHOADES, C., and BROWNING, P. *Normalization at what price? Mental Retardation,* 1977, *15,* 24.

RHODES, W. C. *Behavioral threat and community response.* New York: Behavioral Publication, 1972.

RIVERA, G. *Willowbrook.* New York: Random House, 1972.

Robak v. U.S., 658 F. 2d 471 (7th Cir. 1981).

ROBINSON, N. M., and ROBINSON, H. B. *The mentally retarded child* (2nd ed.). New York: McGraw-Hill, 1976.

RODMAN, D. H., and COLLINS, M. J. A community residence program: An alternative to institutional living for the mentally retarded. *Training School Bulletin,* 1974, *71,* 52–61.

Roe v. Wade, 410 U.S. 113(1973).

ROOS, P. Reconciling behavior modification procedures with the normalization principle. In W. Wolfensberger, *Normalization: The principle of human services.* Toronto: National Institute on Mental Retardation, 1972.

ROOS, P. Parents of mentally retarded people. *International Journal of Mental Health,* 1977, *6,* 96–119.

ROOS, P. Parents of mentally retarded people. *International Journal of Mental Health,* 1978, *6,* 96–119.

ROOS, P. Custodial care for the "subtrainable"—Revisiting an old myth. *Law & Psychology Review,* 1979, *5,* 1–14. (a)

ROOS, P. The law and mentally retarded people: An uncertain future. *Stanford Law Review,* 1979, *31,* 613–624. (b)

ROOS, S. The future of residential services for the mentally retarded in the United States: A Delphi study. *Mental Retardation,* 1978, *16*, 355-356.

ROSENBAUM, S., and WEITZ, J. *Children and federal health care costs: A national survey of the impact of federal health budget reductions on state maternal and health services during 1982.* Washington, D.C.: Children's Defense Fund, 1983.

ROTHMAN, D. *Discovery of the asylum: Social order and disorder in the new republic.* Boston: Little, Brown Co., 1971.

ROTHMAN, S. M. *Who speaks for the mentally retarded person?—An historical and social view.* Paper presented at the annual meeting of the American Association on Mental Deficiency, Detroit, May, 1981.

RUBIN, S., and QUINN-CURRAN, N. Lost, then found: Parents' journey through the community service maze. In M. Seligman (Ed.), *The family with a handicapped child: Understanding and treatment.* New York: Grune & Stratton, 1983.

Ruby v. *Massey,* 452 F. Supp. 361 (D. Conn. 1978).

RUSCH, F. R., and MITHAUG, D. E. *Vocational training for mentally retarded adults.* Champaign, Ill.: Research Press, 1980.

SABATINO, D. A. Are appropriate educational programs operationally achievable under mandated promises of P.L. 94-142? *Journal of Special Education,* 1981, *15*, 9-23.

SAENGER, G. *The adjustment of severely retarded adults in the community.* Albany: Interdepartmental Health Resources Board, 1957.

SALKEVER, D. D. Children's health problems: Implications for parental labor supply and earnings. In V. R. Fuchs (Ed.), *Economic aspects of health.* Chicago: University of Chicago Press, 1982.

SALVIA, J. Perspectives on the nature of retardation. In J. T. Neisworth and R. M. Smith (Eds.), *Retardation: Issues, assessment and intervention.* New York: McGraw-Hill, 1978.

SALZBERG, C. C., and LANGFORD, C. A. Community integration of mentally retarded adults through leisure activity. *Mental Retardation,* 1981, *19*, 127-131.

SANTIESTEVAN, H. *Deinstitutionalization: Out of their beds and into the streets.* Washington, D.C.: American Federation of State, County, and Municipal Employees, 1975.

Santosky v. *Kramer,* 102 S Ct. 1388 (1982).

SARASON, S., CARROLL, C. F., MATON, K., COHEN, S., and LORENTZ, E. *Human services and resources networks.* San Francisco: Jossey-Bass, 1977.

SARASON, S. B., and DORIS, J. *Educational handicap, public policy, and social history: A broadened perspective on mental retardation.* New York: Free Press, 1979.

SCHALOCK, R. L., HARPER, R. S., and GARVER, B. Independent living placements: 5 years later. *American Journal of Mental Deficiency,* 1981, *86*, 170-171.

SCHALOCK, R. L., HARPER, R. S., and GENUNG, T. Community integration of mentally retarded adults: Community placement and program success. *American Journal of Mental Deficiency,* 1981, *85*, 478-488.

SCHEERENBERGER, R. C. *Estimated incidence of mental retardation in the state of Illinois for 1966.* Springfield, Ill.: Division of Mental Retardation Services, 1966.

SCHEERENBERGER, R. C. *Deinstitutionalization and institutional reform.* Springfield, Ill.: Charles C. Thomas, 1976.

SCHEERENBERGER, R. C. Public residential services for the retarded. In N.

Ellis (Ed.), *International review of research in mental retardation* (Vol. 9). New York: Academic Press, 1978.

SCHEERENBERGER, R. C.   Public residential facilities: Status and trends. *Mental Retardation*, 1981, *19*, 59–60.

SCHEERENBERGER, R. C.   Public residential services, 1981: Status and trends. *Mental Retardation*, 1982, *20*, 210–215.

SCHEERENBERGER, R. C.   *A history of mental retardation.* Baltimore: Paul H. Brookes Publishing Co., 1983. (a)

SCHEERENBERGER, R. C.   *Public residential services for the mentally retarded: 1982.* Washington, D.C.: National Association of Superintendents of Public Residential Facilities for the Mentally Retarded, 1983. (b)

SCHEERENBERGER, R. C., and FELSENTHAL, D.   *A study of alternative community placements.* University of Wisconsin, 1976.

SCHILLING, R. F., SCHINKE, S. P., BLYTHE, B. J., and BARTH, R. P.   Child maltreatment and mentally retarded parents. Is there a relationship? *Mental Retardation*, 1983, *20*, 201–209.

SCHIPPER, M. T.   The child with mongolism in the home. *Pediatrics*, 1959, *24*, 132–144.

SCHODEK, K., LIFFITON-CHROSTOWSKI, N., ADAMS, S. C., MINIHAM, P. M., and YANAGUCHI, J.   The regulation of family involvement in deinstitutionalization. *Social Caseworker: The Journal of Contemporary Social Work*, 1980, *25*, 67–73.

SCHONELL, F. J., and RORKE, M.   A second survey of the effects of a subnormal child on the family unit. *American Journal of Mental Deficiency*, 1960, *64*, 862–868.

SCHONELL, F. J., and WATTS, B. H.   A first survey of the effects of a subnormal child on the family unit. *American Journal of Mental Deficiency*, 1956, *61*, 210–219.

Schroeder v. *Perkel,*   432 A. 2d 834 (N.J. 1981).

SCHROEDER, S. R., and HENES, C.   Assessment of progress of institutionalized retarded adults: A matched control comparison. *Mental Retardation*, 1978, *16*, 52–54.

SCHWARTZ, C.   Normalization and idealism. *Mental Retardation*, 1977, *15*, 38–39.

SCULL, A. T.   *Decarceration, community treatment and the deviant: A radical view.* Englewood Cliffs, N.J.: Spectrum Books, Prentice-Hall, 1977.

Secretary of Public Welfare v. *Institutionalized Juveniles,*   442 U.S. 640 (1979).

SEGAL, R.   Trends in services for the aged mentally retarded. *Mental Retardation*, 1977, *15*, 25–27.

SEGUIN, E.   *Idiocy: And its treatment by the physiological method.* New York: William Weed, 1866.

SELTZER, M. M.   Correlates of community opposition to community residences for mentally retarded persons. Boston University, School of Social Work. Unpublished paper, 1983.

SHAPIRO, H.   Jewish religious education for retarded children. *Mental Retardation*, 1964, *2*, 213–216.

SIGELMAN, C., BELL, N., SCHOENROCK, C., ELIAS, S., and DANKER-BROWN, P.   *Alternative community placements and outcomes.* Paper presented at the annual meeting of the American Association on Mental Deficiency, Denver, May, 1978.

SIGELMAN, L., ROEDER, P. W., and SIGELMAN, C.   Social service innovation in the American States: Deinstitutionalization of the mentally retarded. *Social Science Quarterly*, 1981, *62*, 503–515.

SIMONS, J. M., and DWYER, B. Education of the handicapped. In M. F. Williams (Ed.), *Government in the classroom. Proceedings of the Academy of Political Science, 1978.*

SINGER, J., BOSSARD, M., and WATKINS, M. Effects of parental presence on attendance and input of interdisciplinary teams in an institutional setting. *Psychological Reports, 1977, 41,* 1031–1034.

SINGER, J. E., WESTPHAL, M., and NISWANDER, K. P. Sex differences in the incidence of neonatal abnormalities and abnormal performance in early childhood. *Child Development, 1968, 39,* 103–112.

SIROTNIK, K. A. What you see is what you get: Consistency, persistency, and mediocrity in classrooms. *Harvard Educational Review, 1983, 43,* 16–31.

SITKEI, E. C. After group home living—What alternative? Results of a two year mobility follow up study. *Mental Retardation, 1980, 18,* 9–13.

SKARNULIS, L. Less restrictive alternatives in residential services. *American Association of the Severely Profoundly Handicapped Review, 1976, 3,* 42–48.

SKEELS, H. Adult status of children with contrasting life experience: A follow-up. *Monograph of the Society for Research in Child Development, 1966, 13.*

SKEELS, H. M., and DYE, H. B. A study of the effects of differential stimulation on mentally retarded children. *Proceedings and Addresses of the American Association on Mental Deficiency, 1939, 44,* 114–136.

SKELTON, M. Areas of parental concern about retarded children. *Mental Retardation, 1972, 10,* 38–41.

Skinner v. Oklahoma, 315 U.S. 535 (1942)

SMITH, D. *Recognizable patterns of human malformations* (2nd ed.). Philadelphia: W. B. Saunders, 1976.

SMOSKOSKI, F. The mentally retarded are different. *Mental Retardation, 1971, 9,* 52–53.

SNYDERMAN, S., and DAVIES, J. Maple syrup urine disease. In *Birth defects compendium* (2nd ed). New York: A. R. Liss, Inc., 1979.

SOEFFLING, M. Families for handicapped children: Foster and adoptive placement program. *Exceptional Children, 1975, 41,* 537–543.

SOFRENKO, A. Z., and MACY, T. W. Living arrangements of MR/DD persons discharged from an institutional setting. *Mental Retardation, 1978, 16,* 269–270.

SOSKIN, R. M., and VITELLO, S. J. A right to treatment or a right to die? *Amicus, 1979, 4,* 120–127.

SPAKES, P. Family impact analysis: Its promise for social welfare. *Social Caseworker: The Journal of Contemporary Social Work, 1983, 28,* 3–10.

SPARROW, S. S., BALLA, D. A., and CICCHETTI, D. V. *Vineland Adaptive Behavior Scales.* Circle Pines, MN.: American Guidance Service, 1984.

Speck v. Finegold, 439 A. 2d 110 (Pa. 1981).

SPITZ, H. H. The role of input organization in the learning and memory of mental retardation. In N. R. Ellis (Ed.), *International review of research in mental retardation* (Vol. 2). New York: Academic Press, 1966.

Springdale School District v. Grace, 656 F. 2d 300 (8th Cir. 1981), vacated and remanded, 102 S. Ct. 3504 (1982), reinstated 693 F. 2d 41 (8th Cir. 1982).

SPRINGER, A., and STEELE, M. W. Effects of physicians' early parental counseling on rearing of Down Syndrome children. *American Journal of Mental Deficiency, 1980, 85,* 1–5.

STANFORD RESEARCH INSTITUTE INTERNATIONAL. *Three states' experiences with individualized education program (IEP) requirements similar to P.L. 94-142* (Research Report EP RC 23). Menlo Park, Calif.: Author, 1980. (a)

STANFORD RESEARCH INSTITUTE INTERNATIONAL. *Local implementation of P.L. 94-142: Second year report of a longitudinal study* (SRA Project 7124, Education Research Center). Menlo Park, Calif.: Author, 1980. (b)

STARK, J. H. Tragic choices in special education: The effects of scarce resources on the implementation of P.L. 94-142. *Connecticut Law Review*, 1981, *47*, 256-263.

STEDMAN, D. J., and EICHORN, D. H. A comparison of the growth and development of institutionalized and home-reared mongoloids during infancy and early childhood. *American Journal of Mental Deficiency*, 1964, *69*, 391-401.

STEDMAN, D. J. Introduction. In J. Paul, D. Stedman, and G. Neufeld (Eds.), *Deinstitutionalization: Program and policy development.* Syracuse, N.Y.: Syracuse University Press, 1977.

STENE, J., STENE, E., STENGEL-RUTKOWSKI, S., and MURKEN, J. Paternal age in Down Syndrome: Data from pre-noted diagnosis. *Human Genetics*, 1981, *59*, 119-124.

STERNLICHT, M. Variables affecting foster care placement of institutionalized retarded residents. *Mental Retardation*, 1978, *16*, 25-28.

STERNLICHT, M., and SIEGEL, L. Institutional residence and intellectual functioning. *Journal of Mental Deficiency*, 1968, *12*, 119-127.

STONE, N. W. A plea for early intervention. *Mental Retardation*, 1975, *13*, 16-17.

STRAIN, P. S., and KERR, M. M. *Mainstreaming of children in schools: Research and programmatic issues.* New York: Academic Press, 1981.

STREISSGUTH, A. P., LANDESMAN-DWYER, S., MARTIN, J. C., and SMITH, D. W. Terotagenic effects of alcohol in human and laboratory animals. *Science*, 1980, *209*, 353-361.

STUCKEY, P. E., and NEWBROUGH, J. R. Mental health of mentally retarded persons: Social-ecological consideration. In H. C. Haywood and J. R. Newbrough (Eds.), *Living environments for developmentally retarded persons.* Baltimore: University Park Press, 1981.

SUMMERS, J. A. The definition of developmental disabilities: A concept in transition. *Mental Retardation*, 1981, *19*, 259-265.

SUNDBERG, N. D., SNOWDEN, L. R., and REYNOLDS, W. M. Toward the assessment of personal competence and incompetence in life situations. *Annual Review of Psychology*, 1978, *29*, 179-221.

Sundheimer v. *Kolb*, No. 15502/78 (Supreme Court, Bronx, N.Y., March 21, 1979).

SUELZLE, M., and KEENAN, V. Changes in family support networks over the life cycle of mentally retarded persons. *American Journal of Mental Deficiency*, 1981, *36*, 267-274.

SUTHERLAND, G. R. Fragile sites on human chromosomes: Demonstration of their dependence on the type of tissue culture medium. *Science*, 1977, *197*, 265-266.

TARJAN, G. Some thoughts on sociocultural mental retardation. In H. C. Haywood (Ed.), *Social-cultural aspects of mental retardation.* New York: Meredith, 1970.

Tatro v. *State of Texas*, 625 F. 2d 557 (5th Cir. 1980).

TAYLOR, S., et al. *Title XIX and deinstitutionalization: The issue for the 80s.* Syracuse, N.Y.: Syracuse University, The Center for Human Policy, 1981.

TENNANT, L., HATTERSBY, J., and CULLEN, C. Some comments on the punishment relationship and its relevance to normalization for developmentally retarded people. *Mental Retardation*, 1978, *16*, 42-44.

THEODORE, S. M. *The retarded child in touch with God.* Boston: The Daughters of St. Paul, 1966.

THIELE, R. L., PAUL, J. L., and NEUFELD, G. R. Institutionalization: A perspective for deinstitutionalization program development. In J. L. Paul, D. J. Stedman, and G. R. Neufeld. *Deinstitutionalization: Program and policy development.* Syracuse, N.Y.: Syracuse University Press, 1977.

THOMAS, M. A., and REESE, S. J. *Making programmatic decisions during a time of fiscal retrenchment: The case of related services for handicapped youth.* Santa Monica, Calif.: The Rand Corporation, 1982.

THOMPSON, T., and CARY, A. Structural normalization: Intellectual and adaptive behavior changes in a residential setting. *Mental Retardation,* 1980, *18,* 193–197.

THRONE, J. Normalization through the normalization principle: Right ends, wrong means. *Mental Retardation,* 1975, *13,* 23–25.

THRONE, J. M. Deinstitutionalization: Too wide a swath. *Mental Retardation,* 1979, *17,* 171–175.

THURLOW, M., BRUININKS, R., WILLIAMS, S., and MORREAU, L. *Deinstitutionalization and residential services: A literature survey* (Project Report No. 1). Minneapolis: University of Minnesota, Information and Technical Assistance Project on Deinstitutionalization, 1978.

Tokarcik v. *Forest Hills School District,* 665 F. 2d 443 (3rd Cir. 1981).

TOWNSEND, P. W., and FLANAGAN, J. J. Experimental preadmission program to encourage home care for severely and profoundly retarded children. *American Journal of Mental Deficiency,* 1976, *80,* 562–569.

TRACTENBERG, P. L., and JACOBY, E. Pupil testing: A legal view. *Phi Delta Kappan,* 1977, *59,* 249–254.

TREDGOLD, A. F. *A textbook on mental deficiency.* Baltimore: Wood, 1937.

TREDGOLD, R. F., and SODDY, K. *A textbook of mental deficiency* (9th ed.). Baltimore: Williams & Williams, 1956.

TUCKER, J. A. Ethnic proportions in classes for the learning disabled: Issues in non biased assessment. *Journal of Special Education,* 1980, *14,* 93–105.

TURNBULL, H. R. (Ed.), *Consent handbook.* Washington, D.C.: American Association on Mental Deficiency, 1977.

TURNBULL, A. P., and TURNBULL, H. R. Parent involvement in the education of handicapped children: A critique. *Mental Retardation,* 1982, *20,* 115–122.

TURNBULL, H. R., and TURNBULL, A. P. *Parents speak out: View from the other side of the two-way mirror.* Columbus: Charles E. Merrill, 1979.

TURNER, G., and TURNER, B. X-linked mental retardation. *Journal of Medical Genetics,* 1974, *11,* 109–113.

Turpin v. *Sortini,* 174 Cal. Rptr. 128 (Cal. Ct. App. 1981), rev'd., 643 P. 2d 954 (Cal. 1982).

UNITED NATIONS DECLARATION OF THE RIGHTS OF MENTALLY RE-TARDED PERSONS. C.A. Res. 2856, 26 U.N. GAOR, Supp. (No. 29) 93–94, U.N. Doc. A/8429(1971).

UPSHUR, C. C. An evaluation of home-based respite care. *Mental Retardation,* 1982, *20,* 58–62.

U.S. DEPARTMENT OF EDUCATION, DIVISION OF ASSISTANCE TO STATES, BUREAU OF EDUCATION FOR THE HANDICAPPED. *Progress toward a free appropriate public education. Semi-annual update in the implementation of Public Law 94-142: The Education for all Handicapped Children Act.* Washington, D.C.: Department of Health, Education and Welfare, August 1979.

U.S. DEPARTMENT OF EDUCATION, STATE IMPLEMENTATION STUDIES BRANCH OF THE OFFICE OF SPECIAL EDUCATION. *To assure the free appropriate public education of all handicapped children.* (Second annual report to Congress on the implementation of Public Law 94-142, the Education for All Handicapped Children Act). Washington, D.C.: Author, 1980.

U.S. DEPARTMENT OF EDUCATION. *To assure the free appropriate public education of all handicapped children. Fourth annual report to Congress on the implementation of Public Law 94-142: The Education for All Handicapped Children Act.* Washington, D.C.: Author, 1982.

U.S. DEPARTMENT OF HEALTH AND HUMAN SERVICES. *Better health for our children: A national strategy. The report of the Select Panel for the promotion of child health (Vol. 1): Major Findings and Recommendations.* Washington, D.C., 1981.

U.S. v. *Mattson,* 600 F. 2d 1295 (9th Cir. 1979).

U.S. v. *Solomon,* 563 F. 2d 1121 (4th Cir. 1977).

U.S. v. *University Hospital of State University of New York at Stony Brook,* No. CV-83-4818 (E.D.N.Y. Nov. 17, 1983).

VAIL, D. *Dehumanization and the institutional career.* Springfield, Ill.: Charles C. Thomas, 1966.

VITELLO, L. B. *The effects of parent training provided in a medical clinic setting.* Unpublished master's thesis, Pennsylvania State University, 1977.

VITELLO, S. J. Beyond deinstitutionalization: What's happening to the people? *Amicus,* 1977, *2*, 40-44.

VITELLO, S. J. Involuntary sterilization: Recent developments. *Mental Retardation,* 1978, *16*, 405-409.

VITELLO, S. J., and ATTHOWE, J. *Deinstitutionalization: Family reactions and involvement.* Paper delivered at the annual meeting of the American Association on Mental Deficiency, Detroit June 1982.

VITELLO, S. J., ATTHOWE, J., and CADWELL, J. Determinants of community placement among institutionalized mentally retarded persons. *American Journal of Mental Deficiency,* 1983, *87*, 539-545.

VITELLO, S. J., and BRUCE, P. Computer-assisted instructional programs to facilitate mathematical learning among the handicapped. *Journal of Computer Education,* 1977, *4*, 26-29.

VLADECK, B. C. *Unloving care: The nursing home tragedy.* New York: Basic Books, 1980.

VOCATIONAL EDUCATION ACT, 20 U.S.C. d 2301 et seq (1963, 1968, 1976).

VOGEL, F., and MOLTULSKY, A. *Human genetics: Problem and approach.* New York: Springer-Verlag, 1979.

VROOMAN, P. C. Does legal advocacy and redistribution by the courts produce better social policies for the mentally handicapped? *International Journal of Law and Psychiatry,* 1980, *3*, 89-96.

WAISBERN, S. E. Parents' reactions after the birth of a developmentally disabled child. *American Journal of Mental Deficiency,* 1980, *84*, 345-351.

WALSH, J. *An assessment of vocational education programs for the handicapped under Part B of the 1968 Amendments to the Vocational Education Act: Executive Summary.* Salt Lake City: Olympics Research Corporation, 1975.

Washington Association for Retarded Citizens v. *Thomas,* No. C79-1235 v (W.D. Wash. 1979).

WEATHERLY, R., and LIPSKY, M. Street level bureaucrats and institutional innovations: Implementing special education reform. *Harvard Educational Review,* 1977, *47*, 171-197.

Weber v. *Stony Brook Hospital,* No. 672 (N.Y. Ct. App. Oct. 28, 1983).

Webster's new twentieth century dictionary, (2nd ed.). Collins World Publishing Co., 1975.

WEHMAN, P., and HILL, J. W. Competitive employment for moderately and severely   handicapped   individuals.   *Exceptional   Children*,   1981,   *47*, 338–345.

Welsch v. *Likins*,   373 F. Supp. 487 (D. Minn. 1974).

WESTINGHOUSE LEARNING CORPORATION. *The Impact of Head Start*. Athens: Ohio University Press, 1969.

WHITE HOUSE CONFERENCE ON FAMILIES. *Listening to America's families: Action for the 80's*. Washington, D.C.: U.S. Government Printing Office, 1980.

WHITTAKER, J. K. and GARBARINO, J. *Social support networks: Informal helping in the human services*. New York: Aldine Publishing Co., 1983.

WIEGERINK, R., and PELOSI, J. Educational planning. In P. Magrab and J. O. Elder (Eds.), *Planning for services to handicapped persons: Community, education, health*. Baltimore: Paul H. Brookes, 1979.

WIEGERINK. R., and SIMEONSSON, R. Public schools. In J. Wortis (Ed.), *Mental retardation and developmental disabilities* (Vol. 7). New York: Brunner/Mazel, 1975.

WIKLER, L. Chronic stresses of families of mentally retarded children. *Family Relations*, 1981, *30*, 281–288.

WIKLER, L., and HANUSSA, D. *The impact of respite care on stress in families of developmentally disabled*. Paper presented at annual meeting of the American Association of Mental Deficiency Meeting, San Francisco, May, 1980.

WIKLER, L., WASOW, M., and HATFIELD, E. Seeking strengths in families of developmentally disabled children. *Social Work*, 1983, *28*, 313–315.

WILLER, B. *Post institutional adjustment of the retarded returned to their natural families*. Paper presented at the annual meeting of the American Association on Mental Deficiency, Denver, May 19, 1978.

WILLER, B. S. *Return to the natural family*. Unpublished manuscript, 1981.

WILLER, B., and INTAGLIATA, J. *Deinstitutionalization of mentally retarded persons in New York State* (Final report). Buffalo: State University of New York at Buffalo, Division of Community Psychiatry, 1980.

WILLER, B. S., INTAGLIATA, J. C., and ATKINSON, A. L. Crisis for families of mentally retarded persons including the crisis of deinstitutionalization. *British Journal of Mental Subnormality*, 1979, *25*, 38–49.

WILLER, B. S., INTAGLIATA, J. C., and ATKINSON, A. L. Deinstitutionalization as a crisis event for families of mentally retarded persons. *Mental Retardation*, 1981, *19*, 28–29.

WITT, S. J. Increase in adaptive behavior level for mentally retarded persons. *Mental Retardation*, 1980, *19*, 75–79.

WITTER, F., and KING, T. M. Cigarettes and pregnancy. In R. Schwarz, and S. J. Yoffe (Eds.), *Drug and chemical risks of the fetus and newborn*. New York: Alan R. Liss, 1980.

WOLF, L., and ZARFAS, D. E. Parents' attitudes toward sterilization of their mentally retarded children. *American Journal of Mental Deficiency*, 1982, *2*, 122–129.

Wolf v. *Legislature of the State of Utah*,   Civil No. 182646 (3rd Jud. Dist. Ct. Utah, Jan. 8, 1969).

WOLFENSBERGER, W. Will there always be an institution? I. The impact of epidemiological trends. *Mental retardation*, 1971, *9*, 14–20. (a)

WOLFENSBERGER, W. Will there always be an institution? II: The impact of new service models. *Mental Retardation*, 1971, *9*, 31–37. (b)

WOLFENSBERGER, W. *The principle of normalization in human services*. Toronto: National Institute on Mental Retardation, 1972.

WOLFENSBERGER, W. Citizen advocacy for the handicapped, impaired and disadvantaged: An overview. In W. Wolfensberger and H. Zauka, *Citizen advocacy*. Toronto: National Institute on Mental Retardation, 1973.

WOLFENSBERGER, W. The origin and nature of our institutional model. In R. B. Kugel and A. Shearer (Eds.), *Changing patterns in residential services for the mentally retarded*. Washington, D.C.: President's Committee on Mental Retardation, 1976.

WOLFENSBERGER, W. A call to wake up to the beginning of a new wave of "euthanasia" of severely impaired people. *Education and Training of the Mentally Retarded*, 1980, *15*, 171–173.

WOLFENSBERGER, W. Social role valorization: A proposed new term for the principle of normalization. *Mental Retardation*, 1984, *21*, 234–239.

WOLPERT, J. *Group homes for the mentally retarded: An investigation of neighborhood property impacts*. (Study prepared for the New York State Office of Mental Retardation and Developmental Disabilities). Albany, N.Y.: 1978.

WOLRAICH, M. L. Communication between physicians and parents of handicapped children. *Exceptional Children*, 1982, *48*, 324–329.

WOO, S. L. C., LIASKY, A. S., GÜTTLER, F., CHANDRA, T., ROBSON, K. J. H. Cloned human phenylalanine hydroxylase gene allows prenatal diagnosis and carrier detection of classical phenylketonuria. *Nature*, 1983, *306*, 151–155.

WORTIS, J. Poverty and retardation. In J. Wortis (Ed.), *Mental retardation: An annual review (Vol. 1)*. New York: Brunner/Mazel, 1970.

WRIGHT, A. R., COOPERSTEIN, R. A., RENNEKER, E. G, and PADILLA, C. *Local implementation of P.L. 94-142: Final report of a longitudinal study*. Menlo Park, Calif.: Stanford Research Institute International, 1982.

WRIGHT, A. R., PADILLA, C., and COOPERSTEIN, R. D. *Local implementation of P.L. 94-142: Third year report of a longitudinal study*. Menlo Park, Calif.: Stanford Research Institute International, 1981.

Wyatt v. *Stickney*, 344 F. Supp. 387 (M.D. 1972), aff'd *Wyatt* v. *Aderholt*. 503 F. 2d 1305 (5th Cir. 1974).

Wyatt v. *Ireland*, No. 3195-N (M.D. Ala. 10-25-79).

YANKELOVICH, D. New rules in American life: Searching for self-fulfillment in a world turned upside down. *Psychology Today*, 1981, *14*(11), 35–91.

YANKELOVICH, D., SKELLY, F., and WHITE, A. H. Results of a survey on abortion. Reported in Abortion: Women speak out: An Exclusive Poll, *Life*, November 1981, pp. 15–51.

Youngberg v. *Romeo*, 102 S. Ct. 2452 (1982).

ZAHARA, R. *Behavior modification and normalization: A process of checks and balances*. Paper presented at Region VIII AAMD Conferences, October, 1975.

ZARAFU, I. W. Neonatal stress in mental retardation. *Pediatric Habilitation*, 1980, *1*, 305–320.

ZEAMAN, D., and HOUSE, B. J. The role of attention in retardate discrimination learning. In N. R. Ellis (Ed.), *Handbook of Mental Deficiency*. New York: McGraw-Hill, 1963.

ZETTEL, J. Implementing the right to a free appropriate public education. In J. Ballard, B. Ramirez, and F. J. Weintraub (Eds.), *Special education in America: Its legal and governmental foundations*. Reston, Va.: The Council for Exceptional Children, 1982.

ZETTEL, J. J., and BALLARD, J. The Education for All Handicapped Children Act of 1975 (P.L. 94-142): Its history, origins, and concepts. In J. Ballard, B. Ramirez, and F. Weintraub (Eds.), *Special Education in America: Its legal and governmental foundations*. Reston, Va.: The Council for Exceptional Children, 1982.

ZIGLER, E. Developmental versus difference theories of mental retardation. *American Journal of Mental Deficiency,* 1969, *73*, 536–555.

ZIGLER, E. National crisis in mental retardation research. *American Journal of Mental Deficiency,* 1978, *84*, 1–8.

ZIGLER, E., and BALLA, D. Impact of institutional experience on the behavior and development of retarded persons. *American Journal of Mental Deficiency,* 1977, *82*, 1–11.

ZIGLER, E., and BALLA, D. On the definition and classification of mental retardation. Unpublished paper, 1982. (Available from Department of Psychology, Yale University.)

ZIGLER, E., and MUENCHOW, S. Mainstreaming: The proof is in the implementation. *American Psychologist,* 1979, *34*, 993–996.

ZIGLER, E., and VALENTINE, J. *Project head start: A legacy of the war on poverty.* Riverside, Ca.: Free Press, 1979.

ZIMMERMAN, S. L. Families of developmentally disabled: Implications for research and planning and provision of services. In R. H. Bruininks and G. C. Krantz (Eds.), *Family care of developmentally disabled members: Conference proceedings.* Minneapolis: University of Minnesota, August 1979.

ZIPPERLIN, H. Normalization. In J. Wortis (Ed.), *Mental retardation and developmental disabilities* (Vol. 7). New York: Brunner/Mazel, 1975.

ZONCA, A. Personal advocacy: A model to equalize consumer power. In T. Appolloni, J. Cappuccilli, and T. Cooke (Eds.). *Achievements in residential services for persons with disabilities: Toward excellence.* Baltimore: University Park Press, 1980.

INDEX

Aanes, D., 31, 105, 111
Abortions, 72-73
Accidents, 153-154
Accreditation standards, 41
Activism, judicial, 32-35, 52-54
Adams, G.L., 73
Adams, M., 99
Adams, S.C., 86
Adaptions assumption, minimal, 79-80
Adaptive behavior, 5-6, 12, 108
Addison, M., 51, 125
Admissions to institutions, 38, 39
Adoption Assistance and Child Welfare
    Act of 1980, 81
Adoptive families, 99-100
Advocacy, 32, 51-52, 121-32
Age, maternal, 149
Age, prevalence of MR by, 20-21
Aiello, J.R., 107
Akesson, H.O., 28
Alberto, P.A., 50
Albright, L., 115
Aldefor, R., 84
Allen, D.F., 72
Allen, R., 72
Aloia, G.F., 15
Alonzo, B., 115
Alternative placement, 84-87
American Association on Mental Deficiency,
    1, 5, 6-12, 28
American Bar Association, 127
Amniocentesis, 72, 136
Andron, L., 91
Anencephaly, 141
Aninger, M., 104
Anthony, P., 64
Apartment living, 103-4
Appolloni, A. H., 111
Arnold, I. L., 111
Association for Retarded Citizens, 32, 121
Atkinson, A.L., 83, 86
Atthowe, J., 85-86, 105, 107, 110
Auletta, K., 165
Autosomal gene disorders, 137-40

Backlash, 41-47, 62-69
Baken, J.W., 82
Baker, B.L., 37, 102-4
Balla, D., 11, 12, 28, 46, 104, 106, 107
Ballard, J., 54
Bank-Mikkelsen, N.E., 29n
Baroff, G., 10, 11, 19, 99
Barth, R.P., 94
Bass, M.S., 89
Baumeister, A.A., 3, 8
Baxter, D., 90
Beck, C.H., 151
Becker, H., 13

Beckman, P., 78
Begab, M.J., 25, 74, 147
Bell, T., 67
Bellamy, G.T., 117
Belmont, L., 18
Belous, R.S., 70
Benoit, E.P., 3, 83
Bensberg, G.T., 126
Bercovici, S., 21, 90
Berger, B., 87
Berger, P.L., 87
Berkiansky, H.H., 45
Berkowitz, M., 117
Berkowitz, R., 142
Biklen, D., 46, 96, 107
Biogenic determinants, 134-42
Biological concepts, 2-4
Birenbaum, A., 74, 78, 80, 105
Bjaanes, A.T., 30, 102, 105, 107
Bjerkaldal, T., 148
Bland, W., 106
Blanton, R.L., 4
Blatt, B., 29, 32, 41, 96, 107
Blunden, R., 3, 16
Blythe, B.J., 94
Boarding homes, 105-6
Bogdan, R., 15, 96
Bogen, D., 105
Boggs, E., 83, 123
Bolinsky, H., 104
Borchart, K.R., 111
Borderline retarded, 9
Borlee, E., 149
Bornberg, A., 137
Boroskin, A., 83
Borthwick, S., 41, 61
Bossard, M., 86
Bostick, G., 83
Bouckaert, A.C., 149
Bowe, F., 163
Bowers, L., 89, 91
Boyd, P.A., 34
Braddock, D., 41, 45, 81
Bradley, J., 101
Bradley, V.S., 45, 46, 96, 97, 102
Brandon, M.W.G., 93
Breslin, E.R., 65
Brewer, G.D., 118
Brockmeir, W.E., 85
Brockwell, C., 119
Brolin, D.E., 115
Brooks, S., 111
Browder, A., 103, 111
Browder, J.A., 99, 101, 103
Brown, J.L., 105
Brown, J.S., 106
Brown, W.T., 137
Browning, P., 31

Bruce, P., 160
Bruininks, R., 27, 38, 39, 51, 78, 80, 104, 106, 107, 110-14, 117-19
Budoff, M., 62, 66, 67
Buist, N., 139
Burda, M., 41
Bureau of the Education of the Handicapped, 59
Burger, W.E., 43
Burnstead, D.C., 107
Burt, R.A., 33
Buss, W., 61
Butler, E.W., 30, 79, 102, 105, 107
Butterfield, E., 28, 106

Cadwell, J., 105, 107
Caldwell, B.M., 80
Campbell, F.A., 94, 154
Campbell, S., 75
Care. *See also* Deinstitutionalization; Families; Services
costs of, 37-38, 79, 80-82
types of, 30, 78-83, 110-11, 148-52
Career-education concept, 115
Carney, M.F., 65
Carroll, C.F., 97
Carson, K.L., 109
Cary, A., 105
Cavalier, A.R., 44
Centerwall, S.A. and W.R., 28
Central nervous system impairment, 2-4
Chambers, G.M., 135
Chan, K.S., 147
Child Abuse Prevention and Treatment Act of 1974, 154
Childrearing and childbearing, 91-95
Children's Defense Fund, 157
Chitkara, U., 72
Chromosomal anomalies, 134-37
Chorionic villis biopsy, 136
Cicchetti, D.V., 12
Ciccone, J., 79, 109
Citizen advocacy, 125-26
Civil Rights of Institutionalized Persons Act, 128
Clarke, A.D. and A.M., 133
Classification system, 4-6, 8-12, 14, 58
Clausen, J., 10, 12
Cleveland, D.W., 74, 80
Clewell, W.H., 143
Clinical perspective, 2-12, 17
Close, O.W., 105
Cognitive stimulation, inadequate, 154-55
Cohen, M.M., 138
Cohen, S., 97, 111
Cole, R.W., 66, 67
Collins, M.J., 111
Colombatto, J.J., 84
Community based services, 39-40

Community Development Block Grant Program, 37
Community education, 112
Computer assisted instruction, 160
Congenital hypothyroidism, 138-39
Conley, R., 56
Conroy, J.W., 39, 40, 45, 85-86
Continuum of care. *See* Services
Cooley, F.B., 37
Cooperstein, R.A., 66
Corcoran, E.L., 119
Cost(s). *See also* Economic issues
-benefit analysis, 144-45
of care, 37-38, 79, 80-82
of education, 56-57, 65-67
Counseling, 109-10, 135-36, 139
Coval, T.E., 34
Craig, P.A., 68
Crawford, J.L., 107
Creal, D., 78
Cretinism, 138-39
Cronbach, L.J., 23
Cross, A.H., 78
Cruickshank, W., 50
Cullen, C., 30
Culture of poverty, 147-48
Culver, M., 79
Curci, R., 58
Curry, L., 59, 62

Daniels, B.S., 37
Danker-Brown, P., 126
Darling, R.B., 74, 80
Datel, W.G., 37
Davies, J., 140
Davies, S.P., 4, 27, 49, 99, 104
Davis, K., 156
Davis, S., 115
Day, H.M. and R.M., 118
DD Act, 34, 36, 42, 124-25
Dean, D., 117
Defect position, 16
Definition, 6-12, 18-20
Deinstitutionalization, 23-47. *See also* Services
alternative placement and, 84
backlash, 41-47
defined, 23-24
family participation in process, 86
historical precursors, 24-28
home care and, 78-83
impact of, 38-41, 82-85
impetus for, 28-38
mainstreaming and, 69
de Leone, R.H., 147, 148
Delivery systems, service, 119-20
Demaine, J.C., 105
Demography, prevalence of MR by, 20-22
Dempsey, J.J., 88

Deno, E., 113, 114
Dependency, 165
de Silva, R., 104
Deutsch, A., 25
Developmental disability, 11
Developmental expectations, 30–31
Developmentally Disabled Assistance
    and Bill of Rights Act of 1975, 34, 36,
    42, 124–25
Developmental model, 15, 30–31
Developmental perspective, 15–17
Developmental services, 112–19
DeVizia, J., 102
Dexter, L.A., 13
Diagnosis, 71–77, 142–44
Diet, premature births and, 149
Diet therapy, 138, 139
Dingman, H.F., 18–19
Discharges from institutions, 38–39
Discriminatory testing, 53–54
Diseases, infectious, 150, 152, 154.
    See also Genetic disorders
Doll, E.A., 5, 6
Dominant-gene disorder, autosomal,
    137–38
Doris, J., 13, 48, 49, 70, 73
Doth, D., 38, 104, 106, 117
Down syndrome, 75, 134–36, 145
Due process, 42, 56, 61–62
Duff, R., 75
Dugdale, R., 4–5, 27
Dunlap, W.R., 74, 80
Dunn, L.M., 50
Dunn, R., 66, 67
Dussault, W.L.E., 125
Dwyer, B., 59, 62, 67, 69
Dybwad, G., 107
Dye, H.B., 5

Economic issues, 45–46, 65–67, 144–45.
    See also Costs
Edelman, M.W., 58
Edgerton, R.B., 11, 15, 17, 21, 28, 46, 90,
    105–6, 108
Educable mentally retarded, 14, 49–51
Education. *See also* Mainstreaming
    appropriate, 58–61, 64
    cascade system of placement, 114
    costs of, 56–57, 65–67
    Howe's experimental school, 25–26
    in institutions, 60–61
    mass, 155
    parent, 110
    professional and public, 112, 161–63
    right to, 52–53, 54, 63–64
    special, 113–15
Education for All Handicapped Children
    Act of 1975, 37, 54–58, 60–62, 64–67
Eheart, B.K., 79, 109

Eichorn, D.H., 28, 78
Eisenberg, L., 150
Eklund, E., 123
Elkind, D., 71
Ellis, J., 131
Ellis, L., 103, 111
Ellis, N.R., 16, 17, 43, 83
Employment, 118. *See also*
    Vocational training
Encephalocele, 141
Environmental influences, 152–55
Enzyme replacement therapy, 144
Epidemiology, 17–22
Epple, W.A., 104
Erickson, J.D., 148
Erikson, K.T., 13
Euthanasia, 75–77, 166
Expectations
    developmental, 30–31
    over birth of child, 71–72
Exposes on institutions, public, 29
Eyman, R.K., 28, 41, 46, 102, 105,
    106
Eysenck, H.J., 5

Faflak, P., 104
Falendar, C., 110
Families, 70–95
    adoptive, 99–100
    alternative placement and, 84–87
    counseling for, 109–10
    diagnosis and, 71–77
    foster, 81, 100–103
    home care and, 78–83
    respite care for, 110–11
    rights of mentally retarded and, 89–95
    shift in social policy toward, 87–88
Fanning, F., 108
Farber, B., 15, 20, 71, 78, 79, 165–66
Farran, D.C., 94
Featherstone, H., 71
Feinstein, C.S., 45
Felding, C.F., 151
Felsenthal, D., 105
Ferleger, D., 34
Fernald, W.E., 25, 27
Ferrara, D., 85
Fetal alcohol syndrome, 149–50, 151
Fetal surgery, 143–144
Fetoscopy, 143
Finkelstein, N.W., 5, 6, 10, 19, 147
Fiorelli, J.S., 104, 114
Fisher, M.M., 16
Flanagan, J.J., 83, 110
Fletcher, J., 72
Floor, L., 90
Flynn, J.R., 68
Foley, T., 139
Forssman, H., 28

Foster, R., 6, 12
Foster families, 81, 100–103
Fotheringham, J.B., 78, 93
Foutz, T.K., 145
Fowle, C.M., 79
Fragile-X syndrome, 136–37
Francis, S.H., 28
Franklin, D.S., 100
Freedman, R., 82, 96, 103, 105, 111
Freeman, H., 102
Freeman, H., 102
French, R.W., 119
Freud, A., 94, 99
Friedman, P.R., 33
Friedrich, W.L. and W.N., 71
Frith, G.H., 68
Fritz, M., 103
Frohboese, R., 44, 84–86
Fuchs, V.R., 147
Furry, W.S., 65
Future prospects, 159–66

Gacka, R.C., 68
Gallagher, J.J., 50, 78
Galligan, B., 107
Garbarino, J., 120
Garber, H., 94, 154
Gardner, H., 110
Gardner, P., 44, 45
Gath, A., 71, 79
Genetic counseling, 110, 135–36,
    139
Genetic disorders, 134–42
Genetic engineering, 144
Genetic predisposition, 140
Genung, T., 86
Geographical location, prevalence of MR by,
    22
Gesell, G., 76
Gettings, R.M., 39, 45
Gilhool, T., 31, 34
Glazer, N., 120–21
Glean, R., 60
Glenn, L., 31
Gliedman, J., 68, 74, 118
Glossary, 167–69
Goddard, H.H., 4–5, 27
Goffman, I., 15, 24, 30
Gold, M.W., 117
Goldberg, I., 27, 50
Goldstein, J., 94, 99
Goldstein, S., 59, 62
Gollay, E., 82, 96, 103, 105, 110, 111, 113,
    115, 119
Goodlad, J.I., 68
Goodman, L., 60, 69, 111
Gorham, K.A., 84
Gorlin, R.G., 138
Gottlieb, B.W., 58

Gottlieb, J., 48, 58, 68
Gould, S.J., 4
Grannum, P., 142
Griswold, W.R., 151
Grossman, F.K., 79, 80
Grossman, H.J., 5–9, 20
Group placements, 104–7
Grubb, W.N., 158
Guard, K.A., 106
Guardianship services, 124–25
Guralnick, M., 109
Gustafson, J.M., 75
Guze, B., 80

Haagensen, L., 31
Haavik, S.F., 90, 94
Habilitation, right to, 33–34, 42–44
Haddad, H.M., 136
Hainey, J., 137
Hallahan, D.P., 7
Halpern, C., 33
Hansen, A., 41
Hansen, H., 18
Hansen, M., 110
Hanussa, D., 111
Harper, R.S., 86, 104
Harrington, M., 147
Harrington, S., 110
Hastings, A.H., 68
Hatfield, E., 47
Hattersby, J., 30
Hauber, F., 38, 104, 106, 117
Haywood, H.C., 164–66
Heal, L.W., 37
Health care, 112–13, 148–52
Health Planning and Resources
    Development Act, 36–37
Heber, R., 5, 8, 94, 110, 154
Helsel, E.D., 28
Hendrix, E., 31
Henes, C., 105
Hernstein, R.S., 5
Herpes virus, 150, 152
Herr, S., 44, 122, 126, 128
Hill, B.K., 38, 39, 102, 104, 106, 117
Hill, J.W., 117
Hinkle, H., 91
Hobbin, J.C., 142
Hoddinott, B.A., 78, 93
Hoffman, C., 110
Holburn, C.S., 123
Hollingsworth, J.S., 74, 80
Holmes, O.W., 91
Holt, K.S., 78, 79
Home and Community Medicaid Waiver, 81
Home care, 78–83. *See also* Families
Hook, E.B., 135
Horejsi, C.R., 78, 112
Horner, R., 117

House, B.J., 17
Housing and Community Development
   Act of 1974, 37
Howe, E.M., 82
Howe, S., 25–26
Huberty, T.J., 12, 58
Hull, K., 111
Humane care, 30
Hunt, J.M., 5
Hurley, R., 147
Hydrocephaly, 141, 142
Hypertension, 150–51
Hypothyroidism, congenital, 138–39

Imershein, A.W., 120
Impairment, organic, 2–4
Imre, P.D., 20
Incidence, 18, 140–41
Individualized educational program, 55,
   58–59, 69
Individual placements, 99–104
Infectious diseases, 150, 152, 154
Ingalls, R.P., 21
Inman, D., 117
Institutional litigation, 42–44, 128
Institutions, 25–29, 40–44. *See also*
   Deinstitutionalization
   admissions and discharges, 38–39
   debate over, 106–7
   education in, 60–61
   indictment against, 28–29
Intagliata, J., 37, 82, 83, 86, 102–3, 105,
   106, 113
Integration, normalization and, 31–32,
   161
Intelligence-quotient (IQ), 4–5, 7–8, 9–12,
   18–19, 53–54, 58
International developments, 163
Interventions, social, 155–57
Ionizing radiation, fetal exposure to, 150
Isett, R.O., 84

Jacobson, J.W., 11, 113
Jaffe, F.S., 72
Janicki, M.P., 11, 104, 105
Jastak, J. F., 5
Jencks, C., 13
Jenkins, E.C., 137
Jensen, A.R., 5, 21
Jervis, G.A., 2
Jipson, F., 20
Johnson, F., 33
Joint Commission on the Accreditation
   of Hospitals, 41
Jones, J.R., 115
Jones, P.A., 45
Jones, R.L., 15
Judge, C., 137
Judicial activism, 32–35, 52–54

Juriloff, P., 65
Justice, R.S., 101, 103, 106
Justice Department, 127–128

Kahn, A., 121, 123
Kakalik, J.S., 65, 118
Kamerman, S.B., 71, 87, 121, 123
Kamin, L., 5
Kanner, L., 17, 22, 25, 27
Katz, E., 111
Katz, S., 119
Katzman, S., 94
Kauffman, J.M., 7, 63
Kauffman, M.E., 28, 48, 50
Keating, D.J., 85
Keenan, V., 79, 109
Kelly, B.R., 30, 107
Keniston, K., 71, 147
Kennedy, J.F., 35, 166
Keogh, B.K., 73, 110
Kerenyi, T., 72
Kerr, M.M., 50
Keys, V., 83
Kiely, M., 11
King, T.M., 149
Kirp, D., 13, 61, 62
Klaber, M.M., 65, 106
Klein, M.S., 104, 107
Kleinberg, J., 107
Klinefelter's syndrome, 136
Knobloch, H., 148
Knowlton, M., 103
Koegel, P., 21
Koller, J. R., 12, 58
Krantz, G. G., 78
Kraus, S., 113
Krause, J., 63
Krisheff, C.H., 99
Krummel, C., 119
Kukic, M.B., 48
Kuriloff, P., 61
Kurtz, N., 82, 96, 111
Kurtz, R., 21, 125, 126, 161
Kushlick, A., 3, 16

Labeling, 14–15, 165
LaFranchi, S., 139
Lakin, D.C., 27–28, 38, 104, 106,
   107, 117
Landesman-Dwyer, S., 51, 105, 107, 15(
Langford, C.A., 119
Larsen, L., 60
Larson, P., 139
Laski, F., 34
Latib, A., 86
Lavelle, N., 73, 110
Lazerson, M., 158

Lazzarini, A., 138
Lead-Based Poisoning Prevention
    Act of 1971, 153
Leadership, national, 166
Lead poisoning, 152-53
Least restrictive alternative, principle of,
    34-35, 53, 61
LeChat, M.F., 149
Lee, P.R., 72
Legal advocacy, 126-31
Legal issues in prevention, 145-46
Legal Services Corporation, 129-30
Legislative action, 35-37, 54-56
Lei, T.J., 79, 105
Leinhardt, G., 68
Leland, H., 6, 12
Lemanowicz, J.A., 45
Lemkau, P.V., 20
Lesch-Hyhan syndrome, 140
Levi, A.M., 119
Levinson, E.J., 20
Levitan, G.W., 7
Levitan, S.A., 70
Levy, F., 107
Lewis, J., 14
Lewis, O., 148
Lieblum, S., 138
Lifestyle, home care and, 78-79
Liffiton-Chrostowski, N., 86
Lilly, M.S., 56
Lindheim, B.L., 72
Linn, B., 89, 91
Linstone, H.A., 160
Lippincott, M.K., 44
Lippman, L., 27
Lipsky, M., 62, 66
Litch, S.A., 155
Litigation
    over childbearing and childrearing,
        91, 92, 94
    deinstitutionalization and, 32-35
    over education, 52-54, 57, 58, 60-64
    over foster-family-care assistance, 81
    institutional, 42-44, 128
    over medical care, 75-77
    wrongful birth and life suits, 145-46
Lorentz, E., 97
Lubin, R., 11
Lubs, H.A., 137
Luckasson, R., 131
Luckey, R.E., 51, 118, 119
Luria, A.R., 3, 17
Lyon, R., 106

McAllister, R.J., 79
McCarver, R.B., 44
McClung, M., 62
McCord, W. T., 30-31, 109

McCormack, M.K., 28, 138
McDevitt, S.C., 90
McDonald, A.C., 109
McGee, J.J., 43, 44
McGowan, B., 121, 123
McKhann, G., 139
McKusick, V., 138
McLain, R., 102, 105, 106
MacLean, W.E., 3
McLeod, W., 107
MacMillan, D.L., 12, 15, 22, 61, 82
MacMillan, E.S., 76
McNally, R. J., 7
MacPhee, H.M., 5
Macy, T.W., 46
Madden, N.A., 68
Mahoney, M., 142
Mainstreaming, 48-69
    backlash, 62-69
    defined, 48-49
    historical precursors, 49-50
    impact of, 57-62
    impetus for, 50-57
Maloney, M.P., 11, 14, 21
Maple syrup urine disease, 139, 140
Marguiss, J., 104
Marinelli, J., 56
Marion, R.L., 73
Marriage, 89-91
Martin, E.W., 67
Martin, J.C., 150
Marvin, W.E., 105
Mason, B., 34
Massaril, F., 100
Maton, K., 97
Mattinson, I., 91
Mayeda, T., 45, 104, 107
Medical care, withholding of, 75-77
Mendoza, S.A., 151
Menninger, K.A., 90, 94
Menolascino, F. J., 27, 34, 43-45
Mental retardation (MR)
    AAMD definition, 6-12
    clinical perspective, 2-12, 17
    developmental perspective, 15-17
    epidemiology, 17-22
    social system perspective, 13-15
Mental Retardation Facilities and Community
    Mental Health Centers Construction
    Act of 1963, 35
Mercer, J., 2, 10, 11, 13, 14, 19, 21, 50,
    78, 83
Mesibos, G.B., 31
Methodologies, prevalence of MR and, 20
Meyer, R.J., 85-86
Mickelson, P., 93
Mickenberg, N., 131
Miller, C., 102, 105, 106

Miller, N., 74, 80
Miniham, P.M., 86
Minimal adaptions assumption, 79–80
Minority children, 14, 19
Mission, C., 149
Mitchell, D., 39, 45
Mithaug, D.E., 117
Mnookin, R.H., 101
Moe, R., 115
Moen, M., 105
Moltulsky, A., 136
Moore, M., 123
Moore, S., 83
Morell, B., 80, 86
Moroney, R.M., 78, 80, 87
Morreau, L.E., 80, 110–13, 114, 118, 119
Moser, H.W., 133–35
Mosher, E.K., 68, 69
Moss, J.W., 117
Muenchow, S., 23
Multifactorial genetic inheritance, 140–42
Muma, J.R., 8
Murken, J., 135
Murphy, A., 109
Murphy, J.G., 37
Murphy, W., 139
Myths, 162–63

Naeye, R.L., 151
Naisbeth, J., 121
National Adoption Exchange, 100
National Association of Superintendents
    of Public Residential Facilities
    for the Mentally Retarded, 24, 106
Neal, J., 103, 111
Neufeld, G.R., 24
Neufeld, R., 121
Neural-tube defects, 141–42
Neurofibromatosis, 137
Newbrough, J.R., 24
Nihira, K., 6, 12, 102
Nihira, L., 102
Nirje, B., 31
Niswander, K.P., 21
Normalization principle, 29–32, 89, 161
Norms, social, 13–14
Novak, L., 125
Nursing homes, 106
Nutrition, maternal and child, 149

O'Brien, J., 31
O'Connor, G., 101, 103–6, 111
Ogbu, J.U., 148
Olshansky, S., 74
O'Regan, G., 102
Orelove, F.P., 67, 68
Orenstein, A., 62
Organic impairment, 2–4

P.L. 88-164, 35
P.L. 89-313, 57
P.L. 92-233, 35–36
P.L. 92-603, 36
P.L. 93-112, 37, 56
P.L. 94-103, 34, 36, 124–25
P.L. 94-142, 37, 54–58, 60–62, 64–67
P.L. 96-247, 128
P.L. 96-272, 81
P.L. 97-35, 81
Padilla, C., 66
Pagel, S.P., 106
Palley, A., 68
Palmer, D.J., 109
Parents, 32, 51–52, 59, 67–69, 73–75, 110.
    See also Families
Parker, R., 45
Parron, D., 150
Pasamanick, B., 148
Pathological model, 2–4
Patrick, J. L., 12, 58
Paul, J.L., 24, 121
Payne, J.E., 85
Payne, J.S., 10
Pelosi, J., 56
Penrose, L.S., 136
Perske, R., 31, 74, 104
Phenylketonuria, 138, 139, 144
Pignofrio, A., 84
Pindborg, J.J., 138
Pittenger, J.C., 65
Pizzo, P., 109, 120
Placement, 83–86, 99–107. *See also* Services
Plamondon, A., 94
Poisoning, lead, 152–53
Polivka, C.H., 105
Polivka, L.J., 105, 120
Polloway, E.A., 10, 58
Postnatal period, diagnosis in, 73–77
Poverty, culture of, 147–48
Pratt, M.W., 107
Premature births, 148–52
Prenatal period, diagnosis in, 72–73
President's Committee on Employment
    of the Handicapped, 118
President's Committee on
    Mental Retardation, 133
Prevalence, 18–22
Prevention, 133–58
    biogenic determinants and treatment,
        134–42
    issues in, 144–46
    new medical diagnoses and treatment,
        142–44
    sociocultural determinants and, 147–57
    synergistic approach to, 157–58
Prevention: To Be Born Well (Litch), 155
Price, M., 69

Professionals, 51–52, 67–69, 88, 161–63
Protection and advocacy systems, 122–23, 128, 130–31
Psychological concepts, 4–6
Pueschel, S.M., 109

Quellette, E.M., 150

Ramey, C.T., 5, 6, 10, 19, 94, 147, 154
Rauth, M., 68
Ray, J.S., 110
Raynes, N.V., 107
Re, M.A., 105
Readmissions, 39
Reagan, R., 46
Reagan administration, 65, 76, 156
Rebell, M.A., 66
Recessive-gene disorders, autosomal, 138
Recreation, 118–19
Reed, E.W. and S.C., 140–41
Reese, S.J., 60, 66
Reform, institutional, 40–41
Regression/recoupment problem, 60
Rehabilitation Act of 1973, 37, 56, 76
Rehnquist, W.H., 64
Reid, E.S., 74
Reiss, S., 7
Reiter, S., 119
Related services, 60
Religious instruction, 119
Renneker, E.G., 66
Replacement therapy, enzyme, 144
Reschly, D., 11, 12, 15, 19, 20, 58
Research, 28–29, 46–47, 163–64
Residential services, 97–108, 165
Respite care, 110–11
Retarded Infants Services, 102
Return homes, 82–83
Reynolds, W.M., 107
Rh blood incompatibility, 150, 151–52
Rhoades, C., 31
Rhodes, W.C., 26
Rights
    to education, 52–53, 54, 63–64
    familial, 89–93
    to habilitation, 33–34, 42–44
Rillow, J., 82
Risk of incidence, 140–41
Rivera, G., 29
Robinson, H.B. and N. M., 11
Rodman, D.H., 111
Roeder, P.W., 46
Roos, P., 15, 30, 41, 43, 44, 74
Rorke, M., 80
Rosen, M., 90
Rosenbaum, S., 157
Rosett, H.C., 150
Rosman, N.T., 150

Ross, R.T., 83
Roszkowski, M., 84
Roth, W., 68, 74, 118
Rothman, D., 25
Rubin, J., 117
Rueda, R., 147
Rusch, F.R., 117
Ryckman, D.B., 79
Rynders, J.E., 51

Sabatino, D.A., 62
Sackett, G., 51
Sales, B.D., 44, 84–86
Salkever, D.D., 79
Salvia, J., 3, 12
Salzberg, C.C., 119
Santiestevan, H., 45
Sarason, S., 13, 48, 49, 70, 73, 97
Schalock, R.L., 86, 104
Scheerenberger, R.C., 20, 25, 37–40, 46, 80, 82, 96, 104–6
Schilling, R.F., 94
Schinke, S.P., 94
Schipper, M.T., 80
Schmelkin, L., 58
Schmidt, D.W., 90
Schodek, K., 86
Schoen, C., 156
Schonell, F.J., 78, 80
School access, 57–58. *See also* Mainstreaming
School year, extended, 60
Schroeder, S.R., 105
Schwartz, A.A., 113
Schwartz, C., 31
Scull, A.T., 37
Segal, R., 106
Segregation, 161, 165
Seguin, E., 2
Self-advocacy, 131–32
Self-help networks, 120–21
Seltzer, G.B., 37, 102–4
Seltzer, M.M., 37, 44, 102–4
Services, 96–132
    advocacy, 121–32
    community based, 39–40
    delivery system, 119–20
    for families of return homes, 83
    related, 60
    residential, 97–108
    social, 87, 108–21
Severely retarded children, 51, 62
Sex, prevalence of MR by, 21
Sexual expression, 89–93
Shapiro, H., 119
Shapiro, I.G., 118, 119
Sheehy, S., 117
Shellhaas, M., 6, 12
Sheltered workshop programs, 117–18
Siegel, L., 28

Sigelman, C., 46, 126
Sigelman, L., 46
Sigford, B.B., 27, 107
Silverman, R., 142
Silverstein, A.B., 28, 46, 102, 105, 106
Simeonsson, R., 49
Simons, J.M., 59, 62, 67, 69
Singer, J., 21, 86
Single-gene disorder, 137–40
Sitkei, E.C., 105
Sitkei, E.G., 104
Skarnulis, L., 105
Skeels, H., 5, 93
Skelly, F., 72
Skelton, M., 78, 93, 110
Slay, T., 109
Smith, D., 135, 136, 150
Smith, J.D., 58
Smith, P.M., 90
Smoskoski, F., 31
Snowden, L.R., 107
Snyderman, S., 140
Social interventions, 155–57
Social norms, 13–14
Social policy on family care, 87–88
Social programs, 155–57
Social Security Act provisions
    for deinstitutionalization, 35–36
Social services, 87, 108–21
Social system perspective, 13–15, 17
Social vulnerability, 164–66
Sociocultural determinants, 147–55
Socioeconomic status, 21–22, 61–62
Soddy, K., 2
Soeffling, M., 102
Sofrendo, A.Z., 46
Solnit, 94, 99
Soskin, R.M., 75, 94
Spakes, P., 80
Sparrow, S.S., 12
Spaulding for Children of New Jersey, 100
Special-education services. *See*
    Education; Mainstreaming
Spina bifida, 76, 141, 142
Spitz, H.H., 17
Spreat, S., 84
Springer, A., 109
SSI (Supplemental Security Income), 36
Stanford-Binet Scores, 8, 9, 10
Stark, J.H., 65
State Protection and Advocacy Systems,
    124
Statistical model, 4
Stay homes, 78–82
Stedman, D.J., 23, 28, 78, 84
Steele, M.W., 109
Stein, Z., 18
Steindorf, D.R., 82
Stene, E., and J., 135

Stengel-Rutkowski, S., 135
Stereotype, 15
Sterilization, 91–93
Sternlicht, M., 28, 103
Stivers, L.E., 120
Stone, N.W., 110
Strain, P.S., 50
Streissguth, A.P., 150
Strickland, B., 59, 62
Stuckey, P.E., 24
Sturge-Weber syndrome, 138
Sturm, M.L., 91
Subsidies, 80–82, 100
Suelzle, M., 79, 109
Sulzbacher, F.M., 105
Summers, J.A., 11
Sundberg, N.D., 107
Supportive services, 87, 109–12
Surgery, Fetal, 143
Sutherland, G.R., 137
Sutter, P., 107
System of Multicultural Pluralistic Assessment
    (SOMPA), 14–15
Systems advocacy, 123

Tarjan, G., 3, 18–19
Taylor, J., 83
Taylor, S., 45, 96
Tay-Sachs disease, 139, 140, 144
Teachers, 68–69, 162
Technology, 159–60
Ted Brink, T.D., 12, 58
Tennant, L., 30
Terman, L., 4
Testing, I.Q., 4–5, 7–8, 9–12, 18–19,
    53–54, 58
Theodore, S.M., 119
Thiele, R.L., 24
Thomas, M.A., 60, 65, 66
Thompson, D.E., 107
Thompson, T., 105
Thorsheim, M.J., 102
Throne, J., 30, 31, 107
Thurlow, M., 114
Thurlow, M.I., 114
Thurman, S.K., 104, 114
Title XVI, 36
Title XIX, 35–36
Title XX, 36
Townsend, P.W., 83, 110
Trainable mentally retarded, 50
Training, vocational, 115–18
Transportation services, 111
Treatment, 16, 142–44. *See also* Prevention
Tredgold, A.F., 2, 4, 5
Trends, 21–22, 159–66
Triest, G., 111
Trisomy, 21, 135
Tuberous Sclerosis, 137–38

Tucker, J.A., 58
Turnbull, A.P., 59, 62, 71, 110
Turnbull, H.R., 59, 71, 90, 110
Turner, B. and G., 136
Turner's syndrome, 136

Ultrasonography, 142–43
Upshur, C.C., 111

Vail, D., 24
Valentine, J., 155
Vitello, L.B., 110
Vitello, S.J., 46, 75, 85–86, 91, 105, 107,
    110, 160
Vladeck, B.C., 106
Vocational Rehabilitation Act of 1973,
    37, 56, 76, 118
Vocational training, 115–18
Vogel, F., 136
Vrooman, P.C., 129
Vulnerability, social, 164–66

Wagner, J.L., 68
Wai, F., 45
Waisbern, S.E., 80
Walker, S., 84, 85
Ward, M.P., 11, 14, 21, 115
Warren, N., 106
Wasow, M., 47
Watkins, M., 86
Watts, B.H., 78
Weatherly, R., 62, 66
Wechsler Scales, 8, 9, 10
Wehman, P., 117
Weiner, L., 150
Weitz, J., 157
Westphal, M., 21
White, A.H., 72
White, J.W., 120
Whiteman, M., 5
Whitling, C.A., 106

Whitlock, A., 111
Whittaker, J.K., 120
Wiegerink, R., 49, 56, 121
Wiener, S., 137
Wikler, L., 74, 111
Wilkin, L., 136
Willer, B.S., 37, 82, 83, 86, 102–3, 105,
    106, 113, 118, 119
Williams, S.M., 80, 110–13, 114, 118, 119
Willowbrook State School, 29, 33, 82
Witt, S.J., 107
Witter, F., 149
Wolf, L., 93
Wolfensberger, W., 15, 24, 26, 30, 81, 100,
    103, 107, 123, 125, 166
Wolpert, J., 45
Wolraich, M.L., 109
Wortis, J., 147
Wright, A.R., 66
Wrongful birth and life suits, 145–46
Wyngaarden, M., 82, 96

X-linked disorders, 140

Yanaguchi, J., 86
Yankelovich, D., 72, 78
Yekutiel, E., 119

Zahara, R., 30
Zarafu, I.W., 152
Zarfas, D.E., 93
Zeaman, D., 16, 17
Zettel, J.J., 54
Zigler, E., 11, 12, 16, 23, 28, 46, 106, 133,
    155, 158, 164
Zimmerman, S.L., 81
Zipperlin, H., 78, 161
Ziring, P.R., 82
Zisfein, L., 90
Zonca, A., 132
Zoning issue, 35, 44–45